THE MAID AND THE QUEEN

THE MAID
and
THE QUEEN

The Secret History of Joan of Arc
and
Yolande of Aragon

NANCY GOLDSTONE

Weidenfeld and Nicolson
LONDON

First published in Great Britain in 2011
by Weidenfeld & Nicolson

1 3 5 7 9 10 8 6 4 2

© Nancy Goldstone 2011

A CIP catalogue record for this book
is available from the British Library.

ISBN: 978 0 2978 6336 6

Printed and bound by CPI Group (UK) Ltd,
Croydon, CR0 4YY

The Orion Publishing Group's policy is to use papers that are natural,
renewable and recyclable and made from wood grown in
sustainable forests. The logging and manufacturing processes are expected
to conform to environmental regulations of the country of origin.

Weidenfeld & Nicolson

Orion Publishing Group Ltd
Orion House
5 Upper Saint Martin's Lane
London, WC2H 9EA

An Hachette UK Company

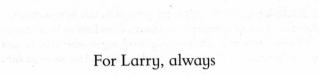

For Larry, always

CONTENTS

PART I

𝔅efore 𝔍oan

PART II

𝔍oan of 𝔄rc

PART III

After Joan

MAPS

ILLUSTRATIONS

NOTE ON SOURCES

THOSE UNFAMILIAR with the study of medieval history may wonder how it is possible to write with any certainty about events that occurred so long ago. Fortunately, the fifteenth century boasted a stunning wealth of primary source material that has survived to the present day. There is Joan's own extensive testimony, and that of her inquisitors, from her Trial of Condemnation, as well as the depositions from the many eyewitnesses who knew the Maid and who were actively involved in the events of the Hundred Years War, which were recorded in the judicial proceedings associated with her rehabilitation. There are also numerous extant works by chroniclers of the period and a significant trove of government reports, letters, royal proclamations, and accounts. For those interested, this evidence is cited at the back of the book in the form of detailed chapter notes and bibliography.

All of which is a long way of saying that, as provocative and even astonishing as it sometimes may appear, what you are about to read actually happened.

INTRODUCTION

The town of Blois, on the banks of the Loire, twenty-five miles southwest of Orléans, April 1429—The narrow streets of this small provincial city, ordinarily quiet, were suddenly crowded with traffic. Wagons piled high with foodstuffs and other provisions jostled for space with lordly knights on horseback and commoners laden with sheaves of grain. Cattle, sheep, and other livestock, some tethered to carts, others herded into hastily erected pens, spilled into the surrounding fields, filling town and countryside alike with the clamor of their bleats and bellows. Within the city's walls an army was massing, the last stragglers of foot soldiers and crossbowmen trickling in to join the convoy of supplies while they awaited their orders.

The kingdom of France—as represented by the dauphin, the heir to the throne—had been invaded by England. The dauphin's position was extremely precarious. Over the last few years, the French army had sustained a series of losses so devastating that the English now held most of the northwest portion of the realm, including the all-important capital city, Paris. The dauphin's forces, by contrast, had been pushed back and were primarily concentrated in the territory south of the Loire. Perpetually on the defensive, the French troops, from the commanders down to the lowest common soldiers, were exhausted and demoralized. An aura of hopelessness had settled over the dauphin's court like a black robe of mourning.

Determined to seize the advantage and shatter what was left of their opponents' spirit, the English had sent home for reinforcements and raised a supplementary army that they used to launch a powerful new offensive. The attack struck at the very heart of the dauphin's support and terrain—the walled city of Orléans. To lose Orléans meant that England would finally pierce the barrier of the Loire, allowing its soldiers to penetrate deeply into the southern countryside that served as a buffer zone between the French royal court and the front line. To lose Orléans meant there would be nothing and no one to stop the English from surrounding the dauphin and his government and precipitating their surrender or capture. To lose Orléans meant the almost certain defeat of France.

Sensible of the larger peril, the loyal inhabitants of that vital city had for six months heroically withstood the cruel siege conditions imposed upon them by the enemy. After an initial bombardment, the English commanders, finding themselves unable to scale the walls or break through Orléans's defenses, had elected simply to surround their target, dig into entrenched positions, and wait for their opponents to either submit or starve to death.

To give voice to this struggle and provide an accurate depiction of events for posterity, the townspeople kept a daily chronicle of their ordeal, known as the *Journal of the Siege of Orléans*. "The Sunday . . . hurled the English into the city six score and four stones from bombards and great cannon, of which there was one stone weighted 116 pounds," the entry for October 17, 1428, began. "This same week did the English cannon damage or destroy twelve mills. . . . The Sunday following the twenty-fourth day of October the English attacked and took . . . the end of the bridge. . . . Thus there was no defence because none dared any longer stay in them," read subsequent reports.

As the months wore on and one by one the access routes into the city were successfully blockaded, stockpiles of provisions began to run dangerously low. Only small parties of horsemen, six or seven at a time, managed to smuggle any food at all into Orléans during the height of that terrible winter. Desperate to survive, the inhabitants launched a daring attempt to hijack a delivery of supplies bound for their English tormentors, but despite their superior numbers the French regiments were routed. The resulting defeat was so humiliating that it was recorded in the official journal as the infamous "day of the herrings," a reference to the enemy's inferior rations— salted herring in barrels—that the city had fought for but nonetheless failed to secure. As punishment for this exploit, the English tightened the grip on their victims so strongly that by spring the people of Orléans "found themselves squeezed in such necessity by the besieging enemies that they knew not whom to have recourse to for a remedy, excepting (or, unless it be) to God."

Now, in nearby Blois, what remained of the French army stoically girded itself for one final gamble in the long struggle to fend off, or at least buy time against, the seemingly invincible English. The pens of noisy barnyard animals, the carts full of wheat, the milling soldiers—all were elements of a signal relief operation organized to resupply Orléans and stave off the specter of mass starvation. The driving force behind this initiative was a leading member of the French aristocracy and one of the dauphin's oldest and most trusted advisers. A veteran of two decades of partisan French politics and civil war, the de facto head of the loyalist party, this high counselor had worked tirelessly for months to bring together not only the necessary provisions but also the most experienced warriors in France with whom to confront the English and save Orléans.

Only a power broker this masterful, a descendant of royalty possessed of the requisite administrative, diplomatic, and logistical skills, could have hoped to succeed at so demanding a task. Although this statesman's influence over the events of her time was unparalleled, neither her achievements nor her dominance has ever been recognized. Even her name has been forgotten. She was Yolande of Aragon, queen of Sicily, the dauphin's mother-in-law.

As perhaps the most astute politician of her age, Yolande of Aragon had been one of the first members of the royal council to recognize the danger represented by the English presence at Orléans, and the absolute necessity of fighting back. Determined to save her son-in-law's kingdom, which included her own lands and estates, she had summoned every weapon in her considerable arsenal—money, spies, coercion, and persuasion—to bring the rest of the French government in line with her point of view. Only the dauphin, terrified of yet another horrific defeat, had remained unconvinced. To change his mind, Yolande had been forced to resort to a highly unorthodox approach, the repercussions of which would resonate for centuries and ultimately change the course of history.

For leading this relief effort was neither duke nor general nor battle-hardened cavalry captain, but a seventeen-year-old girl dressed in armor and carrying a banner and sword—Joan of Arc, the Maid of Orléans.

• • •

THE ENIGMA OF JOAN OF ARC, the brave peasant girl who heard the voices of angels and restored the dauphin to his rightful place on the throne of France, remains as irresistible today as when she first appeared some six centuries ago. How had the Maid, a lowly commoner, gained an audience at the royal court? How had she, an illiterate young woman from a tiny village at the very edge of the kingdom, come to know so much about the complex political situation in France, and indeed, to see into the deepest recesses of her sovereign's heart? What clandestine sign had Joan revealed that convinced the dauphin of her authenticity and inspired him to follow her counsel? How had a seventeen-year-old female with no experience in warfare managed to defeat the fearsome English army, raise the siege of Orléans, and crown the king at Reims, feats that had eluded experienced French commanders twice her age?

The answers to these questions have remained hidden, not because the mystery surrounding Joan cannot be penetrated, but because their solution is inextricably tied to the life of another woman entirely, that of Yolande of Aragon, queen of Sicily. Viewed through the prism of Yolande's experiences and perspective, Joan's story abruptly makes sense, like a fragment torn from a page in a book that has been rediscovered and taped back into place. Pry open the Queen's secrets and there will be found the Maid's.

And so this is the saga of not one but two extraordinary women. It is a story filled with courage, intrigue, madness, and mysticism, which spanned a period measuring more than half a century. Best of all, although it is a work of history, at its heart lies a classic French novel, testimony to the enduring power of literature. Because Yolande's long, eventful life bookended Joan's short, tumultuous one, several decades and many chapters pass before the Maid finally makes her appearance. But it is only in this way—by the patient unraveling of the many curious twists and turns that came before, and which ultimately led to Joan's thrilling introduction to the royal court—that what had been deliberately suppressed for so many centuries may finally be revealed.

Six hundred years is a long time to wait for answers to so prominent a mystery. For those who wonder after reading these pages how it is possible that the evidence of Yolande's involvement in the story of Joan of Arc has never before been adequately explored, I can only respond that there is no more effective camouflage in history than to have been born a woman.

Joan of Arc, the Maid of Orléans.

For full fayne I wold do that might you please,
yff connyng I had in it to procede;
To me wold it be grete plesaunce and ease,
yff aught here might fourge to youre wyl in dede.

(Most gladly would I do that which might you please,
had I the cunning in it to proceed;
It would bring me great pleasure and ease,
if I might here forge something to your liking indeed.)

—*The Romance of Melusine,*
fifteenth-century English translation

Consider the effect and essence of the said science [poetry],
which is known . . . as the Joyous or Gay Science and by
another as the Science of Invention; that science which,
shining with the most pure, honorable and courtly elo-
quence, civilizes the uncouth, vitalizes the slothful, softens
the coarse, entices the learned . . . [and] *disclosing the hidden,
sheds light on things obscure.*

—edict of John I, king of Aragon,
establishing the festival of the Gay Science,
issued at Valencia, February 20, 1393

secret *n* (14c) **1 a:** something kept hidden or unexplained:
MYSTERY

—*Merriam-Webster's Collegiate Dictionary,*
11th edition

PART I
Before Joan

A queen awards prizes at court.

CHAPTER 1

The Kingdom of the Gay Science

⚜

HE SECRET HISTORY OF JOAN OF ARC begins with circumstances and events that occurred long before her youth. In the Middle Ages, antiquity crowded into the present, noisily demanding to be heard. The exploits of Alexander, Caesar, and Charlemagne were not heroic deeds to be admired at a distance but tangible goals to be emulated. Evidence of the miraculous, officially sanctioned by the Church, permeated everyday existence, blurring the distinction between reality and imagination. So it is fitting that Joan's story originates not with her own birth in 1412 but three decades earlier with that of her remarkable patron, Yolande of Aragon.

Yolande was everything Joan wasn't: of the highest rank, in contrast to Joan's humble commoner status; surrounded by wealth and privilege, as compared with the Maid's poverty; educated, where Joan was illiterate; worldly, in the face of Joan's simplicity. She was born in Barcelona on August 11, 1381. Her father, John,* was the eldest son and heir of one of the most respected and feared monarchs of the age, Pedro IV, king of Aragon. Through a combination of ruthlessness and bellicosity exceptional even by medieval standards, Pedro had amassed an empire that extended from the

---

*He is more commonly known as Joan, which is the Catalan spelling of Juan. Under the circumstances, however, this seemed unnecessarily confusing, so I have anglicized his name.

Western Europe,
Circa 1400

SCOTLAND

IRELAND

DENMARK

ENGLAND

London

NETHERLANDS

Atlantic Ocean

English Channel

Brussels

HOLY ROMAN
EMPIRE

N

FLANDERS

LUX

BOHEMIA

Paris

BAR

LORRAINE

BAVARIA

ANJOU

BURGUNDY

AUSTRIA

FRANCE

SAVOY

Milan

Venice

HUNGARY

NAVARRE

PROVENCE

PAPAL
STATES

BOSNIA

CATALONIA

CORSICA

Rome

PORTUGAL

CASTILE

ARAGON

Barcelona

Naples

Valencia

GRANADA

MAJORCA

Mediterranean Sea

SARDINIA

KINGDOM
OF NAPLES

SICILY

Pyrenees across the Mediterranean and included Aragon, Valencia, Barcelona, Catalonia, Majorca, Sardinia, Sicily, and Malta. He had reigned for
forty-five years by the time his granddaughter was born, and showed no
signs of fatigue, even recently completing his memoirs, modestly entitled
*The Book in which are contained all the great deeds that have occurred in Our House,
during the time of Our life, commencing with Our birth.*

To have so strong and accomplished a parent is not always an undiluted
blessing, and Yolande's father evidently felt the weight of paternal expectations. Rebellion comes in many forms; John chose disengagement. He
shunned territorial aggression and political intrigue in favor of the chivalric
pursuits of hunting, dances, and banquets. John threw himself into romance,
not war. When his first fiancée was fatally stricken by illness en route to the
wedding, John rode furiously to be by her side in order to hold her hand on
her deathbed even though he had never met her before. In a society that
equated a monarch's virility with military prowess, the kingdom of Aragon
boasted a crown prince who displayed a keen interest in the ways of fashion,
dabbled in music and literature (John could read and write in several lan-
guages), and had developed a distinct fondness, much to his countrymen's
disgust, for poetry.

He was also a devoted Francophile. John's first two wives hailed from
France, and when the second one died unexpectedly in 1378, he defied his
father, who demanded that he marry a princess of Sicily, and instead wedded
another Frenchwoman, Yolande of Bar.*

Theirs was a genuine love match, highly unusual for the period, a union
based upon a harmony of interests and temperament rather than strategic or
material gain. Like John, Yolande of Bar had been raised in an atmosphere
of gentility, culture, and glamour, and she too was a direct descendant of
royalty. Her mother, Marie of France, was the beloved sister of Charles V,
the French king; her father, Robert I, duke of Bar.

The duchy of Bar was of immense strategic importance to the French.
Because of its location at the extreme eastern perimeter of France, Bar was
under constant threat from its neighbor, the duke of Lorraine, a vassal of the
Holy Roman Emperor. The resulting rivalry split Bar's political identity in
half. The majority of the inhabitants living to the west of the Meuse River,

---

*Not to be confused with Yolande of Aragon, the subject of this biography. Yolande of Bar was
Yolande of Aragon's mother. Children were often named after their parents in the Middle Ages.

which flowed down the center of the duchy, considered themselves French, while those to the east identified with the empire. To maintain the loyalty of Bar was vital; that was why Marie, a French princess, had been given in marriage to its duke.

Marie had two passions in life: hunting and books. She read voraciously and accumulated not only novels and romances, but also works of theology, history, and poetry. Even more significantly, Marie gave her progeny, the girls included, the same superior education that she herself, as a member of the French royal family, had received.

Yolande of Bar was the eldest of Marie's eleven children. She too loved to hunt and especially to read. Yolande's admiration for troubadours, songs, and poetry approached the reverential. By the time of her engagement to John of Aragon in October 1379 at the age of fourteen (he was twenty-nine), she had grown into a particularly charming and vivacious adolescent. She even won over her father-in-law, who had reluctantly given his permission in a glum letter in which he scolded John for having thrown away the opportunity for a glorious reign by jilting the Sicilian heiress.

Yolande of Aragon, the woman who would have such an effect on Joan of Arc's life, was her parents' firstborn and only surviving child. Her seven younger brothers and sisters all perished in infancy or early childhood. Perhaps to assuage the terrible grief over so many deaths, life at court was especially convivial. "But this was taken to such exaggerated lengths that all life was spent in dances and ladies' assemblies," wrote a disapproving chronicler of the period.

In 1387, when the princess Yolande was six years old, her grandfather finally died and her father, John, inherited the throne. To mark the occasion, a novel cultural initiative was launched: to render Aragon famous throughout Europe as the principal center for the study and practice of the art of the troubadour, known as "the Gay Science." So many new public schools dedicated to the teaching of poetry were established that it seemed to the disapproving Aragonese baronial class that "what in bygone days had been a very respectable exercise, a relief from the travails of war in which many excellent knights . . . distinguished themselves, became debased to such a degree that all men appeared to be minstrels." A grand festival was instituted annually, at which high government officials were solemnly appointed as judges, with precious jewels awarded for the best verses.

To grow up, as Yolande of Aragon did, in this peculiarly artistic atmosphere was a unique experience in Christendom. Other European courts patronized troubadours and encouraged the literary arts, of course, but nothing like this. The point was not simply to learn to read, write, and perform verses, stories, or songs, but to incorporate the art into daily existence—to *live* poetry.

Not that there wasn't precedent for this approach. During the Middle Ages, the stories of passion and chivalry found in songs and literature routinely inspired real-life mimicry. It was not at all unusual, for example, for a knight to try to impress a lady by embarking on a quest in her name. Courts of love, where women acted as judges, deliberating over quarrels between sweethearts and meting out rewards or punishments according to the verdict handed down, were commonplace.

The difference in Aragon during Princess Yolande's childhood and adolescence was one of degree. Her parents' notions of the poetic ideal trespassed not only into the reality of everyday life but into a spiritual realm more commonly associated with worship and theology. ("All earthly things are moved by her; she influences the heavenly bodies in their courses," her father wrote of the Gay Science.) One result of this indoctrination was a predilection for literature that would accompany Yolande of Aragon into adulthood. She would spend her life surrounded by books, eventually compiling a substantial library. Upon the death of the old duke of Berry in 1416, Yolande purchased one of the most famous works in his collection, his *Belles Heures,* a magnificently illustrated manuscript made expressly for the duke during his lifetime.* (In this transaction, Yolande demonstrated not only her love of beautiful volumes, but also her familiarity with the wily ways of booksellers. The executors for the duke of Berry's estate set the value of the tome at 700 Parisian pounds, but "after having for a long time viewed and examined these Hours, [Yolande] kept them and paid to the executors the sum of only 300 Tours pounds.") When the duke of Orléans was captured by the English during the battle of Agincourt in 1415, Yolande had his entire library transferred to her castle at Saumur so that it would not fall into the hands of the enemy.

But her fascination with fiction extended beyond her desire to read and own books. She once lost herself so thoroughly in a performance by minstrels

---

*This copy of the *Belles Heures* is now part of the collection of the Cloisters Museum in New York, where it is on permanent display.

that it wasn't until the act was over that she discovered she'd had her pocket picked by a particularly audacious thief who got away not only with her purse but also with her personal seal, bearing her name and coat of arms. Her tendency to view religion in terms of parables too survived childhood. This credulity was reflected in an episode made famous by the chronicler Jehan de Bourdigné. While she was out riding one day with a large entourage, including her ladies-in-waiting, other members of her household, and four or five spaniels, Yolande's hunting dogs caught a scent and began barking and worrying at a group of bushes in front of her. Suddenly they flushed out a rabbit, which jumped for safety into her lap. Yolande immediately stopped the procession, called off the dogs, and, cradling the rabbit in her arms, asked her servants to explore the area. They discovered a large stone very close to the hare's burrow, on which all agreed appeared an image of the Virgin Mary holding the baby Jesus in her lap, just as the rabbit was then ensconced in Yolande's. Convinced that the incident was miraculous in nature, Yolande had a chapel erected at the spot to commemorate the event.

But there was one book in particular that was destined to have such a profound effect on Yolande of Aragon that it would influence the future of France itself. The book was called *The Romance of Melusine,* and it was written by Jean of Arras in 1393, when Yolande was twelve years old. What was so interesting about *The Romance of Melusine* was that it was a work of fiction commissioned and written specifically to address a political controversy.

JEAN OF ARRAS was a secretary to the duke of Berry, brother of both Charles V, king of France, and Yolande's grandmother, Marie, duchess of Bar, and one of the most powerful nobles in France. As a ranking member of the royal family, the duke of Berry had been given the task of administering that portion of southern France that included Poitou, whose capital city was Poitiers. He was known for being a rather grasping fellow, with a tendency to appropriate other people's property for his own use. In the 1380s, the duke of Berry decided that he needed a more impressive residence at which to stay on those occasions when he left Paris to visit his southern territories, so he seized a particularly ancient and imposing castle that had long been in the possession of a local family by the name of Lusignan, had his soldiers throw out the current owners, and moved in.

The duke had failed to reckon, however, with the political strength of his evictees. The Lusignans came from a leading clan of aristocrats, the counts of La Marche, who had persistently exercised power in the area. Their ancestry was extremely prestigious—a century earlier, a Lusignan had married a former queen of England, and another had ruled Cyprus—and they did not appreciate having their castle lifted from them as though they were no better than a pack of serfs. They mounted a vigorous opposition to the duke's action, and such was the weight of their name and the esteem in which the family was held locally that the rebellion threatened to spread and undermine French authority generally in the region.

The duke of Berry was in a bind. To retreat from his initial position and return the castle to its rightful owners would be a demonstration of weakness that could set a precedent for further acts of insubordination. Besides, he liked the castle. It was the nicest one in the area, and he felt that since his pedigree and authority were superior to those of the Lusignans, who were after all his subjects, he should have it. On the other hand, he did not relish having to go to war over it. This meant he had to come up with a good reason for the appropriation. Luckily for the duke, the Lusignan family had something of a history of sedition, having occasionally conspired with England against France in the preceding centuries. If they could somehow be linked to the English in the present day, the summary acquisition of their castle would not appear as usurpation but as the rightful return of property to the French crown. In 1387, the duke of Berry charged his secretary, Jean of Arras, with undertaking this delicate task of propaganda, and *The Romance of Melusine* was the astonishing result.

Melusine, set in the not too distant past, told the story of Raymondin, youngest son of the earl of the Forest. The earl was an impecunious aristocrat who had sired many children and was therefore receptive to his cousin Aimery's suggestion that Aimery adopt Raymondin. Aimery, the count of Poitiers, was an extremely wealthy and learned man, who was schooled in civil and canon law, science, and especially astrology. He was also very fond of hunting.

Accordingly, Raymondin came to live with Aimery in Poitiers. He was very respectful and served his cousin to the best of his abilities, and in turn was treated as a beloved son. All went well until one day, five or six years later, when Aimery and a large retinue of knights, including Raymondin, went off to hunt in the forest.

Once in the wood, the hunters encountered a wild boar and the chase was on. In the excitement of the pursuit, Aimery and Raymondin rode faster than the others and were soon separated from the group. The boar drew them deeper and deeper into the wilderness. As night fell, they realized they were lost.

As they were searching for a way out of the wood, Aimery studied the stars, which shone very brightly that night, and marveled at what they told him. He explained to Raymondin that the heavens augured a strange enterprise: "The adventure is this: that if, at this present hour, a subject were to kill his lord, he would become the richest, most powerful, and most honored of all his line, and from him would issue such a noble lineage that it would be spoken of and remembered until the end of the world." Upset by this portent (with good reason, as it turned out), Aimery turned to Raymondin and exclaimed, "O Lord God! Why doth fortune make a man prosper by ill-doing?"

Instead of replying, Raymondin, to ease the earl's distress, stopped his horse and built a small fire so they could rest in comfort. As they were warming themselves by the flames, the wild boar they had been chasing earlier suddenly burst out of the wood and attacked. Aimery bravely stepped forward to strike down the boar with his sword but missed his aim. Raymondin's blow went similarly astray, but to disastrous results; glancing off the boar's back, Raymondin's sword instead pierced Aimery, who went down. The wild beast charged again, and to save himself Raymondin pulled his blade out of Aimery and struck down the creature. Safe at last, he turned back to the earl, only to find Aimery dead of the wounds inflicted by his sword.

Distraught, Raymondin at first considered suicide, but, remembering that this was a sin against God, instead climbed into his saddle and rode despondently through the wood, not caring where he went. Eventually, his horse led him to a fountain known to be frequented by fairies. It was at this fountain that Raymondin encountered Melusine.

Melusine was a fairy in the guise of a beautiful woman. She was a mixed-breed—half human, half sprite—of regal lineage. Her father was the king of Albanie (the medieval name for Scotland); her mother, Presine, a fairy. When she was fifteen, Melusine punished her father for betraying her mother, and her mother in turn punished *her* for not showing enough respect to her father—fairies clearly took their parental responsibilities seriously—by casting a spell that turned Melusine into a serpent from the waist down every Saturday. But it wasn't Saturday when Raymondin met her, so he couldn't tell that she was a fairy. To him, she was simply a well-dressed, extremely attractive woman of obviously high aristocratic birth.

At first, Raymondin, lost in his own grief, failed even to notice Melusine, but she soon succeeded in securing his attention by calling him by name and recounting the source of his sorrow, much to his astonishment. Then, in a speech extraordinary for its prescience, Melusine offered her aid to Raymondin:

"In God's name, Raymondin, I am, after God, the one who can help and advance you the most in this mortal world, in whatever adversity befalls you. . . . And may you know that I well know that you think me some phantom or diabolical creation in my deeds and words, but I assure you that I am sent by order of God . . . and a true Catholic. . . . May you also know with certainty that without me or my advice you cannot accomplish your goals . . . for I will make you the most noble, most sovereign and greatest member ever of your lineage, and the most powerful mortal on earth."

Melusine's intimate knowledge of his predicament, her insistence that she was a messenger from God and a true daughter of the Church, and above all the confidence she projected persuaded Raymondin of her legitimacy. He agreed to marry her, accepting her condition that as long as they lived he was never to follow her on a Saturday but to leave her alone in privacy. After their marriage, as she had pledged, Raymondin, through his wife, became one of the greatest lords of his time. As one of her first acts as a married woman, Melusine built a mighty castle, with high towers and a strong dungeon, which she christened "Lusignan" after the latter part of her name; it was the first of many cities, towns, and castles in Poitou, including Parthenay and La Rochelle, that Melusine founded and gave to Raymondin. With Melusine's aid, as prophesied by the stars, Raymondin eventually took over his cousin Aimery's lands and estates, and became an even wealthier and more powerful lord than the former count of Poitiers.

Also as promised, Melusine gave Raymondin many sons, ten in all, ensuring an unbroken line of descendants. They were all strong, well made, and healthy, but, being of fairy ancestry, were also born with strange defects. The eldest had a "huge mouth and large great nostrils"; another had a complexion like fire; still another possessed only one eye ("though he could see more clearly than a person with two eyes, for all their plenty"). The sixth son, Geoffrey, had an immense tooth, while the eighth, Horrible, was born with three eyes and (perhaps understandably) a wicked disposition. These abnormalities in no way inhibited Melusine's sons from prospering in the world; most performed feats of great courage in battle, and consequently married beautiful princesses and became illustrious kings, further adding to Raymondin's prestige. Only Geoffrey of the great tooth and Horrible of the three eyes brought shame upon their parents: Geoffrey by burning down an abbey filled with monks, one of whom was his brother, a member of the Order; Horrible for having so pernicious a temperament that Melusine was ultimately forced to advise her husband to have him killed, lest Horrible perpetually sow the seeds of war and famine among Raymondin's subjects.

But Geoffrey and Horrible were not to be the cause of the family's downfall; that distinction belonged to Raymondin. For despite all Melusine had done for him, eventually there came a Saturday when Raymondin, prodded by his father, the earl of the Forest, could no longer resist the urge to spy on her. Making a small hole in the door of her room with his sword, he peered through and, catching his wife in the bath, discovered her to be a large snake from the waist down. When in anger he later confronted her with this information, calling her a serpent, she cried:

"Evil was the hour and season wherein I first saw thy treason and falseness! Thine unmeasurable language has condemned me to eternal pain. . . . Had you kept your covenant truly, I should have been a woman at all hours, and, at death, the King of Glory would have borne away my soul, and I should have been buried with great honor. Alas! I must now suffer pain. . . . God pardon you for being the cause of my suffering torment."

Thus tragically betrayed, Melusine assumed the form of a serpent and flew around her namesake castle of Lusignan, as a public warning to others who would violate a solemn oath. "Melusine came to Lusignan and circled it three times, shrieking woefully in a plaintive female voice. Up in the fortress and in the town below, people were utterly amazed; they knew not what to think, for they could see the form of a serpent, yet they heard the lady's voice issuing forth from it." Significantly, before she left, Melusine vowed to appear again in the future, "if not in the air, [then] on the earth or by this fountain," whenever mastery of the castle was about to change hands, as a sign of the lawful rights of the new owner.

By this device did the author, Jean of Arras, cleverly complete the task assigned to him by his employer. For at the end of *The Romance of Melusine,* the fairy reappears in the bedroom of the castle of Lusignan, both as a serpent and as a beautiful woman, "to tell the last English tenant . . . that it must be handed over to its besieger, the duke of Berry," thereby justifying the duke's claim.

Jean of Arras's book was not a completely original work. The legend of the fairy Melusine had been around, in various incarnations, for decades. Jean in fact based his story partly on some old writings purporting to recount Melusine's exploits found in the castle of Lusignan by the duke of Berry when he moved in. But what Jean of Arras did, to brilliant effect, was to seamlessly weave together fact and fiction, past and present, for the express purpose of lobbying public support for a piece of partisan shenanigans. "It is in Jean d'Arras, for perhaps the first time in vernacular European literature, that we find the fairy realm joined to the contemporary, political

Raymondin breaks his vow and spies on Melusine on a Saturday.

world for the purpose of making political allegory," observed Professor Stephen G. Nichols, a specialist in medieval French history and literature.

The Romance of Melusine, written in Latin but translated promptly by the author into French, was a phenomenal success. Because of its overwhelming popularity, versions of the book appeared in England, Spain, and Germany. Nearly a century later it was one of the very first volumes (after the Bible) printed in Geneva in 1478 with Gutenberg's newfangled invention of movable type. In France, Jean of Arras's work acquired such a huge, enthusiastic, and loyal readership that it was almost impossible for a literate person not to be aware of the book. The novel was distributed at festivals as a mark of special favor. Significantly, in 1444 the court of Lorraine ordered the production of a beautifully bound copy that was presented as a gift to Charles VII, king of France. With the arrival of the printing press, *The Romance of Melusine* went through twenty editions in French in the fifteenth century alone.

The great strength of this work was that it managed to flatter both parties in the dispute. The story recognized and celebrated the Lusignans' history of great men and stirring deeds, immortalizing the family by providing them with a genealogy that traced their antecedents to royalty, a tactic that at the same time augmented the duke of Berry's achievement in taking their castle away from them. Moreover, by associating the previous occupant of the fortress with the English, Jean of Arras lent to his patron's otherwise selfish actions the stirring aura of French nationalism. Everyone who read *The Romance of Melusine* at the time it was written understood its political implications, and support for the duke of Berry's position increased proportionately. The duke was very pleased with his secretary.

This book, so admired throughout Europe, was of even greater importance to the princess Yolande of Aragon and her family. For although Jean of Arras had written the romance at the request of the duke of Berry, he had dedicated the work to the duke's sister, Marie, duchess of Bar. "And to the pleasure of my Right high and mighty lord John, son to the king of France, duke of Berry . . . the which history [Melusine's] I have begun after the true chronicles which I have had of him . . . and because his noble sister, Marie, daughter of the king of France and duchess of Bar, had Required my said lord to have the history," Jean of Arras inscribed in the opening to his book. In fact, according to French scholarship, *The Romance of Melusine* was written not only "for the amusement of Marie of France" but also to aid in the "political education of the children" of the duchess of Bar.* Jean of Arras even based two of the characters in the romance on Marie's eldest daughter, the queen of Aragon, and her husband, King John. Everyone associated with Marie—friends and family—received copies.

That the novel was dedicated to her grandmother and that her parents were a source of inspiration to the author would have only increased the value of the work in Princess Yolande's eyes. This was the book of her family.

And so, decades later, when Joan of Arc, claiming to be a messenger from God, appeared at the royal court of Chinon and approached the dauphin with the words, "Very noble lord dauphin, I have come and I have been sent from God to bring aid to you and to the kingdom," the resemblance to Melusine would have been immediate and profound. As a result, Joan did not have to overcome resistance in order to convince Yolande of Aragon of the genuineness of her mission.

On the contrary. Yolande was waiting for her.

---

*Almost all the incidents depicted in *The Romance of Melusine*—the adventures of Melusine's children, for example—refer to actual episodes in French history, many associated with the duchy of Bar. That's why the work was considered such a useful tool for teaching children.

CHAPTER 2

To Be
a
Queen

ESPITE HER PARENTS' preoccupation with troubadour culture, Princess Yolande's education was not limited to poetry, books, and music. She also gleaned the fundamentals of rule and government through firsthand observation of the workings of the court. On his ascension to the throne, her father had inherited a vast empire that required a significant degree of political wrangling with the various representative assemblies, known as *cortes,* from Catalonia, Valencia, and Majorca as well as Aragon.

The administration of so large a territory was a daunting task, and one for which John, who was frequently ill—it has been hypothesized that he suffered from a form of epilepsy—was particularly unsuited. To compensate for the king's deficiencies, his wife inserted herself aggressively into the governing process. In 1388, when John impatiently threatened to disband a particularly fractious meeting of the general assembly, Queen Yolande stepped in and provided the diplomatic initiatives necessary to effect compromise between the crown and its regional representatives. The queen also participated in all the royal councils and accompanied the king on his official visits throughout the realm. "She was very interested in the affairs of state and she wanted always to be at his [the king's] side, using to her advantage the talents of a woman who knew herself to be beloved by her husband," wrote Spanish scholar Rafael Tasis I Marca. Yolande of Bar's activist role, which antagonized many of the functionaries of her husband's court, strongly influenced her daughter's perceptions of the responsibilities associated with government.

But of course the principal civic duty of any medieval princess, particularly one who hailed from so prestigious a realm as Aragon, was to attract the marital attentions of a similarly illustrious suitor, and thereby produce a match that would bring honor, wealth, and territory, or at least some combination of the three, to the kingdom. This obligation Yolande of Aragon managed to fulfill while still a child. For no sooner had her father succeeded to the throne in 1387 than two high-ranking ambassadors, representing the king of Sicily, appeared at the royal court to formally request the princess's hand. The king of Sicily being only ten years old at the time, the ambassadors were actually sent by his mother, the formidable Marie of Blois. If the councillors to the court of Aragon thought Yolande of Bar an ambitious woman who meddled too much in affairs of state, in Marie of Blois they were about to get an education as to what a resolute and indefatigable female could achieve in the political arena when she set her mind to it.

MARIE OF BLOIS was the widow of Louis I, duke of Anjou, count of Provence, and (even though he was French to his core) king of Sicily. Louis I was another of Charles V's many siblings, which meant he was also the brother of the duchess of Bar.* In the complicated mess that was the genealogy of the French royal family, this made him the queen of Aragon's uncle, so Marie of Blois was Yolande of Bar's aunt.

Until the last years of his life, the kingdom of Sicily, which in the fourteenth century encompassed most of Italy south of Rome, was little more to Louis I than a drawing on a map. But in 1381, his distant cousin Joanna I, queen of Naples, Jerusalem, and Sicily, had been threatened with invasion and, desperate for allies, had offered to make Louis her heir if he came to her aid. This proposition was too tempting to be refused, and so the following year Louis, adding the prestigious denomination "King of Sicily" to his title, had raised a tremendous army and crossed into Italy. Large armies move slowly, however, and by the time he made it down to Naples, Joanna I was dead and the kingdom held by a rival militia. Louis attempted to take

---

*Charles V, king of France, had three brothers—Louis I, duke of Anjou; Jean, duke of Berry; and Philip the Bold, duke of Burgundy—and three sisters—Joan, queen of Navarre; Marie, duchess of Bar; and Isabelle, duchess of Milan.

his legacy by force, but his troops had been decimated by sickness and star-vation on the long march south and he was unable to secure a military vic-tory. Refusing to surrender the inheritance he had risked everything to claim, he retreated to the eastern coast of Italy and sent to France for rein-forcements. Louis's persistence was admirable but his luck rather less felici-tous, and he died soon thereafter of a chill contracted at a drafty castle, before the requested supplementary regiments had time to arrive.

By any reasonable standard, Louis I's dream of sovereignty should have died when he did. The French ruling family had no political experience in southern Italy, no knowledge of local customs or the serpentine nature of the various family and baronial alliances necessary to maintain power. They were hazy even on the geography of the place. But none of this stopped Louis's widow, Marie of Blois, from relentlessly pursuing what she consid-ered to be her family's lawful inheritance. She was an intensely practical middle-aged woman and must have known that her chances of succeeding at so ambitious a quest were low. But she had two sons, the eldest of whom, Louis II, was just seven when his father died, and opportunities to claim large, prestigious kingdoms didn't materialize every day. Marie had no intention of letting this one slip by without a fight.

The first step was to get little Louis II officially recognized as count of Provence. This was itself a difficult task, as most of the towns in the county, hearing of the death of Louis I, were in revolt. To achieve her goal, Marie would have to force the rebellious Provençal barons, grown men all, to go down on one knee and do homage to her son.

And so at the age of forty Marie pawned her valuables, everything she owned right down to the gold and silver dinner service, and bought herself an army. It wasn't a large army—only "400 lances," which translated into about fifteen hundred men—but Marie counted on its being just formidable enough to give the opposition pause. Then, with her son by her side, and her remaining money from this transaction conveniently stashed in silver coins in her saddlebags, she led her force into Provence.

She stopped in village after village, introducing Louis II to the local officials and noblemen, graciously listening to their grievances and, more important, dispensing privileges and largesse. With her gifts of silver and her ever-present soldiers hovering ominously by her side, Marie proved herself a master of the art of carrot and stick. Her reputation swelled as town after town, baron after baron, came over to her side and paid homage to her son. "And for certain this lady was very astute in her ability to determine who could serve and help her . . . and for magnanimity and courage of heart she exceeded many of the princes of her time and for this reason was greatly feared, prized, and esteemed," observed Jehan de Bourdigné. The rebellion fizzled in the face of Marie's steely-eyed determination, personal charm, and large cache of cash. By the fall of 1387, Louis II's authority was firmly established and at the age of ten he was able to enter the capital city of Aix, where he was accorded all of the rights, dignities, and income due to the official count of Provence.

Having secured her son's inheritance, Marie looked to similarly settle his future. No sooner was Louis II formally invested with his title than his mother made her first overture to the court of Aragon, sending two high-ranking Provençal knights to King John to ask for the hand of the princess Yolande in marriage. John was interested enough to send an envoy to Provence to discuss the details, and even seems to have committed himself, in a general way, to the alliance.

Having come this far, Marie continued to lobby aggressively for her son's advancement, and especially for his legitimate installation as king of Sicily. By this time, Charles V was dead, and his son, Charles VI, had ascended to the throne of France. Charles VI was very fond of his young cousin and lent authority to Marie's cause, first by knighting Louis II at a grand celebration held in Saint-Denis, and then by agreeing to attend a coronation for the boy in Avignon, seat of the papal court.

At last, on All Saints' Day, November 1, 1389, in a solemn ceremony witnessed by an august assembly including the king of France and his reti-nue, the pope crowned twelve-year-old Louis II king of Sicily, Naples, and Jerusalem.* With the public support of the French crown came aid of a more tangible nature, and the following August, Marie had the satisfaction of watching her son, accompanied by a papal legate, sail out of Marseille at the head of a fleet of warships bound for Naples, with the intention of conquer-ing his kingdom.

She would not see him again for nine years.

NEGOTIATIONS BETWEEN Marie of Blois and the court of Aragon for a marriage between her son and Princess Yolande had continued throughout

---

*In France, this title was always referred to as simply "King of Sicily"—the rest was understood.

the period preceding Louis II's embarkation for Italy. An alliance with King John was critical to the success of Marie's plans. The crown of Aragon controlled much of the Mediterranean, including the island of Sicily itself. Marie could not take the risk that powerful Aragon would try to thwart her son's title to his adopted kingdom by sending an army to fight against him. A way had to be found to neutralize Aragonese ambitions in southern Italy. To unite both parties' interests by arranging a marriage between Louis II and Yolande of Aragon seemed the perfect solution.

But while such a union was certainly to be desired by Marie of Blois and her family, the advantages to Aragon were less obvious, particularly as Louis II's uncles, the dukes of Berry and Burgundy, demanded a dowry of at least 200,000 francs. This seemed a large sum to pay for a thirteen-year-old king who had yet to secure his realm. Yolande was an only child, and a very pretty one at that, and her parents were convinced that their daughter's royal lineage, powerful connections, and considerable personal charms merited a brilliant match. The marriage negotiations with Provence ground to a halt. To extricate the crown of Aragon from whatever legal difficulties might arise from the verbal assurances given in the past, when she was eleven years old, Yolande signed a document disavowing any promise made by her or her ambassadors on the grounds that these had been wrung from her before she reached thirteen, the age of consent.

In this way was the ground laid for the appearance of a rival suitor, and in due course he presented himself. In 1395, when Yolande was fourteen, emissaries from the recently widowed Richard II, king of England, arrived at her parents' favorite castle at Zaragoza to solicit the princess's hand. A nuptial agreement with the twenty-eight-year-old Richard, who actually ruled his kingdom, and had the sort of financial, diplomatic, and military resources that might prove useful to Aragon in the future, was much more in keeping with her parents' views of their daughter's station in life, and they entered into negotiations enthusiastically.

This marriage, with its implied expectation of an alliance at the highest levels between France's perpetual enemy, England, and the powerful kingdom of Aragon, was sufficiently disquieting to provoke an energetic response from the French king. Charles VI hastily offered the hand of his own daughter, Isabelle, supplemented by a massive dowry of 500,000 francs to Richard. Despite the French princess's extreme youth—she was six years old—Charles VI's proposal was accepted by the English, and Isabelle and a down payment of 200,000 francs were conducted to London, there to await the bride's reaching the venerable age of thirteen or fourteen, at which point it would be legally permissible for her patient middle-aged husband to consummate the marriage, the trigger at which the remaining 300,000 francs of the dowry would be paid.*

Any hopes for the appearance of a third royal suitor were dashed the following year when King John, out riding in yet another hunt—perhaps not the happiest choice of sport for a man with epilepsy—was thrown, or more likely fell, from his horse and died. Yolande of Bar did everything she could to retain ownership of both her crown and the royal castle at Zaragoza, even going so far as to claim that she was pregnant with the king's posthumous male heir. But after a few months this ruse was inevitably discovered, and the queen was forced to give way to the new king of Aragon, John's younger brother, Martin.

The responsibility for choosing Princess Yolande's future husband now fell to her uncle, and the issue was revisited almost immediately when yet another ambassador, this one representing the French court, appeared in Zaragoza. The indefatigable Marie of Blois had prevailed upon the French king to help her bring about the union of her house with that of Aragon, and to please her Charles VI sent one of his most trusted knights to lobby for the marriage of Yolande to Louis II. The new king of Aragon, with an unmarried sixteen-year-old girl on his hands, was receptive to the idea, but negotiations again foundered, this time because the bride herself opposed the match. Her objection to Louis II did not seem to be personal—after all, she'd never met the man—but rather political. Yolande, having been raised in Aragon, identified with her native kingdom. Louis II's interests in Sicily clashed with those of her homeland. If she married him, she knew she would be expected to support French ambitions in Italy over those of Aragon, and this she did not wish to do.

Yolande's willingness to set herself in opposition to this marriage, and so attempt to exert some control over her future, demonstrated both considerable spirit and a sophisticated understanding of the political situation. But against a veteran campaigner like Marie of Blois she was outmatched. With the return of the now twenty-two, still unmarried Louis II to Provence in

---

*Three years later, when his French bride was still only nine, an heirless Richard would be summarily deposed by his cousin Henry IV. He should have married Yolande.

July 1399—remarkably, his forces had managed to hold the capital city of Naples for nine years until he was ousted by an adept rival—Marie sent her ambassadors again to Aragon on her son's behalf, and this time succeeded. With his niece rapidly approaching an age when she would no longer be considered quite as desirable as a bride, King Martin came to terms with the Provençal envoys. His relief in having the matter settled may be inferred from the alacrity with which he agreed to pay the 200,000-franc dowry. Princess Yolande was forced to publicly retract her objection to the marriage.

The wedding, to be held in Arles, was planned for the following December. The bride, accompanied by a splendid retinue, left Zaragoza in the fall of 1400 and began the long journey to Provence. King Martin, with more pressing business to attend to, declined to leave Aragon for the ceremony, and delegated one of his cousins as his surrogate.

Yolande of Aragon's reputation for handsomeness preceded her. The Monk of Saint-Denis, writing of her at the time of her marriage in the monastery's official chronicle, rhapsodized, "This princess captivated all eyes with her exceptional beauty, the charms of her face and the dignity that emanated from her whole person. In a word, she was a genuine treasure of graces. The wise said that Nature had enjoyed creating her and bestowed on her every possible perfection; she lacked only immortality. I will not attempt to describe her beauty; suffice to say that she was beyond compare." She was "one of the most beautiful creatures that one could see," agreed the chronicler Jean Juvenal des Ursins, who knew her.

Anxious to set eyes on so admirable a paragon of feminine charm (or more likely suspicious that the accolades were a little too effusive to be true), the prospective bridegroom found himself too impatient to wait at Arles for Yolande to appear as protocol demanded. Instead, Louis II raced to Montpellier, which was along the wedding party's route. There he disguised himself and hid among the crowd that had massed to view the royal procession in all its magnificence. The princess of Aragon and her entourage passed through as planned; Louis was able to get a good long look at his intended without being observed himself; and, finding (no doubt to his intense relief) that she passed muster, galloped back to Provence with a light heart in plenty of time for the official reception.

Yolande of Aragon arrived in Arles on December 1, 1400. She made a grand entrance into the city, a canopy of gold cloth embroidered with her coat of arms and those of her future husband held over her head by four syndics. She was received by her husband-to-be and future mother-in-law "with all expressions of honor and joy," and was married the next day by a cardinal in front of an audience that included many high-ranking members of the Church and the Provençal aristocracy. Afterward, the newlyweds repaired to their castle to receive the homage of the local baronage, and the following days were given over to feasting and merrymaking, to mark the momentous and glorious nature of the occasion.

Marie of Blois had succeeded in corralling the daughter-in-law of her choice. Little did she know that in doing so, she had also saved France.

FOR A MARRIAGE that had begun with the wife's repeated refusal of the husband, Yolande of Aragon and Louis II got along very well together. They would be married for seventeen years and there was never a hint of

Portrait of Louis I of Anjou and his wife, Marie of Blois,
Yolande of Aragon's formidable mother-in-law.

scandal or infidelity about either one of them. They seem actually to have loved each other.

Of course, the readiness with which Yolande and Louis II fell into a harmonious conjugal relation might easily be traced, at least in the beginning, to their opulent, carefree, and highly agreeable lifestyle. The revenue from the rents and taxes on Louis's holdings in Anjou, Maine, and Provence were substantial, and this income, in combination with Yolande's impressive dowry, vaulted the young couple into the realm of the extremely wealthy. They owned more castles than they knew what to do with, and these were so conveniently placed that every year they could spend the hottest months of the summer in Anjou in the north and then migrate south for the cold of winter to warm and sunny Provence. Louis II's castle in Angers, the capital city of Anjou, was one of the largest and most important fortresses in France. It was capable of housing an entire army and was composed of seventeen massive stone towers, each of which rose nearly one hundred feet in the air. The area enclosed by the outside walls was so expansive that Louis II's father, Louis I, had been able to erect his own luxury palace within the fortress's grounds—a castle within a castle—and to decorate its main hall with a magnificent tapestry that measured a full seventy-five feet in length depicting the Revelation of Saint John the Divine. Louis II and Yolande also owned an exquisite castle in Saumur, whose storybook looks and crenellated towers were immortalized in a famous illustration in *The Very Rich Hours of the Duke of Berry*. Additionally, they possessed several castles in Provence, including the strategically placed stronghold of Tarascon and a more elegant citadel in Aix.

Naturally, the upkeep on all of these estates required a substantial investment. Adding no doubt to the felicity of the nuptial experience, Louis II generously allotted his wife an annual allowance of 10,000 gold francs, an immense sum. With this, Yolande paid the expenses of her numerous household: chamberlain, valets, kitchen staff, greengrocers, stablemen, riders, guards, kennel keepers (for her hunting dogs), tailor, furrier, shoemaker, chaplain, and secretary. She also kept ten maids of honor and three ladies-in-waiting, all of whom were chosen from among the most aristocratic families within their respective provinces. Further reconciling Yolande to the rigors of early married life was the need to dress in accordance with her husband's royal status. The new queen of Sicily's clothes were breathtaking—silks and velvets in brilliant hues of ruby, azure, emerald, and violet; cloth of gold trimmed in the rich fur of white ermine; tiaras and brooches encrusted with pearls, diamonds, and sapphires, and for official state occasions, a crown of gold. Extravagant cone-shaped hats called turrets and extra-wide sleeves were all the fashion in the fifteenth century, and no one's turret rose higher or sleeves trailed longer than Yolande of Aragon's. Her wardrobe was so splendid that she provoked a number of sermons by disapproving clergymen on the evils of earthly vanity.

Many similarly happy marriages in the Middle Ages foundered when the wife failed to produce an heir quickly, but here too the king and queen of Sicily were blessed. Yolande's first child, born in 1403, was a son, Louis III, followed quickly by a daughter, Marie, in 1404. Her second son, René, who would inherit his mother's passion for literature, was born in 1409; then came another daughter, Yolande, in 1412; and, finally, a third son, Charles, in 1414. Although she did lose a third daughter in infancy, in general Yolande was spared her own mother's terrible childbearing ordeal as her five remaining progeny all survived into adulthood. No wonder, then, that the king and queen of Sicily, surrounded by wealth and privilege, and with a hereditary line firmly established, were envied for their affectionate relationship, so much so that the chronicler Jehan de Bourdigné recorded that "it was joyful to see the warm, fervent love between these two young people."

But these advantages were accompanied by significant responsibilities. It was understood that Louis II's primary task was to raise an army, return to Naples, and recapture the kingdom of Sicily. For all the titles, the clothes and the jewels, the great estates and deferential treatment, a king who could not control his realm was not really a king, and Louis II was determined to bend southern Italy to his rule.

That meant that the administration of his other properties—the great French duchies of Anjou and Maine in the north and the independent county of Provence in the south—would have to be left to his wife. Yolande would be expected not only to collect customs and rents, but to sit on governing councils, settle disputes among the baronage, make decisions concerning the raising or lowering of taxes (subject to approval by the French throne in the case of Anjou and Maine), keep the peace, and ensure the loyalty of her husband's subjects during his many absences. And she had to do all of this for large tracts of territory that were separated by nearly four hundred miles, a journey that took the fastest courier a full two weeks to cover on horseback. It took even longer for the household to make this trip: whenever they moved from Anjou to Provence or back, Yolande and Louis eschewed the overland route and instead traveled with all of their possessions, family members, and servants by barge either up or down the Loire and Rhône (depending on whether they were coming or going), a cruise that could take as long as eight weeks. Yolande was also obliged to help Louis II raise and outfit an invasion force, after which it was her responsibility to continue to supply him through the port of Marseille, or to marshal additional ships and troops in the event of unforeseen difficulties.

Emotionally and intellectually, Yolande's upbringing was of great help in tackling these numerous duties. Even more important, she did not come to her marriage as an unprepared child of thirteen or fourteen, but rather as a secure and poised young woman of nineteen who understood the nature of rule.

But it is one thing to understand how power works in a general way through observation, quite another to master the details, especially for regions as diverse culturally, economically, and politically as Anjou and Provence. The inhabitants of Louis II's northern territories did not even use the same calendar as those of his Provençal subjects.* The feudal customs were different and the privileges granted to each baronage varied from place to place, sometimes from town to town. In Provence, exports of salt from the mines of Hyères provided a large source of income and had to be monitored; in Anjou there were rents on manors to be collected. Competent officials had to be identified and appointed to ensure the smooth functioning of each local government, and the opinions and grievances of the various regional councils had to be duly noted and addressed.

A daunting undertaking for any young woman, but in this instance too Yolande's path was smoothed by careful instruction from a highly experienced mentor: her mother-in-law, Marie of Blois. For the first four years of their marriage, Louis's mother was a dominant presence in the life of the young couple, and her daughter-in-law clearly benefited from the older woman's knowledge and contacts. There was no aspect of governance with which Marie was not familiar, and her grasp of finance was impressive. "For twenty-two years she had indeed administered with such order and foresight the income derived from Provence, Anjou, and Maine, that she was

---

*In Anjou they used the French calendar, which began the New Year at Easter. In Provence they used the Italian calendar, which started the New Year on January 1.

able to support, in the name of her eldest son Louis, the war for Naples begun by his father, and to provide this son with the upkeep needed to maintain his royal status," confirmed the official chronicler for the monastery of Saint-Denis. "Her intimate counselors insist that she had amassed from the revenue of these domains a private treasure of 200,000 écus of gold." Even on her deathbed, Yolande's mother-in-law left the young couple with a sage (and prophetic) example of her uncanny ability to anticipate and compensate for future adversity. "When her last hour approached, she devoutly received the final sacraments of the Church; after which she called her son to her and revealed to him this secret," wrote the Monk of Saint-Denis, referring to Marie's extensive savings. "The young prince, justifiably surprised, gently demanded why, during the time where he had recently been in distress, she had not been more generous with him. She responded that she had been afraid that he would be taken prisoner, and that she had always wanted to have money in reserve, to save him from the shame of having to beg his ransom from everybody and anybody."

This issue of ransom was central to fifteenth-century warfare. The expenses associated with raising and maintaining armies were prohibitive, and a favorite way to recoup costs was to capture a royal antagonist and hold him hostage for a crippling sum. As usual, Marie had seen clearly to the core of this issue: with so much money at stake, not even the closest of friends or allies could be relied on for funds; only members of the immediate family would care enough to bankrupt themselves to ransom a loved one. Her son's royal rank ensured that this threat of capture and ransom would dog him whenever he undertook to assert his rights to southern Italy, and she was warning him, and by implication Yolande, of the need to be prepared for this eventuality. This last admonition on the part of her mother-in-law was one that would resonate with Yolande of Aragon.

Marie died peacefully in June 1404. It was well for Yolande that she had had the benefit of this remarkable woman's counsel. For not even Marie of Blois could have anticipated the terrible darkness, the pernicious violence, the wanton destruction and bloodshed that would overtake the once-mighty kingdom of France in the coming decades. A storm of epic proportions was brewing, brought about in equal parts by insanity, ambition, and greed, and this tempest would rage until Joan of Arc, an obscure peasant girl of extraordinary courage, suddenly stepped out of the shadows to quell it.

CHAPTER 3

The Mad King
of
France

⚜

ISTORY IS COMMONLY depicted as a tangled skein
of cause and effect, design and fate, so interwoven as
to make it impossible to isolate any one factor as key
to the progression of human affairs. But this was not
the case in France during the first two decades of the
fifteenth century, where almost every disturbance
in the political arena can be traced back to one fundamental determinant: the insanity of Charles VI. Here was a madness so
pervasive, so destabilizing, that it afflicted not only a king but a kingdom.

Possibly the most poignant aspect of the whole predicament was the
potential Charles VI exhibited at the start of his reign. He inherited his
throne in 1380 when he was just eleven and his younger brother, Louis, later
duke of Orléans, eight. The old king, Charles V, had managed to recover
most of the territory lost to England during the first half of the Hundred
Years War and so was able to leave his eldest son a relatively strong and peaceful kingdom. The specter of conquest by England, which had haunted France
in the middle of the century, faded, and in the boy king's youthful energy
there was every hope for the future.

Charles VI was a charming scamp, high-spirited, fun-loving, and socia-
ble. Christine de Pizan, who knew him, described Charles as a tall, well-
built young man, attractive even with his prominent nose. (Both Charles
and his younger brother Louis, duke of Orléans, inherited their father's dis-
tinctive proboscis.) Unlike Charles V, who had been sickly, preferring books

and scholars to physical activity, Charles VI was an athlete who loved nothing better than a good joust, a trait that augured well for his ability to protect his kingdom in times of strife. His personality too differed markedly from Charles V's in a manner that, in hindsight, betrayed his later affliction: the son was quixotic and impetuous where the father had been coldly calculating.

Because the new king was still so young, until he came of age France was ruled by his uncles, the dukes of Berry and Burgundy, acting as regents. Unfortunately, they used this transitional phase to seize as much money, power, and territory as was possible. During this period, for example, the duke of Berry stole the castle of Lusignan.

But while the duke of Berry was certainly avaricious, he was also timid. As a result, he was no match for his brother the duke of Burgundy, who displayed no such weakness. "The Duke of Burgundy," declared the chronicler Jean Froissart, "was the greatest personage in France next to the King." Known as Philip the Bold for his predatory policies, the duke of Burgundy busied himself during Charles VI's minority with extending his influence to the north and east of France. He had earlier married the countess of Flanders, heir to one of the richest provinces in Europe, and so gained an interest not only in her domain but in Belgium and the Netherlands as well. Nearer to his home demesne of Burgundy in eastern France, he sought an alliance with his neighbor, the duke of Bavaria, with the intention of encircling France along its outer boundaries. As his power grew, he could then by degrees close in on his nephew's territories.

Initially, Charles VI's youth and inexperience allowed Philip the Bold to manipulate him easily. When in 1382 the citizens of Flanders rebelled, Philip advised Charles to lead an army to Ghent to put down the rebellion. Fourteen-year-old Charles thought this an excellent idea. His first introduction to warfare! A real battle! He and his uncles and a large force of men-at-arms all trooped north to Flanders, where the royal knights, with their chain mail, maces, and iron-tipped spears, made short work of the rebel force, made up as it was of ordinary townspeople whose only protection was iron hats. "The clattering on the helmets by the axes and leaden maces was so loud that nothing could be heard for the noise of them," the chronicler Froissart noted. In the wake of this resounding victory most of the neighboring towns surrendered or paid Charles an exorbitant sum to go away.

Having reasserted his authority to the north, Philip the Bold then looked

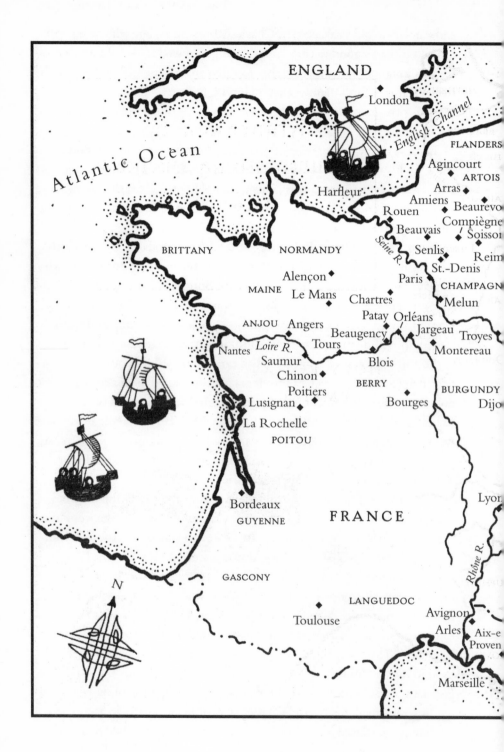

ENGLAND

London

Atlantic Ocean

English Channel

FLANDERS

Agincourt

ARTOIS

Harfleur

Arras

Amiens

Beaurevo

Rouen

Compiègne

BRITTANY

NORMANDY

Beauvais

Soisson

Seine R.

Senlis

Reim

St.-Denis

Alençon

Paris

MAINE

Le Mans

Chartres

CHAMPAGN

Melun

ANJOU

Angers

Patay

Orléans

Jargeau

Troyes

Loire R.

Beaugency

Nantes

Tours

Montereau

Saumur

Blois

Chinon

BERRY

Poitiers

BURGUNDY

Lusignan

Bourges

Dijo

La Rochelle

POITOU

Lyor

Bordeaux

FRANCE

GUYENNE

Rhône R.

N

GASCONY

LANGUEDOC

Avignon

Toulouse

Arles

Aix-e

Proven

Marseille

NETHERLANDS

BRABANT

Brussels

HAINAUT

Meuse R.

France and the
Surrounding Duchies,
Circa 1430

Luxembourg

LORRAINE

BAR

Metz

Nancy

Vaucouleurs

Neufchâteau

Domrémy

HOLY ROMAN

EMPIRE

BOHEMIA

BAVARIA

AUSTRIA

SAVOY

DAUPHINE

Milan

Venice

HUNGARY

PROVENCE

to use his nephew to help augment his power to the east. Here he was aided by the former king's last request. As he lay dying, Charles V had called the dukes of Berry and Burgundy to him. "I feel I have not long to live. Seek out in Germany an alliance for my dear son, Charles, that our connection with that country may be strengthened hereby." Again, fortune smiled upon Philip the Bold: the duke of Bavaria happened to have a daughter, Isabeau, two years younger than Charles VI and reputed to be quite pretty.

The only problem was that Isabeau's father was against the marriage on the grounds that there was too great a difference in rank between his daughter and the king of France. The court of Bavaria, where Isabeau had been raised, was a quiet little backwater, comfortable but not ostentatious. The girl was unprepared to take on the responsibilities of a royal retinue, let alone navigate the complex political milieu associated with the most powerful kingdom in Europe. The duke preferred Isabeau to marry one of his own nobles and stay closer to home—a less brilliant alliance, certainly, but on the whole a more sensible one.

Her father's reluctance did not at all deter the duke of Burgundy from pursuing the union, although it did force him to engage in a bit of subterfuge. He was aided by the duchess of Brabant, a relative of the duke of Bavaria, who recognized in Philip the Bold a possible military ally. The duchess prevailed upon Isabeau's father to send the girl to her for a short visit, and then to another highly respectable relation, the duchess of Hainaut. As a treat for Isabeau, the two women intended to escort her to the fair at Amiens, and from there, on a more somber note, to make a pilgrimage to the nearby shrine of Saint Jean. Faced with so meritorious a request, the duke of Bavaria acceded to his cousin's wishes. He even agreed to allow Isabeau's portrait to be painted for the duchess.

Isabeau traveled to Brussels in the early summer of 1385. She was fourteen years old. She visited for three days with the duchess of Brabant before going on to see the duchess of Hainaut, with whom she stayed for three weeks. During this period, the duchess of Hainaut, an extremely worldly woman, took it upon herself to transform Isabeau, at least on the outside, from an awkward country girl into a vision of medieval beauty, elegance, and sophistication. Out went all of Isabeau's dowdy Bavarian clothes and in came chic Parisian gowns, headdresses, and jewels worthy of a princess. For three weeks the girl was drilled in manners and comportment, including how to sit, stand, eat, walk, dance, and curtsy. Isabeau's complete ignorance of the French language meant that the duchess of Hainaut did not have to work on her accent or on witty repartee; she simply instructed her not to speak.

In the meantime, Charles VI, now sixteen and very interested in girls, was shown Isabeau's portrait, along with those of the duchesses of Lorraine (another territory the duke of Burgundy was interested in) and of Austria, and asked whom he preferred to marry. Apparently her rivals for the king's affection did not represent much competition in the looks department, as Charles immediately chose Isabeau. Upon being told that she and her relatives would attend the fair at Amiens, he arranged to be present at the same time and then sent two of his closest knights to the duchesses of Hainaut and Brabant to arrange an interview.

The rendezvous was held on a Friday in the presence of a large audience. It took the duchesses of Brabant and Hainaut most of the day to get Isabeau ready, but finally she arrived at the king's apartments dressed and accessorized as splendidly as art and money could achieve. Charles, who had spent a long, fraught, teenaged male night thinking about her portrait, was in that state of anticipation that lent itself mightily to the success of the enterprise. Isabeau made her way gracefully through the crowd of courtiers before coming to stand (silently) before the king. Charles was completely smitten. Later that evening, as he was preparing for bed, he instructed his emissaries, "Tell my uncle, the Duke of Burgundy, to make haste and conclude the affair." So eager was Charles for the wedding night that he refused to wait to be married at Arras, as his uncle desired, and instead had a beautiful gold crown delivered to Isabeau on the spot. The two were married three days later at the local cathedral in Amiens without benefit of a nuptial contract or a dowry, an unheard-of omission for a royal alliance.

And so a provincial girl of fourteen, who likely could not read or write, and who had never been exposed to the workings of a large government, let alone the intrigues and shifting political currents of possibly the most sophisticated and cosmopolitan court in Europe, became queen of France. Nor did Isabeau have the benefit, as had Yolande of Aragon, of an experienced older woman who could act as a mentor or guide through the labyrinth of customs and relationships that constituted her new realm's entrenched power structure. Charles's mother was dead, and soon after the wedding the duchesses of Brabant and Hainaut abandoned her for their own courts, well satisfied with their efforts. At least some of the blame for the trouble to come may be laid at the feet of these two cynical women, who taught the new queen of France how to arrange her hair but not to rule.

In the beginning, though, as Isabeau was not called on to do much more than buy expensive clothes, look regal, and have fun, her inexperience did not work against her. The marriage was a happy one. Isabeau's temperament suited that of her new husband; both loved banquets, dancing, and late nights filled with company and wine; they were also united in their love of fine clothes and elaborate, opulent, and frequently raucous entertainments. For her coronation, Charles arranged a three-day extravaganza in Saint-Denis, complete with fountains that spouted honeyed spiced wine, a large choir of children dressed as angels, and a highly theatrical street performance that boasted costumed actors reenacting the battle of the crusaders against King Saladin.

Charles too reacted well to the marriage, and matured greatly in the years immediately following his wedding. By 1388, when he was still only nineteen, he was able to dismiss the regency government administered by his uncles. This was a very popular move, as there had been a disastrous (and expensive) military campaign against England subsequent to the initial victory in Flanders for which his uncles the dukes of Berry and Burgundy were universally blamed. At the urging of Charles's younger brother, Louis, a very precocious sixteen-year-old, the king sent his disgruntled uncles graciously but firmly back to their own provinces "with many thanks for the trouble and toil they had had with him and the realm." Charles immediately surrounded himself with his father's former counselors, all experienced and prudent men who governed, if not wisely, at least with moderation, and for the next four years there was peace in France.

And then came the summer of 1392.

IRONICALLY, the year had begun advantageously for Charles; in retrospect, it may well have marked the high point of his reign. He was in full control of his government, he was beloved by his people, and on February 6 he had fulfilled perhaps the most important task of a monarchy when the queen finally gave birth to a son who survived infancy. "The bells were ringing and in order to announce to all of France the new and joyous event that had taken place in the city, couriers were dispatched in all directions, charged in the name of the king to spread the happy news of the birth of the prince throughout the kingdom," the Monk of Saint-Denis recorded in the official chronicle.

By this time Charles was twenty-three and monitored the administration of his government "with much diligence." Diligence often required traveling long distances under unsanitary conditions, and in March when he went to Amiens on a diplomatic mission, he and several other members of his retinue fell ill with what seems to have been typhoid fever. Charles was so sick that he had to be taken by litter south to Beauvais, where it took him nearly two months to recuperate. He was not back in Paris until the very end of May.

Soon after his return, while he was still in a weakened state, a disquieting episode occurred in the capital. His chamberlain, Pierre de Craon, had recently been removed from his post, which Pierre attributed to a heated exchange with the constable of France, a man very high in the king's favor. Nursing his grudge, Pierre and several of his men ambushed the constable on his way home from dinner with the king on the evening of June 13. They tried to kill him but succeeded only in wounding him. Charles was in the act of undressing for bed when he was informed (mistakenly) that his constable had been murdered; so upset was he that he did not bother to change but threw on only a cloak and went himself to investigate. He discovered the injured man in a nearby baker's shop, where he had been carried after the attack. The constable had sustained many wounds and was covered in blood. Charles had known this man since childhood; the constable had watched over him faithfully since he first ascended to the throne. The sight of his longtime protector and father figure in so pitiable a state upset the king deeply.

"The first words the King said were, 'Constable, how fares it with you?' 'Dear sire,' he replied, 'but so so, and very weak.' 'And who has put you in this state?' 'Pierre de Craon and his accomplices have traitorously, and without the smallest suspicion, attacked me.' 'Constable,' said the King, 'nothing shall ever be more severely punished than this crime. . . . They shall pay for it as if it were done to myself.'"

Charles ordered the assailant pursued, but Pierre had already fled the city. Eventually it was determined that he had sought refuge with the duke of Brittany, although the duke denied this. A furious Charles summoned an army and made preparations to attack Brittany and retrieve the criminal. He personally led his force out of Paris but made it only as far as Le Mans. There he became so ill that he was unable to sit upon his horse. "He had been the whole summer feeble in mind and body, scarcely eating or drinking anything, and almost daily attacked with fever, to which he was naturally inclined, and which was increased by any contradiction or fatigue," observed Froissart. Even more worrying, the Monk of Saint-Denis reported that while at Le Mans, the king would sometimes talk nonsense and behave in a manner "unbecoming to royalty." Despite his obvious weakness, at the end of three weeks, over the objections of his physicians, Charles insisted upon persevering, and once more mounted his horse to lead his forces to Brittany.

By this time it was August and very hot. Charles was in full armor. As the army left Le Mans, they passed a local leper colony where they picked up a deranged vagrant who shadowed the king for half an hour, shouting, "Go no further, great king, for you are to be quickly betrayed!" before being run off by the royal guard. The army continued on its way through first a forest and then out onto a dry stretch of flat land, at which point there was quite a bit of dust kicked up by all the horses, so the king and two pages rode a little ahead of the procession to escape the dirt. The pages were young, and one of them, struggling to keep awake in the heat, let fall the lance he was carrying. It clattered against the armor of the other page, startling the king.

At once, Charles brandished his sword and turned on the boys. "Advance, advance on these traitors!" he cried. The pages, terrified, spurred their horses to get away, but the king, hallucinating and believing himself to be under attack, continued to strike out at those around him, including his brother, the duke of Orléans, who somehow managed to elude him. Others were not so lucky, however. Charles killed five of his own men before his sword broke and he was wrestled from his horse by one of his knights.

The company immediately turned around and took him back to Le Mans, where he lay completely unresponsive for two days, staring blankly at his uncles and unable to speak when they came to visit. Only on the third day did Charles recover his senses and realize what he had done. He was sent south to recuperate. He did not return to Paris until October.

THIS WAS THE BEGINNING of Charles VI's thirty-year struggle with what today doctors would likely diagnose as schizophrenia. During its most acute stages, which occurred annually and sometimes persisted for months at a time, Charles lost all sense of reality. He did not know who he was and

Charles VI suffers his first psychotic episode, attacking his own men.

denied being king. When he saw his own coat of arms, or those of the queen, he performed a bizarre little jig and then tried to efface them. He insisted that his name was George and that he had a different coat of arms altogether. During these episodes he was often uncontrollable, and would dash wildly through the castle, trying to find a way out, shrieking that his enemies were all around him. Eventually, his household had to block all the outside door-ways so he did not run out into the street in this condition. During his most extreme bouts of madness Charles would refuse to bathe or change his apparel, often for as long as five months. He had to be tricked or frightened into removing his clothes, and when he did, his servants found his body covered in sores and smeared with his own excrement. Sometimes he threw his clothes into the fire. Sometimes he urinated on them. Often he made obscene gestures or babbled incoherently.

Although frequently he would recognize his household servants, he almost never knew his wife and children. The sight of Isabeau, in particular, upset him; he couldn't bear to have her around him. According to the Monk of Saint-Denis, "when . . . she [Isabeau] approached to lavish attention on him, the king repulsed her, whispering to his people: 'Who is this woman obstructing my view? Find out what she wants, and stop her from annoying and bothering me, if you can.'" Instead, to calm him, he was provided with a mistress who lived with him at his favorite Parisian domicile, the Hôtel Saint-Pol, and by whom he eventually had a child.

But then, sometimes after days, but more often after weeks or even months of raving, the hallucinations would disappear as abruptly as they had come. Charles would remember who and what he was and return to his wife and children. He would also once again resume rule. This was the great undoing of France. For although he appeared sane during these periods, the king was likely never really free of the disease, and his confusion and uncertainty, particularly about what had occurred in the kingdom during the intervals of his lunacy, made him highly susceptible to suggestion and the slightest persuasion. He became like one of those characters in a fairy tale who, stricken by Cupid's arrow, or sprinkled with magic powder, or placed under a wizard's spell, falls in love with the first person he sees upon waking. Eventually it became widely known among his relatives that whosoever succeeded at gaining entry into the king's presence immediately upon his emergence from one of his cycles of madness could obtain pretty much anything he or she wanted out of him.

As soon as it became clear that Charles was mentally incapacitated, his uncles, especially the duke of Burgundy, moved quickly to once again take control of the kingdom. Unlike the period of the king's minority, however, they were not openly named as regents. Because Charles was sometimes sane enough to govern, he was never removed from power, and his subjects continued to consider him to be the only legitimate ruler of France. Consequently, every policy that was implemented by his uncles or anyone else had to be done in the king's name, whether the king was aware of the action or not. It could also be reversed by the king whenever he was rational enough to do so. Additionally, any commandment issued by the king, even if it conflicted openly with a prior commandment, was automatically accepted as law.

This confusing state of affairs was further exacerbated by the introduction of a new and powerful rival to the duke of Burgundy. The king's younger brother, Louis, duke of Orléans, married and with a family of his own to protect, was now old enough to jealously guard his prerogative. Louis was ambitious not only for power but for wealth, and was determined that his holdings should be on a par with—or preferably exceed—those of his uncles. In 1401, he took advantage of the duke of Burgundy's absence from Paris to cajole his brother the king into ceding to him two important properties that Philip the Bold coveted. Furious, the duke of Burgundy responded by raising an army and marching on Paris. Civil war was only averted at the last minute through arbitration undertaken by the queen, the king being at the time locked up, raving, in the Hôtel Saint-Pol.

This was Isabeau's first real foray into politics, and from the result she evidently decided it was better to wield power than to be at the mercy of someone else's army, because the next year, when the king emerged from his annual period of madness, she made sure that *she* was the first person he saw. Consequently, in 1402, Charles ruled that if there was ever a disagreement in the future between two of the royal peers and he himself wasn't available, the queen was authorized to settle the dispute as she saw fit. She was also empowered, in the king's absence, to conduct or intervene in any business associated with governing the realm. To help her with these new responsibilities, Isabeau was allowed to consult as many or as few of the royal princes or the members of the council as she felt she needed. By these edicts, then, was the queen essentially made ruler of France.

But Isabeau's avarice clouded her judgment and made her an easy target for her enemies. She took or wheedled as much treasure as she could from her husband. She was very fond of her brother and promoted his interests openly, much to the dismay of her subjects, who did not wish to see their hard-earned taxes lavished on a Bavarian. She has also been painted throughout history as having extremely lax sexual mores and as openly conducting an affair with her brother-in-law, the duke of Orléans, during the periods of her husband's madness. Although recent scholarship suggests that these allegations came later as part of a deliberate effort by the English to undermine the legitimacy of the dauphin, there is no question that Isabeau cast about for allies and settled on her husband's brother as a man she could trust. The pair worked together to forward their own interests, often to the detriment of their subjects' pocketbooks. "They [Isabeau and the duke of Orléans] could be reproached also with insulting the people's misery by spending heavily from the payments of others. Indifferent to the defense of the kingdom, they put all their vanity in riches, all their joy in the pleasures of the flesh. In a word, they so forgot the rules and duties of royalty that they became an object of scandal for France," complained the Monk of Saint-Denis.

Naturally, the king's uncles were not particularly happy that the queen (and by implication the duke of Orléans) was in control of the government. Evidently, Isabeau wasn't quick enough the next time, because in 1403, after a private meeting with the dukes of Berry and Burgundy, the king amended his earlier ruling to state that in the event of his absence from court, the queen *and* his uncles were responsible for the administration of the realm, and that in the event of a disagreement, a decision would be taken by the majority and "sounder part" of the royal council—in other words, the duke of Burgundy.

And so it went, back and forth, back and forth. Sometimes the duke of Burgundy had the upper hand, sometimes the queen, sometimes the duke of Orléans. One ordinance cancelled out another. For example, again in 1403, by virtue of yet a later royal declaration, which stated very clearly that it could not be invalidated, the duke of Orléans was named regent in the event that Charles died while his heir was too young to rule. Four days later, in the presence of the duke of Burgundy, the king invalidated this edict.

Then, on April 27, 1404, Philip the Bold died and the balance of power shifted decisively in the duke of Orléans's favor. Within six weeks, Charles had agreed to betroth his widowed daughter Isabelle (whose husband, Richard II, had been deposed and most likely murdered by his successor, Henry IV of England) and her immense dowry of 500,000 francs to Louis's eldest son. Louis was also named lord of Pisa, a title that carried with it a special award of 40,000 francs, and received a number of French cities, gifts that Philip the Bold would no doubt have challenged vigorously had he been alive to do so. And the next year the duke of Orléans did even better, adding nearly 400,000 francs to his estate as a result of grants from the royal treasury, including a 20,000-franc bequest that the duke put entirely to the purchase of a particularly fine gemstone that had caught his eye.

This level of ostentation and affluence did not go unnoticed by the rest of the kingdom. A vehement protest was raised when the duke of Orléans's obviously improved financial circumstances necessitated an increase in taxes to replenish the treasury. Some of the populace's anger directed against the king's brother spilled off onto Isabeau as well, especially when it was revealed that she had secreted a fortune in gold in a convoy subsequently dispatched to Bavaria. The rampant public dissatisfaction with the queen and the duke of Orléans allowed a newcomer to rise to power: Philip the Bold's son, John the Fearless, the new duke of Burgundy.

John the Fearless was thirty-three years old, as energetic, competent, and assured as his father had been, but also more direct and prone to impatience. He assumed that he held a degree of power and influence that he had not yet quite achieved, and this caused him to overreach politically. He was like an understudy who, from long years of observation in the wings, knew all the lines but whose performance once on stage lacked the nuance of the more seasoned principal actor.

John began, much to the approval of the general populace, with a call for an audit and overhaul of the realm's finances. To counter the threat, Isabeau and Louis banded together against him and largely prevailed. For the next two years, John the Fearless struggled with a notable lack of success to displace the duke of Orléans from his position of authority in France. John tried to reform the treasury; Louis thwarted him by deftly replacing those members of the royal council loyal to John with his own supporters. John received authority from the king to negotiate a general peace with England; Louis undermined his efforts by ordering the admiral of the French fleet to launch an assault against English ships in the Channel. Even more unsettling, funds that the king had promised would be paid to the account of the duke of Burgundy never arrived, an administrative omission that John attributed, not unreasonably, to the duke of Orléans's influence.

It is unclear at what point exactly the duke of Burgundy decided to take a shortcut to power, but certainly by the fall of 1407 he had given up on the conventional avenues by which influence is acquired in favor of a more direct approach. On November 23, 1407, the duke of Orléans had dinner and spent the early evening alone with the queen at her private residence at the Hôtel Barbette in Paris. Isabeau had two weeks earlier given birth to a son who had died almost immediately, and was so affected by this death that she had taken to her bed. Louis was there to try to console the queen for her loss. After dinner, they were interrupted by a messenger purporting to come from the king, who claimed that the duke of Orléans was needed. Louis said good night to Isabeau and left her apartments in the company of a nominal retinue, with six valets bearing torches to light the way, a German page, and two young knights-in-training, who shared a horse and rode ahead of the duke. As this little procession turned a dark corner, after his sword-bearers had passed, a group of seventeen armed men rushed out of the shadows to attack Louis. Thinking his identity unknown to his assailants, to save himself he cried out, "I am the Duc d'Orléans!" but "It is you we want," came the cold reply, and a scuffle ensued. The apprentice knights were too far ahead to be of use; by the time they had turned the horse around it was over. It had taken only moments for a prince of the royal blood and his German page to be stabbed to death and their corpses left to lie on the streets of Paris. To distract pursuers, the assassins set fire to a nearby building and then escaped furtively into the blackness of the winter night.

CHAPTER 4

Civil War

EWS OF THE MURDER of the duke of Orléans spread rapidly through Paris. Repulsed by the horrific crime, members of the royal council convened a meeting two days later, on November 25, to arrange for a thorough investigation. Present among these councillors was Yolande of Aragon's husband, Louis II, king of Sicily.

Since his marriage, Louis II had been active in French politics. Possibly because his territorial aspirations were tied to Italy and not France, the king of Sicily had managed to maintain cordial relations with each of the various warring factions within the kingdom. He had been of invaluable aid to Isabeau in her effort to quell the hostility between Philip the Bold and the duke of Orléans, and was treated as a beloved member of the family by Charles VI. Two months before the duke of Orléans's murder, John the Fearless, on the lookout for allies, had affianced his daughter Catherine to Louis's eldest son, four-year-old Louis III. John had provided Catherine with a sizable dowry of 150,000 écus, 30,000 of which had already been paid. The money had made an extremely welcome addition to Louis II's war chest for his upcoming expedition to Naples.

It therefore came as something of a shock to Louis when, during the meeting of the royal council, John the Fearless abruptly took him and the duke of Berry aside and confessed to having ordered the assassination himself. The duke's sudden candor might have been prompted partly by conscience but was mostly of necessity. The royal councillors had just agreed to conduct a house-by-house search for the killers, beginning with their own apartments. Apparently quite a few of the assassins, including their leader, had taken shelter at the Hôtel d'Artois, John the Fearless's primary Parisian residence.

Louis II was a pragmatic man, but not a particularly quick-witted one. The duke of Burgundy's admission, to which he is reported to have responded, "Ah, cousin, you have committed a dastardly act!" left him flailing around in search of the appropriate posture to take. The others, however, roundly condemned John the Fearless and began pressing for his arrest. (The king was indisposed—the duke of Burgundy, no fool, had chosen to murder his rival at a time when Charles had again taken leave of his senses.) Under the circumstances, John the Fearless decided that Paris was perhaps not the optimal location from which to discuss the matter, and the next day he escaped to Flanders, where he proceeded to raise a large army.

The prospect of new violence prompted Louis II and the duke of Berry to adopt a policy of appeasement. They arranged to meet John in Amiens, where they promised to intervene with the king if the duke of Burgundy would only show some remorse by apologizing to the duke of Orléans's widow and children. But John's guilt had hardened him, and he chose to pursue a course of justification rather than admit to error. To the dismay of the two ambassadors, he appeared at the meeting in Amiens accompanied by a force of some three thousand men, rejected all of their proposals, and then proceeded to march on Paris, arriving at the beginning of March 1408.

Here the duke of Burgundy was the beneficiary of a piece of good luck. Just as he and his army had settled into the capital (no one being in a position to stop them), the king was slowly returning to rationality. It was simply a question of who got in to see him first. On March 9, even before Charles had time to make a full recovery, the Burgundian army made sure that John the Fearless was that person.

The interview was held at night in the king's chamber. Although Louis II and the duke of Berry were also present, as were several other prominent noblemen, John and his lawyer did all the talking. The duke of Burgundy stood by Charles's bedside and informed the king of France with a straight face that he had been forced to kill Louis because he had discovered that the duke of Orléans was plotting to murder the king and all of his heirs, and that this had been the only way to save the monarchy. Since this explanation fit in completely with Charles's own paranoid fantasies, the king accepted this extraordinary pronouncement without further investigation. He not only immediately signed a document pardoning John, he also personally authorized a second edict allowing the duke of Burgundy to punish anyone who sought to dishonor him by spreading further rumors or allegations against him.

And so one of the most sensational and despicable murders in French history went unpunished. The bitterness engendered by this evil act ran deeply through the kingdom, severing the realm as effectively as though it had been sliced in two by a sword. Very soon, the breach between those citizens who supported John the Fearless and those who remained loyal to the memory of the murdered duke of Orléans and his heirs would erupt into civil war.

VIOLENCE AND RUIN became endemic to the kingdom in the years following John the Fearless's pardon. In 1410, six of the most important noblemen in France—the dukes of Berry, Brittany, and Orléans (Louis's eldest son, who had inherited his murdered father's title and estates), along with the counts of Armagnac, Alençon, and Clermont—signed a pact pledging to raise an army to go to war against their enemies (understood to be the Burgundians). Members of this faction were called Armagnacs because the new duke of Orléans was married to the count of Armagnac's daughter, and his father-in-law, more experienced militarily and politically, was widely regarded as the leader of the alliance.

True to their word, that summer the six confederates summoned their men-at-arms and descended on the capital, which necessitated the duke of Burgundy's hastily summoning *his* men-at-arms to meet them. "About the end of August, each one brought up so many troops around Paris that everything was devastated for twenty leagues round about," wrote a chronicler who was in the city for these events. Two years later, the duke of Burgundy took the fight to the Armagnacs and besieged his opponents, who were holed up in the city of Bourges. Charles VI, who was having a good spell, actually accompanied John the Fearless on this expedition, as did Charles's eldest son, the duke of Guyenne. "The King of France arrived with his army . . . [and] made a vigorous attack upon the town," wrote the chronicler. "Towards the end of July, when all the poor people had been eaten up, the first by taxation and the others by pillaging, they induced the young Duke of Guienne to negotiate. . . . He promised them . . . that he would reconcile them all to the

King. And so he did, in spite of all objections, for everyone was very tired of the war on account of the extremely hot weather."

But this climate-based peace lasted less than a year. The following spring, the duke of Burgundy used a popular uprising in Paris led by the city's butchers and their cohorts, the flayers—clearly not men to be trifled with— as an excuse to take over the capital. Unhappy with the worsening economic conditions brought on by what was perceived to be extravagant spending by the queen and her eldest son, on April 28, 1413, a mob assembled in front of the duke of Guyenne's palace. Waving a list of names (helpfully provided by the duke of Burgundy), the insurgents demanded the surrender of some fifty members of the royal household accused of improprieties. When the duke of Guyenne refused, the butchers overran the front door, seized the offending noblemen, and took them prisoner. Afterward, the rioters openly delivered their captives to the Hôtel d'Artois, John the Fearless's Paris residence. The sixteen-year-old duke of Guyenne, furious at the offense, confronted his cousin. "Know with certainty that one day you will be sorry," he warned the duke of Burgundy, "and things will not always turn out as you would like."

John's role in instigating a mob attack on the royal family seems finally to have aroused the moral indignation of Louis II, as it was only after this that he and Yolande of Aragon took a step that placed them firmly and irrevocably on the side of the Armagnacs.* In November 1413 they abruptly repudiated the engagement between Louis III and the duke of Burgundy's daughter, Catherine. Ten-year-old Catherine, who had been living with Yolande and her family for the past four years in preparation for the consummation of her marriage, was obliged to pack up and, together with all of her worldly goods, was returned to John the Fearless like last year's coronet.

To be publicly discarded in this fashion was an insult of unfathomable proportions. Furious, the duke of Burgundy severed all relations with the king of Sicily. Nor did he ever forget this humiliation to his family. From this time on, John the Fearless and Louis II were sworn enemies.

But the king and queen of Sicily had already taken steps to compensate for any damage to their position incurred by the rupture. On October 21, 1413, just prior to Catherine's departure, Yolande of Aragon met privately with the

---

*In fairness, Louis II was away in Italy for large portions of the years 1409 to 1411, trying (unsuccessfully of course) to retake Naples, and so did not really have time to concentrate on French affairs until his return.

queen of France at Isabeau's residence in Marcoussis, just south of Paris. The purpose of this interview was to finalize the terms of a marriage contract between Yolande's eldest daughter, nine-year-old Marie, and the king of France's third son, ten-year-old Charles. The mob assault on the duke of Guyenne had frightened Isabeau sufficiently that she was openly seeking new allies as a means of isolating the duke of Burgundy from the rest of the peerage. By this engagement was a new and powerful political alignment created in France.

That Yolande and not her husband was responsible for these negotiations is an indication of how much Louis II now relied on his wife's experience and advice. Yolande was by this time thirty-two years old and the mother of four (soon to be five) children. She had matured into a supremely self-possessed, forceful, and politically astute woman who was not afraid to fight for what she believed to be her rights and property. To help finance her husband's military operations in Naples she had pawned her jewels to his Florentine bankers and managed his estates in Provence and Anjou in his absence. In 1410, while Louis II was away in Italy, Yolande's uncle Martin, king of Aragon, had died without an heir. Yolande sent ambassadors to the special assembly charged with determining the succession to demand that her eldest son, Louis III, be invested with the kingdom. Although the *cortes* eventually chose a different candidate, they were forced to pay the queen of Sicily a settlement of 150,000 florins as compensation for her claim. Despite this substantial remuneration, Yolande never recognized this abrogation of her rights and insisted on adding the honorifics "Queen of Aragon" and "King of Aragon" to her and Louis III's other titles.*

Yolande and Isabeau had no difficulty reaching an agreement at their October meeting, and the engagement of Charles and Marie was celebrated with much pomp and gaiety on December 18, 1413, in Paris. (John the Fearless's support of the butchers had backfired on him and he had been obliged to flee the city in August, so it was safe to hold these festivities in the capital.) It is a simple matter to surmise the partisan nature of this alliance from the guest list; those assembled could just as easily have been attending an anti-Burgundian rally as a sovereign betrothal. The king was again raving and so was unable to attend the engagement of his son. Yolande had brought all

---

*For this reason, in her own time, Yolande was often referred to as "Queen of the Four Kingdoms"—Naples, Sicily, Jerusalem, and Aragon.

of her children with her, and as a special mark of favor Isabeau invited everyone to stay at her favorite palace, the Hôtel Barbette. A number of feasts were given in the children's honor, and Isabeau, pleased by the success of her maneuver, was exceptionally generous in her gift-giving. Yolande received six hanaps—stemmed, oversized wine goblets, almost the size of vases—fashioned of gold and decorated with a rich enamel of transparent ruby to commemorate her daughter's engagement. Even adorable little René, just four years old, was the beneficiary of an expensive diamond and a ring from the queen of France.

The family tarried in the capital until the beginning of February 1414, when word suddenly reached the city that the duke of Burgundy had raised yet another army with the intention of marching on Paris. Louis II elected to stay behind and moved into the Bastille in preparation for defending the city. Yolande, concerned about the safety of her children, made plans to return to her castle at Angers. On February 5, with the duke of Burgundy's forces having already achieved Compiègne, just two days' ride from the city, the queen of Sicily gathered her brood and household together and hastily departed. She took her future son-in-law Charles with her, to be brought up with her own children, just as she had once taken the duke of Burgundy's daughter Catherine into her home. There was nothing at all remarkable in this— nothing except that the quiet, withdrawn little boy Yolande shepherded out of Paris that cold February morning just two weeks short of his eleventh birthday would grow up to be the man Joan of Arc called the dauphin.

UP UNTIL THE MOMENT of his adoption by Yolande and her family, young Charles's life seems to have been one of long periods of neglect and loneli- ness punctuated by sharp bursts of confusion and fear. Born on February 22, 1403, he was the youngest of Isabeau's seven surviving children. He had two older brothers and four sisters and was closest in age to his sister Catherine. As was common for the period, the children were given over to the care of nurses. Even so, the queen of France was reputed to be a particularly removed parent. A chronicler noted that complaints were brought to the king in June 1405 alleging that Isabeau was ignoring her offspring. The king asked his eldest son, the duke of Guyenne, eight years old at the time, about this. How long had it been since his mother had shown him affection, had caressed or kissed him? "Three months," the child replied.

Yolande of Aragon and her husband, Louis II, escort ten-year-old Charles out of Paris.

Worse, the royal progeny were often used as bargaining chips or hostages in the power struggles that consumed the adults. When Charles was two, to escape the duke of Burgundy, the queen attempted to smuggle all three of her sons out of Paris. But John the Fearless got wind of the scheme, brought up an army, and intercepted Isabeau and the children as they were in the act of fleeing. There was a violent scene between John and Isabeau's Bavarian brother, who was also accompanying her, and then the duke of Burgundy and his soldiers, brandishing their swords, grabbed the boys and brought them back to Paris. To prevent further escape, the royal princes were lodged under armed guard for the next four months in the Louvre. It was a period of intense unrest in Paris, and at night the frightened children could hear the shouts and clanging of weapons as well as cries of "Alarm! Alarm!" from the castle sentinels.

When Charles was five, he and his siblings were again secretly removed from Paris by the queen. This time, Isabeau took her children to Melun, where they were barricaded for safety in a fortress surrounded by soldiers. The sojourn in Melun was interrupted by another precipitate departure, when Isabeau was again forced to evade the armies of the duke of Burgundy. The family did not return to Paris until the next year.

And so it went throughout Charles's childhood: the frightening, clandestine escapes from the capital, followed by the inevitable, heavily guarded return, often to the Louvre, and always more warfare, more violence, more blood. At ten, Charles witnessed the hostility of the butchers to his eldest brother and learned to fear the Parisian populace. The king's insanity left him ill equipped to shoulder the demands of fatherhood, and even his youngest son knew better than to expect solicitude from that quarter. Charles's mother, faced with an untenable political situation and desperately in need of allies, focused all of her familial attention on her eldest son, the duke of Guyenne, whose stature as heir to the throne lent her legitimacy, and whose goodwill was consequently necessary to her well-being. Absorbed in these, her own troubles, Isabeau simply had no time for her younger children. What crumbs of affection Charles managed to solicit came from the servants.

And then came his engagement, and with it his transfer to Yolande's care.

For Charles, this must have been like stepping out of the darkness and into the light. Vanished were the fearful trappings of war-ravaged Paris— the angry voices of the soldiers, the threatening hostility of the crowds, the blood and beatings, all the evidence of the casual brutality that afflicted the city. Yolande's castle at Angers was far removed from the front lines of civic unrest. Charles experienced the peace of the countryside. He could fall asleep at night without dread of being shaken awake and forced to flee in the darkness. There were no shouts of "Alarm!" and no rotting dead bodies piled by the side of the road in the morning. In September, he joined in the king and queen of Sicily's annual migration to Provence. He took the long, slow barge ride with the rest of the family to the ancestral castle at Tarascon, and along the way was introduced to the beauty of the southern landscape of France.

From being an annoyance and afterthought, overnight he became valued. Louis III, Yolande's firstborn, was the same age and the two became friends; in later life, Louis III would put aside his own ambitions in order to fight for Charles. Marie, just a year younger, was also a playmate and companion. Although there seems to have been no real physical attraction between them (at least on Charles's part), Marie nonetheless managed to forge a childhood bond with her future husband that over the years became the basis for the marriage. But of all his newfound siblings, it seems to have been little René who most wormed his way into Charles's affections. An appealing child who would grow into an exceedingly charming adult, René possessed an artistic temperament that flourished in his mother's household. He loved stories and books—he would eventually inherit Yolande's extensive library and add to it—but also music, verses, and drawing. Perhaps because previously Charles himself had always been the youngest, he was attracted to René, or possibly he simply found the five-year-old less intimidating in the beginning, when he was still feeling his way in his new surroundings. For whatever reason, the pair established an early friendship and intimacy that survived into adulthood.

But it was to Yolande herself that Charles, craving maternal affection, was most drawn. Yolande's children, too, had nursemaids. René loved his so much that on her death nearly a half century later, he built her a beautiful crypt and had it inscribed with the playful dedication, "For the great love of nourishment." (She had been his wet nurse.) But unlike Isabeau, the queen of Sicily paid attention to her children. She monitored their education and kept them with her whenever she could. There were no raving lunatics shut away in the recesses of Yolande's palace; no cold, absent mother too busy with clothes and feasts and council meetings to notice a ten-year-old; only a warm, gentle, interested woman and happy children. This was Charles's first experience of a loving parent and a normal family life, and he thrived on it.

Yolande focused her attention upon Charles even more than was usual. Her daughter's alliance with the royal family was very important to the queen of Sicily. She and Louis II had burned their bridges with the duke of Burgundy; there was no going back, this relationship *had* to work. Also, it is possible that she felt slightly guilty about having returned Catherine and so compensated for that act by being especially affectionate to Charles. Whatever the reason, Yolande made every effort to ensure that Charles was comfortable in her home and to earn his trust, and the boy, feeling himself loved and appreciated for the first time, opened up to her. He called her his "Bonne Mère"—his good mother—and became very attached to her, relying on her judgment and reflexively turning to her in moments of distress. No one had more influence with Charles than Yolande.

Charles remained with the queen of Sicily without interruption for the next five years. This was the happiest interlude of his life. During that time, the entire family became intimately acquainted with him. As a result, there was no hope or dream, fear or worry, aspiration, fancy, apprehension, trouble, preoccupation, innermost thought, or secret prayer of Charles's, expressed or unexpressed, of which Yolande or one of her children was not aware.

The family remained in Provence until the summer of 1415. Yolande was recuperating from the birth of her fifth child, a son whom she named Charles, yet another flattering sign of the esteem in which Isabeau's son was held by the king and queen of Sicily. Then, in July, this peaceful domestic interlude was suddenly interrupted by the arrival of an official summons for Louis II from the French court. Word had arrived that the English were planning to invade France in the fall. To meet the threat, Charles VI had called upon all of his vassals to gather for a great council meeting at Rouen in October to prepare for war against England's new king, Henry V.

OWING TO THE EFFORTS of William Shakespeare, Henry V has had a very easy time of it throughout history. Handsome actors portray him in film and on stage. His memory is irrevocably intertwined with stirring speeches and lofty sentiments. He is soldier, lover, statesman, general, hero, majesty—the very definition of English daring and English mettle; the ideal king who, with a regiment of only six thousand ill and exhausted soldiers, took on the entire French army, an arrogant force ten times their size, and walloped them at Agincourt. What nobody ever mentions is that Henry's noble assault on France took place at a time when the English king was perfectly aware that his enemies had spent the last eight years in a highly destructive civil war and were consequently in complete disarray, and that his counterpart, the French king, was a man who spent the majority of his time locked up in a castle ranting that he was being pursued by phantom enemies and insisting that he was actually somebody named George.

Henry V was already a seasoned military commander by the time of his ascension to the throne in 1413, having honed his leadership skills during the numerous armed conflicts that had occurred during his father's reign. Since it was generally recognized that Henry IV had usurped the crown from Richard II, there had been quite a bit of civil strife in the beginning. Not unreasonably, Richard's legitimate heirs and their supporters resented this appropriation of the monarchy, and had done their best, through rebellion and warfare, to get it back. In 1403, when he was only sixteen years old, Henry had been enlisted by his father to help put down a revolt involving four thousand entrenched, well-trained Welsh and northern English soldiers. Early in the battle, the inexperienced Henry had taken an arrow full in the face but, to inspire his men, had *left it there* and fought on; afterward, he had to endure a lengthy, unanesthetized operation to remove the arrowhead, which was lodged deeply in his nose. Some makeshift tongs were inserted by degrees into the wound (which had to be widened bit by bit, the deeper the instrument was inserted) by the medical practitioner, a former counterfeiter turned king's surgeon. "Then, by moving it to and fro, little by little (with the help of God) I extracted the arrowhead," the reformed swindler later recounted. The rigors of war must have paled in comparison with the pain inflicted by this procedure, but by this experience did Henry V secure both his inheritance—he and his father won the battle—and his reputation for toughness.

Still, a faint whiff of the sour odor of usurpation dogged Henry V's coronation as it had his father's, and the new king was sensitive to this. (At a meeting between the French and the English in July 1415, when Henry tried to press his government's claims to lands in France, the French ambassador pointed out tartly that Henry was legally on rather thin ice, as the people with whom the archbishop should really be negotiating were the heirs of Richard II.) But Henry understood that nothing distracted from small improprieties at home like a triumph abroad. The question of his legitimate right to the English throne would forever be decided in his favor should he succeed in reclaiming some of these disputed territories in France. He would also never have a better opportunity to strike than at the beginning of his reign, when the Burgundians and Armagnacs were so consumed with killing each other that large portions of France might be available for the taking.

Popular legend as encouraged again by Shakespeare records that the French reaction to this threat was one of scorn: the dauphin (the duke of Guyenne) reportedly sent Henry a box of tennis balls, implying that he should grow up. However, since the duke of Guyenne was only eighteen years old in 1415, while Henry himself was twenty-eight, this seems unlikely. Moreover, the duke of Guyenne was not involved in any of the negotiations preceding Henry's invasion. The whole tennis ball anecdote "simply did not happen," a noted expert on English medieval history stated flatly.

What did happen was that both the Burgundians and the Armagnacs took Henry's militarist stance very seriously, so much so that each side did its best to buy him off by proposing marriage alliances and other monetary and territorial inducements. The duke of Burgundy began the bidding by offering the hand of his daughter Catherine (now conveniently available, having been returned by the king and queen of Sicily), together with the suggestion that he and Henry together launch a campaign to seize the estates and fiefs currently held by the Armagnacs and split the spoils between them. The Armagnacs countered with the proposal that Henry instead marry the French king's youngest daughter, also named Catherine, and threw in the lordship of Aquitaine, together with a whopping dowry of 800,000 crowns. Here the Armagnacs had the upper hand even without the financial and territorial incentives, as Henry was given an enthusiastic report of the princess Catherine's looks by his brother, who had seen her, whereas the duke of Burgundy's Catherine and her older sister (who was married to the duke of Guyenne) were unfortunately described by a fellow Burgundian as "looking like a couple of baby owls without feathers."

But far from forestalling the English king, these negotiations only reinforced Henry's opinion of the weakness and division that existed among his enemies, and convinced him that he could achieve even more concessions by a show of strength. Although he took a sizable force with him, it is unlikely that he was intending a full-scale invasion; it is far more probable that he was simply hoping to make a reconnaissance for future attacks and to take home a quick spoil or two in the process. Whatever his true intent, on August 11, 1415, the king of England, in the company of an army of about twelve thousand men, of whom approximately six thousand were archers, set sail from Southampton, and by August 14 had landed in France near the town of Harfleur.

On the French side, the great council meeting was slow to materialize. By the time the English had landed, the constable of France had managed to assemble a decent-sized army at nearby Rouen, enough to lend Harfleur an additional garrison of three hundred soldiers. But none of the other great lords of France and their respective men-at-arms had yet arrived. The constable took one look at the size of Henry's battalion and sent back urgently to Paris for reinforcements.

Charles VI was well enough to sign another summons on August 28, ordering up fresh troops. The question of the role the duke of Burgundy would play in the conflict was handled with some delicacy. The French army needed as many men as possible, but no one on the Armagnac side trusted the duke of Burgundy to lead his own soldiers into battle. There was too great a temptation, it was felt, that he would fight *with* the English rather than against them. In the end, the duke of Guyenne sent one of his own household to John the Fearless with the polite request that the duke supply five hundred knights and three hundred bowmen to aid the king's effort against the English, but that it was quite unnecessary for the duke himself to put in an appearance.

Despite the increasingly desperate messages from the constable asking for help in defending Harfleur, none of the major participants on the French side managed to get to Rouen with their forces until the middle of October. By that time, Henry V had taken the city, although at a significant cost: during the long siege of Harfleur his army had been decimated by dysentery. Approximately two thousand soldiers had succumbed outright to the disease, and thousands of others had either deserted or were too weak to be of use and had to be sent home. Harfleur fell on September 22, 1415, but by that time all that remained of the English army were nine hundred knights and about five thousand longbowmen.

The French—or rather the Armagnacs, for the duke of Burgundy's forces did not get to Rouen in time—were finally in place, with the duke of Orléans and his troops arriving at the very last minute, around October 21. This left not much time for strategizing, but with the English army so reduced, and the French army so enhanced, there did not seem much need for a coordinated policy. They did decide, however, that for obvious reasons it was unwise for the king himself to participate, and they also insisted that the duke of Guyenne, as the heir to the throne, remain safely behind in Rouen. The only other high-ranking members of the French aristocracy excused from battle were the old duke of Berry, who was seventy-five, and Louis II, king of Sicily, who had contracted a bladder infection that prevented him from remaining for any extended period on his horse.

The constable had scouts in place, watching the enemy's movements. He knew that Henry and what was left of his army had left Harfleur the first week in October and set out for the safety of Calais, then in English hands, in preparation for returning to England. He had reports that the English soldiers were weary, ill, and hungry, and that their supplies were running out. Anxious that the king of England should not get away while the Armagnacs possessed such an overwhelming numerical advantage—there is no accurate estimate of the size of the French force, but the chaplain accompanying the English reported that "their numbers were so great as not to be even comparable with ours"—the French left Rouen as soon as the duke of Orléans arrived, and shadowed Henry's troops, attempting to intercept him. On October 24, they caught up with him in a narrow field near the town of Agincourt, and the next morning advanced into battle.

Much has been made of the fact that neither Charles VI nor his eldest son was present at this historic contest, implying that what was missing from the French performance was an inspiring commander. "There is no doubt that knights and men-at-arms and the whole army would have greater courage in fighting, seeing their lord in his place, ready to live and die with them," Christine de Pizan would later write. But in reality, the presence or lack thereof of a member of the royal family was irrelevant; the French army was in no need of inspiration. The knights and men-at-arms displayed great courage in fighting and were certainly ready to die for their cause, as is proven by the fact that thousands of them did die. What they lacked was cohesion, the ability to adapt to changing combat conditions, and, above all, discipline.

And they were facing the very definition of cohesion and discipline. This core unit of Henry and his men had been fighting together for months. They knew what they were supposed to do and when they were supposed to do it. They waited for signals, and when those signals were given, they acted.

And they had a technological advantage in the longbow. The French had never taken to archery. No nobleman in France hunted with a bow and arrow. In England, the longbow was akin to the national sport. Henry had only six thousand men, but five thousand of them were expert archers. The king of England was aware from personal experience of the destructive potential of a rain of arrows, and he used this knowledge to devastating effect.

The field at Agincourt was muddy and narrow. The French cavalry was not in formation in time and the English were able to stake out an advantageous position that placed the French knights within range of their archers. When the French finally advanced, the English longbowmen just stood there and let fly. They never had to move. Their superiority was akin to having automatic long-range assault weapons. Thousands of arrows rained down on the French; the horses and knights fell in the mud; the advancing men-at-arms fell down on top of them; the next wave of knights, followed by their men-at-arms, rushed in to help and fell victim themselves to the arrows. This process was repeated for hours. Those French who did not die outright from their wounds perished from loss of blood, or, unable to extricate themselves from the growing pile of corpses, they simply suffocated in the mud. The main theater of operation soon turned into a ghastly morass, reminiscent of a huge open-air communal gravesite. Few battles in history compare with Agincourt for the sickening waste of human life. At the end of the day, a nobleman who fought on the side of France reported that ten thousand of his compatriots lay dead in the field at Agincourt, although it is not at all clear that this number included members of the lower classes. By contrast, the English lost a total of 112 men.

Henry V's assessment of the opposition—and of his own countrymen—had been correct. After Agincourt, no one in England ever doubted his right to the throne. The only question was, did he now also rule France?

The battle of Agincourt.

CHAPTER 5

A
New Dauphin

⚜

OLANDE WAS IN ANGERS with the children when she received the news of the annihilation of the French army at Agincourt. Although she must have been relieved to hear that her husband was safe, the number of knights who perished or were taken prisoner that day was stunning. Almost no family of noble French origin was unaffected by this tragedy. The Armagnac ruling faction, in particular, was decimated. The constable had died in the fray, as had the count of Alençon, one of the founding members of the anti-Burgundian league. The dukes of Orléans and Bourbon had survived the fight only to be captured and held for ransom. Yolande herself had two uncles killed in the battle, one of whom was the duke of Bar. Even the duke of Burgundy sacrificed two brothers to the English longbows at Agincourt.

In the aftermath of the defeat, Charles VI and his eldest son, uncertain of Henry's next move, stayed at Rouen, and Louis II remained with them. It soon became clear that the English king intended to continue on to Calais as he had originally planned, and from there to England. Despite his great victory, his men were too tired and sick to press on toward Paris. On November 16, 1415, Henry V and his army sailed from Calais for home, taking with them hundreds of captive French noblemen, including their most important prisoner, the twenty-year-old duke of Orléans.

Those who remained at Rouen understood that the respite from their

English aggressors was only temporary. In the spring, Henry would return, probably with an even larger army, to claim his rights to France. The French crown would have to make deep concessions to prevent the loss of the kingdom altogether. Charles VI, once again on the verge of a psychotic episode, returned to Paris at the end of November, as did the duke of Guyenne, to confer with the surviving members of the royal council. Louis II, still suffering from illness, accompanied them. But before they arrived, a more immediate danger threatened. Messengers reported that the duke of Burgundy was marching toward Paris at the head of a large contingent of men-at-arms.

John the Fearless's reaction to the French slaughter at Agincourt was mixed. While he grieved for his lost brothers, he could not help but notice that the English had conveniently relieved him of his most obstinate adversaries in the opposing political party. The discomfiture of his rivals and the resulting confusion at the royal court presented the duke of Burgundy with an opportunity to seize power that was too tempting to let slip by. The duke of Guyenne had bade him stay away from the battle, and to his great advantage John the Fearless had acquiesced to that request; now, in a position of strength, he came to take Paris.

Despite falling ill with dysentery on December 6, the eighteen-year-old duke of Guyenne took charge of the government. The count of Armagnac, the only leading member of the anti-Burgundian faction not to have participated at Agincourt, was hastily nominated as the new constable of France, and an embassy sent to his estates in the south urgently summoning him, with as many troops as he could muster, to Paris. The duke of Guyenne also sent emissaries to intercept John the Fearless armed with royal orders commanding the duke of Burgundy to break off his campaign and disband his forces, but the duke of Burgundy simply ignored these edicts and continued his march on the capital. On hearing this news, Louis II, strongly suspecting that John had not yet gotten over that unfortunate Catherine business, and that accordingly he stood a good chance of being singled out as a target of the duke's ire, felt a pressing need to leave Paris. The king of Sicily slipped out of his *hôtel* at dawn on December 10 and made a dignified escape to his wife and children at Angers.

The duke of Burgundy and his troops arrived at the outskirts of the city on December 15; the count of Armagnac was reported to be on the road with his forces at about the same time; and three days later, on December 18, just as it seemed that it was impossible for French affairs to become more chaotic, the duke of Guyenne died of his dysentery.

The sudden death of the heir to the throne, followed by the necessary funeral ceremonies, created a temporary hiatus in the political and military frenzy. The duke of Burgundy could not very well march into Paris with an army while the whole kingdom was mourning the loss of the crown prince. Moreover, he had to worry about the position of his daughter, the former duchess of Guyenne, now an unwanted appendage without obvious means of financial support. It wouldn't do to try to bully the royal family at the same time that he was trying to obtain a substantial widow's portion for her.

While the duke of Burgundy hesitated, the count of Armagnac arrived and as the lawfully named constable of France ensconced himself in Paris, then used his troops to sever the supply lines servicing John the Fearless's army. Charles VI's second son, John, who had married the count of Hainaut's daughter and was living with his in-laws in Belgium, was recalled to Paris to take his dead brother's place as heir to the throne. The duke of Burgundy, faced with the problem of an increasingly hungry contingent of men-at-arms and a Parisian population hopefully anticipating the arrival of a new dauphin, was forced to withdraw, leaving the government of the kingdom once again in the hands of his rivals. With the departure of his powerful enemy, the king of Sicily judged the capital once again safe enough to hazard his return. By the middle of January 1416, Louis II was back in Paris, and this time he brought his wife with him.

FOR YOLANDE TO LEAVE the children behind in Angers—she was almost never separated from them—is a measure of how critical was the political situation in which she and her husband found themselves. Louis's recent illness had weakened him considerably, and he was forced to rely more and more upon his wife's diplomatic skills. Yolande was especially useful as a conduit to Isabeau of Bavaria, with whom she had established a personal and political relationship. Like Louis II, Queen Isabeau attended the meetings of the royal council. Over the next few months, with his wife's help, the king of Sicily became the principal power in the government, appointing members of his retinue, including his longtime councillor, Tanneguy du Chastel, as prévôt of the city.

The political alliance between Yolande, Louis II, and the queen of France infuriated the duke of Burgundy. Taking advantage of a short absence by the count of Armagnac from the capital, John the Fearless sent spies into Paris to set in motion a plot to murder Queen Isabeau, Yolande, Louis II, the duke of Berry, Tanneguy du Chastel, and a number of others. The plan was for a group of Parisian middle-class burghers, goaded on by the Burgundian gentlemen who had infiltrated the capital, to steal the keys of the city from the local officials. They were then to arrest and execute the targeted victims, making sure to first humiliate them by making them ride through the streets of Paris on the backs of mules to the derision of the local population. Unfortunately for the duke, this plot was discovered by the royal guard on the evening of April 19, 1416. The captain denounced the conspirators to the royal council; an extraordinary commission was immediately established to investigate; the details of the scheme, including the compromising role played by the duke of Burgundy himself, came to light; and the unhappy intriguers, rather than ruling the city, found themselves hunted down and beheaded.

Ironically, the effect of this treachery was to secure Louis II's hold on the government, a grasp that became even more pronounced upon the death two months later of the old duke of Berry, who had taken the news of the conspiracy very hard. With the king of Sicily's steadily increasing authority, he and Yolande must have felt much more confident of their ability to protect themselves, because they brought thirteen-year-old Charles to Paris to stay with them while they awaited the arrival of his elder brother John, the new dauphin.

But the duke of Burgundy also had his eye on the new dauphin. In October, John the Fearless met secretly with Henry V as a first step toward arranging an alliance with the English that separated and protected Burgundian interests from those of the rest of France. To gain leverage over the dauphin, John the Fearless then threatened to have the count of Hainaut overthrown or murdered by these powerful new allies. This gambit yielded the desired result. In November, the count of Hainaut came to an understanding with the duke of Burgundy. The dauphin John would enter into an agreement with the duke to defend and protect the duke's interests against all who opposed him. John the Fearless further instructed the count of Hainaut to approach the royal council on his behalf and insist that they agree to abide by the terms of this treaty.

Only after this agreement was finalized did the count of Hainaut and the dauphin John finally begin their journey to Paris. The negotiations had taken so long that it was by this time winter, and very cold. In January they reached Compiègne, where they settled to await preparations for the dauphin's grand entry into the capital. During this stopover, the dauphin came down with an ear infection, so in March the count of Hainaut went to Paris alone to confront the royal council with John the Fearless's demands. As might be expected, the Armagnac government did not appreciate the ultimatum, and by the end of March the count had returned empty-handed to Compiègne. Only then did he discover that his son-in-law had fallen seriously ill in his absence. There being no effective treatment against the more aggressive strains of bacteria in the fifteenth century, the infection that had begun in John's ear had spread to his skull.

One week later, on April 5, 1417, to the utter disbelief of the kingdom, the dauphin John died. And just like that, Yolande of Aragon's future son-in-law Charles, the fourteen-year-old boy who worshipped her, was the new dauphin and heir to the throne of France.

YOLANDE WAS NOT WITH CHARLES when the news of John's death reached Paris. Louis II's health had deteriorated significantly with the onset of winter. He had never really recovered from the infection that had prevented him from participating in the battle of Agincourt. By the previous January, he had become so weak that Yolande decided he was better off living quietly at home than in the turmoil of the capital. In fact, the king of Sicily, too, was dying.

Before they had left Paris, Yolande and her husband had made every effort to ensure Charles's safety and political future. Yolande charged the most capable members of her household, including Tanneguy du Chastel, provost of Paris; Robert Le Maçon, Charles's chancellor; and Gérard Machet, his confessor, with the care and protection of Charles in her absence. These were Angevin counselors of long standing whose political experience would prove invaluable. Still, this was a painful leave-taking for Yolande and her husband, as well as for Charles. Louis II must have known that his condition was fatal, because a chronicler reported that "he clasped [Charles] many times in his arms, and recommended that he never trust the duke of Burgundy, but to endeavor nevertheless by all means possible to be on good terms with him." Then Yolande escorted Louis II slowly home to Angers.

He lasted until April 29, 1417, just long enough to learn that the dauphin John had succumbed to illness and that consequently his daughter Marie was now engaged to the heir to the throne of France. Louis II died in bed, surrounded by his wife and children, at the age of forty. In his will, he specifically enjoined his children to obey their mother in all things, and to revere her all their lives, and he added a special clause recommending that the dauphin Charles do the same. Although his eldest son, Louis III, inherited the majority of his estates and titles, Yolande was made executor of his will and regent over all of his fiefs until his son should reach his majority, and she also retained the property associated with her dower, which included the beautiful castle of Saumur and other lands and revenues in Provence.

There is no good time to die, of course, but Louis II picked a particularly unhelpful moment to make his exit. Coming so soon upon the death of the second dauphin, the demise of the king of Sicily provoked a power struggle in Paris between the count of Armagnac and Queen Isabeau, in which Charles, as the new heir to the throne, once again played the pawn. Charles had by chance been visiting his mother and his sister Catherine in Senlis when the news arrived that his older brother had died. Isabeau, taking advantage of Charles's presence in her castle, was determined to keep him with her as a way of safeguarding her own interests. By exerting influence over Charles, her last remaining son, she could take control of the royal council and keep the reins of government in her own hands. So intent was Isabeau upon capitalizing on this opportunity that she called up a large contingent of soldiers to Senlis, ostensibly to help guard her prize, but really as a preliminary step toward advancing on Paris.

The summoning of this force—a clumsy and obvious contrivance—betrayed her intentions and instigated a showdown with the count of Armagnac, who naturally saw himself as the head of the political faction bearing his name, and who had no intention of ceding authority. He and Tanneguy du Chastel struck back. The king had just emerged from a bout of madness and was once again easily influenced by those who approached him first. Through a representative, the count of Armagnac leveled some scandalous accusations against Queen Isabeau's court and suggested that the king reprimand his wife. Following the familiar pattern, the king accepted these allegations without investigation, took the count of Armagnac's advice, and sent an army headed by Tanneguy du Chastel in his guise as provost of Paris (a sort of chief of police) to Senlis to take Charles away from Isabeau and bring him back to his father at the Hôtel Saint-Pol. Also by the king's order, "the Queen was deprived of everything; she was no longer to be one of the Council and her establishment was reduced," reported a chronicler and eyewitness. A seething Isabeau, stripped of all her royal powers, was exiled to Tours, there to contemplate her uncertain future in the company of a court by no means as glittering or opulent as that to which she had become accustomed.

None of this would ever have happened if the king and queen of Sicily had been in Paris; they were the glue that had held together the shaky alliance between the count of Armagnac and the queen of France. But Louis II was dead, and Yolande, as executor of his will, was in no position to leave the duchy of Anjou to try to sort out the mess in Paris. Instead, she did the next best thing: she got Charles out of the capital and back to his adopted family by insisting that the boy, in his capacity as dauphin and representative of the crown, preside over an official state meeting in Saumur. Charles, who by this time was afraid of both his father and his mother, leapt at the chance to return to Yolande. Yolande met him with an impressive retinue calculated to underscore his position as heir to the throne, and brought him back with her to the quiet of her castle at Saumur.

Yolande kept Charles with her that summer for as long as possible. He accompanied her and the rest of the family when she arranged to have her eldest son, Louis III, now duke of Anjou, count of Provence, and king of Sicily, engaged to the daughter of the count of Brittany, another major diplomatic coup. Louis II had wanted this alliance for many years but the duke of Brittany had always hesitated. However, now that Yolande's daughter, Marie, was engaged to the dauphin of France, the duke of Brittany's objections vanished, and he himself came to Angers to negotiate the terms of the nuptial agreement (which included a highly satisfactory dowry of 100,000 francs). Yolande made sure to bring Charles into the proceedings, and the engagement received "the consent of our very dear lord, son and brother, the Dauphin," as a further reassurance to the duke of Brittany of the family's now lofty royal connections.

But eventually Charles had to go back; with his new station in life came official responsibilities. Toward the end of July, an outbreak of civil disorder demanded that the dauphin, who had been accorded the position of lieutenant general of the kingdom by his father, led a military force to Rouen to put down the disturbance. On July 29, 1417, Charles and a small troop of men-at-arms successfully negotiated a peaceful settlement to the uprising, and the dauphin was able to enter the city and was accorded all of the dignities associated with his rank. Unfortunately, at the same moment, Henry V, accompanied by a seriously intimidating army of some twelve thousand soldiers, was midway across the English Channel at the head of a fleet of fifteen hundred ships heading for France.

THE ARRIVAL of this second invasion from England set off the final, calamitous series of events that would result in the French capitulation. No sooner had Henry V's army landed than the duke of Burgundy, in accordance with the secret agreement he had made with the English the previous October, raised a force of his own. While Henry and his men methodically worked their way south down the coast and inward toward Alençon in an effort to secure Normandy, John the Fearless led his army out of the northern stronghold of Arras to march on Paris.

In the midst of the turmoil, Isabeau suddenly reemerged. Still smarting in Tours over her humiliation at the hands of the count of Armagnac, the queen of France, so long a friend to the party associated with the duke of Orléans, abruptly changed sides. She sent a covert messenger to John the Fearless, pledging to join forces with him against the Armagnacs if he would only use his army to rescue her from her exile. As a symbol of her goodwill, she took the valuable gold signet ring off her finger and had it delivered to John, to seal her part of the bargain.

The duke of Burgundy was only too pleased to accommodate the queen. Having the participation of so high a member of the royal family greatly increased the legitimacy of his military action. On November 2, 1417, he conducted a force of eight hundred men-at-arms to Tours to relieve Isabeau of her confinement. Isabeau then accompanied John as he made his way to Paris. While on the road, she wrote letters and issued edicts claiming that the king and the dauphin were being held against their will by evil counselors and "persons of low rank," and called on her subjects to join with the duke of Burgundy to liberate her husband and son from their oppressors. This, of course, was a complete fabrication, but he'd gotten her out and she had to say *something*.

Working together, the queen and the duke tried to breach Paris at the end of November by secretly contriving to have one of the gates to the city left open. But the plot was discovered and thwarted at the last minute by

Tanneguy du Chastel, who arranged for crossbowmen to guard the compromised gate. Frustrated, the duke of Burgundy and the queen of France were forced to withdraw and bide their time while they waited for another opportunity to present itself.

In the interim, the dauphin Charles had returned to Paris and was doing his best to govern. To counteract his mother's propaganda, he too penned letters and edicts in which he informed his subjects that the duke of Burgundy was an accomplice to the king of England and warned them not to believe his words or follow his commands. Still, Charles was not equipped to handle so profound a crisis. He could control neither his father nor the count of Armagnac. The result was chaos. At the beginning of February 1418, just before the dauphin's fifteenth birthday, Charles VI suddenly took it into his head to attack the English, and with the count of Armagnac took an army to Senlis. There weren't any English in Senlis, only Burgundians, but this didn't matter to the king, and the count of Armagnac was of course only too thrilled to besiege the rival political faction. Unfortunately, this partnership between king and count was particularly inept, and two months later they were forced to retreat, having accomplished nothing besides wasting a great deal of money and losing most of their military equipment to the duke of Burgundy. Their incompetence was manifest to the citizens of Paris, who paid for this fiasco with both higher prices and taxes.

The English army, on the other hand, was operating with a devastating effectiveness. By February 1418, Henry V had taken Caen, Bayeux, Alençon, Mortagne, Bellême, and Falaise, and by so doing had securely established the English presence in western Normandy. A chronicler who lived in Paris, who was openly sympathetic to the Burgundians, summed up the situation succinctly: "Indeed, it is perfectly true that some people who had come to Paris from Normandy, having escaped from the English . . . solemnly affirmed on oath that the English had been kinder to them than the Burgundians had, and the Burgundians a hundred times kinder than the troops from Paris, as regards food, ransom, physical suffering, and imprisonment."

Yolande, still in Angers, watched the progress of the English army with alarm. To have Henry V in Alençon, so near Le Mans and the border of her fiefs of Anjou and Maine, was disquieting; if he wasn't stopped he would soon be in a position to launch a full-scale assault on her property. She sent an ambassador to Paris to ask for reinforcements, but Charles VI was busy besieging Senlis and had no men-at-arms to spare.

So Yolande made one last great effort to reconcile the Burgundians and the Armagnacs, to prepare the way for a united front against the English. Working together with the duke of Brittany—they were the two whose territories stood closest to Henry V's army—she called for a parley and actually succeeded in gathering representatives from each faction for a conference near Montereau-Fault-Yonne, about forty miles southeast of Paris. These talks began in March and lasted through the month of May, and at the end of that time, against all odds, an agreement was actually hammered out and a treaty drawn up.

But in fact no one wanted it. After all this time, the divisions ran too deep, and even the reality of an English invasion could not prompt the two sides to compromise. The count of Armagnac rejected the terms outright when the document was brought to Paris in May, and by his subsequent actions it was clear that the duke of Burgundy also had no intention of complying with the conditions of this truce.

For on May 29, 1418, after so many failed attempts on Paris, John the Fearless finally succeeded in breaching the city's defenses. In the early hours just after midnight, Burgundian partisans unlocked the Saint-Germain gate with a stolen key and an army of eight hundred heavily armed warriors swarmed into Paris. Almost immediately, the streets were filled with a rampaging mob, as all the pent-up fury against the incompetence of the Armagnacs' rule burst out of the citizenry. "Then Paris was in an uproar; the people took up their arms much faster than the soldiers did," wrote an eyewitness. "And now Fate joined the Burgundians with the people of Paris and with every kind of weapon; she made them break down their doors and pour out their treasures and plunder; she twisted her wheel malevolently round, avenging herself on their ingratitude, because they did not care about peace. They were very glad to hide in cellars or basements or any corner, those that could."

As soon as the extent of the danger became clear, Tanneguy du Chastel slipped into the dauphin's bedroom at the Hôtel Saint-Pol and awakened him. It was just after two o'clock in the morning. For Charles, this nocturnal rousing must have elicited the old fearsome emotions associated with the nightmare journeys from his childhood, only this time he was old enough to understand the ferocity of the passions unleashed by the attack. In the blackness, from the streets below, came the terrifying sounds of violence and murder. Even more ominously, the shouts of the mob could now be heard plainly from within the palace itself: "Vive le duc de Bourgogne! Long live the duke of Burgundy!" and "Death! Death! The town is ours! Kill them all, kill them all!"

Hastily wrapping the dauphin in a robe—there was no time to dress— Tanneguy led Charles quickly through a back door of the *hôtel*, which opened onto the rue Saint-Antoine. From there, the pair fled to the fortified safety of the Bastille, the most secure structure in Paris, where they were soon joined by Robert Le Maçon, Charles's chancellor. Although the massive walls of the Bastille had protected the sovereigns of France for centuries, both counselors feared that in this instance they would be insufficient to shield Charles from the reach of his Burgundian pursuers. After a brief consultation, a fateful decision was made to take advantage of the chaos in the streets to risk a desperate flight out of the city before the mob detected the absence of their prey. Robert Le Maçon valiantly gave up his own horse to Charles, who, in borrowed clothes and in the company of Tanneguy, stole

The Burgundians massacre the Armagnacs in Paris.

out into the streets under cover of darkness. The intrigue worked; no one recognized the dauphin; and "to the great annoyance of the town of Paris," as a Burgundian chronicler complained later, both men galloped to safety in Melun, outside the reach of the mob.

The wisdom of Tanneguy du Chastel's initiative was to prove only too evident in the days ahead. "The people, bitterly inflamed against the confederates [Armagnacs], went through all the houses in Paris, hunting for them," reported an eyewitness. "All that they found, of whatever rank, whether they had been taken prisoner by the soldiers or not, they hauled out into the streets and killed them at once without mercy, with heavy axes and other weapons. . . . There was not one of the principal streets of Paris that had not had a killing in it. . . . They were heaped up in piles in the mud like sides of bacon—a dreadful thing, it was. Five hundred and twenty-two men died by the sword or other weapons that day in Paris out in the streets, not counting the ones who were killed inside the houses." In fact, in the course of that terrible night and over the next few weeks, some *sixteen hundred* members of the Armagnac party who had remained in Paris, including the count of Armagnac himself, who was discovered hiding in a cellar, would be arrested and eventually massacred by the Burgundians.

By July 13, Queen Isabeau and John the Fearless had sufficiently consolidated their hold on Paris to be able to enter the capital in state. Charles VI, ever erratic, welcomed them warmly, believed everything they said, and gave them everything they wanted; he even reinstated all of Isabeau's powers retroactively, as though she had never been in exile. Perhaps he did not notice the carnage around him—two days before, the citizens of Paris had murdered the last of their Armagnac prisoners, including the count—or, if he did, felt it was a natural extension of his own paranoia. Whatever the reason, from this point on, Isabeau and John the Fearless controlled the Parisian government and the royal council.

And yet the continued absence of the dauphin, the legitimate heir to the throne, threatened to undermine their authority. To have Charles at large was too dangerous; those members of the Armagnac faction who had escaped or who lived outside the capital might use him as a rallying point. To prevent this, Isabeau issued a formal summons ordering Charles to appear in Paris. This was not a friendly invitation. To obey meant risking imprisonment or worse; to refuse gave the queen and the duke of Burgundy the justification they needed to raise an army and so force the dauphin to submit to their rule.

But by this time Charles was safely in Bourges, south of the Loire, under Yolande's protection. With the death of the count of Armagnac and so many others, it was left to the queen of Sicily to undertake the leadership of the opposition to Burgundian rule. Her influence with Charles was so strong during this period that he seems to have been hesitant to act in any capacity without first securing her approval. In a long letter dated June 29, 1418, exactly one month after he had escaped Paris, he wrote to the citizens of Lyon that he would not set a date to visit their city "until we have had the advice of our mother the Queen of Sicily."

As the political leader of the former Armagnac faction it was left to Yolande to answer the summons by Isabeau. Her reply, since lost, was reputed to have been recorded by the chronicler Jehan de Bourdigné:

"We have not nurtured and cherished this one for you to make him die like his brothers or to go mad like his father, or to become English like you. I keep him for my own. Come and take him away if you dare."

DESPITE THIS CONTENTIOUS RESPONSE, Yolande was not in fact interested in promoting further warfare with Isabeau and the duke of Burgundy. Throughout her life, the queen of Sicily consistently demonstrated a preference for diplomacy over military action as a means of resolution. Also, she recognized the English as the primary enemy. However, she had first to get Isabeau and John the Fearless's attention, to make them understand that they could not ignore the dauphin's rights as heir to the throne. Both she and Charles understood that the king would be of no help—"I know very well that they [Isabeau and John the Fearless] will do to my lord [the king] everything they wish," the dauphin remarked to one of his officials—so it became necessary to use the threat of military action to intimidate their adversaries. Accordingly, with Yolande's approval, Charles summoned his vassals and men-at-arms. Some four thousand soldiers answered his call, insufficient, perhaps, to defeat the English, but certainly enough to demonstrate to his mother and the duke of Burgundy that they had to take him seriously.

"Those who get power should be careful how they rule, because one day we'll come back against them," the dauphin warned.*

Having strengthened Charles's bargaining position, Yolande once again insisted on a peace conference, and in August 1418 she succeeded in bringing together representatives from the two warring factions at Saint-Maur-des-Fossés, just outside of Paris. Here, her ambassadors put forward the novel suggestion that the two sides reconcile and join forces in repelling their common enemy, Henry V, who had by this time taken Rouen, and was demanding to marry Charles VI's daughter Catherine and to be officially recognized as the future king of France. The duke of Brittany, who was again the queen of Sicily's ally, managed to obtain a private interview with John the Fearless, and out of this a treaty emerged, which was signed by the duke of Burgundy and sanctioned by the king on September 16.

And then came a surprise: Yolande could not get Charles to sign it. He was beginning to listen to the more militant members of his entourage, like Tanneguy du Chastel, who had been targeted more than once by the duke of Burgundy. Tanneguy, it turned out, preferred not to come to terms with a man who routinely murdered, or tried to murder, his opponents whenever their interests conflicted with his own. But Yolande was in charge and she worked on Charles until finally, the next year, her efforts were rewarded. Over the course of three days, between July 8 and July 11, 1419, the dauphin met the duke of Burgundy face-to-face on a bridge near Melun, and after a series of talks they shook hands and signed a treaty of friendship. The two even exchanged "the kiss of peace." At this time, they also made arrangements to meet later in the year, in order to continue the diplomatic dialogue. All of France breathed a sigh of relief.

Having maneuvered Charles into what she believed to be a position of security, Yolande felt comfortable enough to leave the dauphin in the hands of his advisers and make a journey that she had already been putting off for far too long. It had been two years since her husband's death, and she still had not brought her eldest son, Louis III, to Provence so that he could be formally installed as count in his father's place. Provence was an integral component of Louis III's inheritance; he could not hope to renew the family

---

*Interestingly, this is almost the same threat that his older brother, the duke of Guyenne, had used when confronting John the Fearless after the 1413 uprising of the butchers: "Know with certainty that one day you will be sorry, and things will not always turn out as you would like."

quest to conquer the kingdom of Naples without the county's support. She needed to secure the homage of the principal Provençal barons by going from town to town with her son, just as her mother-in-law, Marie of Blois, had done so many years before with Louis II. And so as soon as she knew that the treaty with John the Fearless had been signed, Yolande left Saumur and began the long journey south, taking Louis III and her two youngest children with her.

When Yolande quitted the dauphin's court, she took the voice of moderation with her, and this would be France's undoing. For in August, Henry V's forces easily took the city of Pontoise and an Armagnac spy informed the dauphin that the duke of Burgundy had treacherously aided the English in this conquest. Although it is impossible to determine if this source was reliable, John the Fearless's past behavior did not recommend him to the good opinion of those in the opposition party. The advisers surrounding Charles, particularly Tanneguy du Chastel, did not hesitate to believe the accusation. In a moment, all Yolande's careful diplomatic groundwork was undone and a desperate plan conceived and put into effect.

As it happened, Charles had already arranged to meet John the Fearless for another diplomatic talk on the bridge of Montereau-Fault-Yonne on September 10, 1419. (Bridges were so often used as venues in these cases because it was generally assumed that it would be more difficult to conduct an ambush out in the open in such a confined space; in the event, this piece of conventional dogma turned out to be of dubious value.) On the appointed day, the two sides met as planned. The duke of Burgundy and the dauphin each stepped out onto the bridge accompanied by ten members of their respective entourages. As dictated by chivalry, John the Fearless went down on one knee before Charles and swept off his large black velvet chapeau in the required gesture of homage, at which point Charles, also following protocol, politely took him by the hand, raised him to his feet, and indicated that he could return his hat to his head. The niceties having been satisfied, Tanneguy du Chastel then shoved the duke of Burgundy from behind, so that another of Charles's entourage could slash at his face more easily with his sword, and then Tanneguy du Chastel finished him off with his axe. In less than two minutes the once feared duke of Burgundy was on the ground with his internal organs spilling out all over the bridge. The whole operation was conducted with such ruthless efficiency that John the Fearless's men did not have time to move before their leader was dead and they themselves surrounded.

This violent act, meant both to improve the position of the dauphin relative to his powerful cousin, and as the long-sought retribution for the murder of the duke of Orléans, did not achieve the desired result; rather it sent Charles hurtling along a downward spiral. As a result of the assassination, Isabeau, mistrustful of her son and fearing reprisals from the English, convinced the king to come to terms with Henry V. In a series of letters issued in May 1420, which became known as the Treaty of Troyes, Henry V was married to the princess Catherine, and then Henry was officially adopted by Charles VI in place of the dauphin as regent and heir to the French throne. The English army moved into Paris and held the capital as well as Normandy, Gascony, and Maine, while the dauphin Charles, distraught and disinherited, was exiled to the provincial court at Bourges.

But to Yolande of Aragon, who would be confronted with the aftermath of this fiasco (and the responsibility for cleaning it up), the parallels to the story line of *The Romance of Melusine* were stunningly obvious. For just like Raymondin, the fictional male protagonist in Jean of Arras's tale, the dauphin, having participated in the murder of his cousin, the duke of Burgundy, was wandering lost and despondent in the forest of southern France. According to this narrative, Raymondin—that is to say, Charles—would eventually inherit all of the duke's estates, establish a royal lineage, and become an even greater lord than his murdered cousin. There was just one element missing to turn this fiction into reality.

Upon her return from Provence, the evidence suggests that the queen of Sicily actively sought a Melusine as part of her strategy for reinstating the dauphin as the legitimate heir to the French throne. It is difficult to trace her movements completely, as for political reasons Yolande exercised discretion, but of one fact there can be no doubt.

She knew her when she saw her.

PART II
Joan of Arc

The earliest surviving image of Joan of Arc,
doodled in the margin of a manuscript.

CHAPTER 6

Childhood in Domrémy

⚜

In my town they called me Jeannette, and since I came to France I have been called Joan. As for my surname, I know of none.

—Joan of Arc, in response to an inquisitor's question at her Trial of Condemnation, 1431

THE COURAGEOUS YOUNG WOMAN who would one day become known all over France as Joan of Arc was born in 1412, three years before the battle of Agincourt, on a small farm on the eastern frontier of the kingdom. Her baptism was not recorded; the evidence for her date of birth comes from Joan herself. "As far as I know, [I am] about nineteen years old," she told her inquisitors in 1431.

Very little is certain about her family. Her father, a farmer who apparently also kept some sheep and cattle, was variously known as Jacques Tart, Tarc, or Darc—Joan herself referred to him as "Jacques Tarc." Her mother, Isabelle, gave birth to four children in addition to Joan: three boys, Jacquemin, Jean, and Pierre, and a girl, Catherine, who died in childhood. Joan seems to have been younger than all three of her brothers; probably she was the fourth child born to Isabelle.

The precise circumstances of her childhood are unclear, but the family was not wealthy, as, according to an eyewitness, Joan "dressed in poor clothes." As for schooling, she had none. "[I] knew neither A nor B," she once confessed. What little religious instruction she had came from Isabelle. "It was from my mother that I learnt Pater Noster, Ave Maria, Credo. Nobody taught me my belief, if not my mother," she told her inquisitors.

There was nothing unusual in any of this. The concept of public education of the lower classes—and especially of girls—would not be embraced for centuries. What was uncommon in Joan's case was her very high level of intelligence, which manifested itself at an early age. Her verbal byplay, which she later wielded against her inquisitors, displayed enormous gifts— untrained and unschooled, she bested and eluded learned men twice her age who sought to ensnare her in her own words. Her power of speech impressed all who saw her, beginning with her own family; early on, she convinced the husband of one of her mother's cousins to aid her in her fantastic quest to seek an audience with the dauphin, even though this meant his risking the scorn of the commander of the local fortress, a form of public humiliation. Most telling was the comment of Albert d'Ourches, a member of the provincial gentry from nearby Vaucouleurs. "This girl spoke terribly well," he said of Joan. "I would really like to have had so fine a daughter." Birth was everything in the Middle Ages. Members of the underclass were uniformly viewed as vulgar and contemptible. It was singular, even for a member of the bourgeoisie, to set aside these prejudices and admire a peasant.

Her mental aptitude evoked comparison to the better-known female mystics of the Middle Ages, such as Hildegard of Bingen, a Benedictine nun who became abbess of her convent in Germany, and who also had visions, and Clare of Assisi. But the medieval saint with whom Joan would seem to have the most in common is Catherine of Siena. Born in the previous century, Catherine had been the youngest of twenty-five children. When she was six, she claimed to have been visited by Jesus and knew from that point that she was destined for the Church. Over the strong objections of her family, who wished her to marry, Catherine succeeded in remaining a virgin and finally entered a convent at the age of seventeen. There she taught herself to read and write in the vernacular and subsequently inserted herself aggressively into international politics by conducting a ferocious letterwriting campaign with the pope and various heads of state, in which she lectured her targeted correspondents on the inadequacies of their foreign policies. Among the royal recipients of Catherine's epistles were Charles V, king of France; Louis I of Anjou (husband of Marie of Blois); Elizabeth, queen of Hungary; and Joanna I, queen of Naples.

Perhaps because Joan's acuity did not have a scholarly or creative outlet—books or a teacher were required for literacy, and she had access to neither—her talent came out in her speech, and in her instinctive perception of the world at large. Her cognitive process was obviously rapid and comprehensive. It was as though she had an internal antenna that picked up all sorts of disparate signals, unconsciously set to work organizing them into a coherent narrative, and then later replayed them in her head, like a song on a radio.

JOAN'S ENTIRE CHILDHOOD and adolescence were spent on her parents' farm and in the tiny village in which she was born. She learned to sew and spin thread and to help her mother around the house; she also worked with the livestock. "When I was quite big and had reached the years of reason, I did not generally guard the animals, but I did help to take them to the meadows," she reported. This pastoral existence seems to have provoked misconceptions about Joan's degree of isolation from events in the outside world. Because of its location—Domrémy was situated on the eastern border separating France from the Holy Roman Empire—historians as a rule have generally assumed the village to be a provincial backwater, a hamlet so poor and far away from Paris that its inhabitants could not hope to understand or care about the complex political and military situation in which France found itself. "Life [in Domrémy] was like the countryside itself, barely undulating, dull, where all strangers were foreigners and potential enemies, and all new ideas suspect," wrote John Holland Smith, one of Joan's biographers. "How had provincial France declined into this miserable condition?"

But to believe this is to ignore one essential aspect of the village's existence. Domrémy was situated in the duchy of Bar, ancestral home of Yolande of Aragon's mother, Yolande of Bar, and an area as vital to the French crown in the fifteenth century as it had been during the reign of Yolande of Aragon's grandmother, Marie of France. As before, half the inhabitants—those who lived, like Joan and her family, to the west of the Meuse River—were loyal to the French king, while those who lived to the east of the waterway gave their allegiance to next-door Lorraine, technically subject to the Holy Roman Emperor. Except, in Joan's day, the duke of Lorraine, a weak, fearful man much given to gout, had allied himself—or rather been bullied into allying himself—with the duke of Burgundy. So Joan and those like her living on the western bank of the Meuse identified those of her neighbors living on the eastern side not as citizens of the empire, but as Burgundians. Far from being removed from the Armagnac-Burgundian controversy that plagued the rest of France then, Domrémy was actually on the front lines of the conflict, literally face-to-face with the enemy across the river. Joan herself affirmed the accuracy of this portrait of her birthplace later, at her condemnation trial. Asked by an inquisitor, "Did the people of Domrémy take the Burgundian side or that of their opponents?" Joan replied, "I knew only one Burgundian there and I could have wished his head cut off—however, only if it pleased God."

In 1419, when Joan was seven years old, a political event of some importance took place in the duchy. The former duke of Bar (Yolande of Aragon's uncle) having been killed four years earlier at the battle of Agincourt, the duchy had devolved upon another of Yolande's uncles, the duke's younger brother, cardinal Louis, bishop of nearby Châlons-sur-Marne. Being a clergyman, however, the new duke of Bar had no children, and could not expect (at least legitimately) to beget any in the future, so to remedy this problem cardinal Louis agreed to adopt a male heir. Concurrent with this adoption, it was also decided that the young man chosen as cardinal Louis's successor would marry Isabelle, the daughter of the duke of next-door Lorraine, with the understanding that after the deaths of the present dukes this couple together would inherit and rule both Bar and Lorraine.

There then only remained the question of whom cardinal Louis should elect to succeed him. In the summer of 1419, just before she left for Provence, Yolande of Aragon deftly used her family ties to put forward her own aspirant and successfully contrived to convince her uncle of the merits of her candidate. The lucky young gentleman chosen to inherit the prestigious and lucrative territories of both Bar and Lorraine was none other than Yolande's second son, artistic little René.

With this one diplomatic stroke, Yolande managed through René not only to hold Bar for the dauphin Charles, but also to make inroads into rival Burgundian territory. The duchy of Lorraine was integral to John the Fearless's political ambitions, and although there is no record of his reaction, he must have been furious to have been outmaneuvered in this fashion by his longtime enemy, the queen of Sicily. "Bar and Lorraine could provide invaluable links between [the Burgundians'] northern and southern blocks of territories and the sudden appearance of a Valois prince [René] loyal to the dauphin Charles was the worst thing that could have happened to their plans for consolidation," medievalist Margaret L. Kekewich observed matter-of-factly. Before his assassination, John the Fearless had hoped that one of his English allies would succeed in winning the duke of Lorraine's daughter and had exerted pressure in this direction, but to no avail. "Yolande had pulled off a double *coup* in the face of stiff competition since Henry V of England had asked for the hand of Isabelle for his brother, the duke of Bedford," Kekewich continued.

And so in the summer of 1419, ten-year-old René left his childhood home in Angers and came to live with his great-uncle in Bar as preparation for one day assuming the lordship of the duchy. He was only three years older than Joan herself. His mother, who was expected in Provence, could not come with him, but she sent him with an entourage of trusted Angevin counselors to ensure his safety and training, just as she had once surrounded the dauphin Charles with advisers loyal to herself and her family while he was still a boy under her care.

On August 13, 1419, a mere month before the deadly rendezvous on the bridge at Montereau-Fault-Yonne that would take the life of John the Fearless, René was formally invested with the duchy of Bar at a solemn ceremony in his great-uncle Louis's castle, and the next year married Isabelle, who was a year younger than he. The wedding took place amid general rejoicing on October 24, 1420, in Nancy, the capital of Lorraine. "Now it is true that the aforesaid cardinal adopted as his heir his nephew René, and gave to him and relinquished the duchy of Bar and many other beautiful dominions; and by means of these fiefs . . . the daughter and heiress of the duchy of Lorraine was given him in marriage," wrote Jean Le Févre, a chronicler of the period. "Because for a long time these dominions [Bar and Lorraine] had endured war and division, and by this marriage would achieve peace and unity under one master." From this time on, René lived with his wife, residing alternately with his great-uncle, cardinal Louis, and his father-in-law, the duke of Lorraine.

Domrémy was a small village, but not so small that its inhabitants did not know the name of their duke or the relation of his adopted heir to the royal family of France. Medieval courts—particularly regional courts like René's in Bar and Lorraine—moved frequently from castle to castle and acted as social and political hubs for the surrounding area. Servants and vassals came and went; food and clothing were supplied by local merchants who chatted with the kitchen help or the ladies of the wardrobe; and the

duke's officials and representatives traveled regularly throughout the countryside to check on rents and taxes. In René's case, the threat from neighboring Burgundian partisans—not everybody was happy about this
marriage—meant that he had a military responsibility to protect his duchy
from enemy incursions, so as he grew older, he and his counselors were in
constant communication with the many knights and men-at-arms who
were stationed in the various fortified castles scattered throughout the
duchy. René, of course, also kept in touch with his own family, particularly
his mother and his sister Marie and her husband, the dauphin Charles. Royal
messengers from Charles's suite at Bourges regularly braved enemy territory
to make the trip to René's various castles in Bar or Lorraine. As a result, the
court life centering around the newly married young couple fairly pulsed
with information—family news, military reports, political updates, snatches
of overheard private conversations, whispers, gossip, rumor, innuendo—
which by degrees made its way out of the aristocratic grand halls down into
the depths of the servants' quarters and finally out into the larger towns of
the countryside.

Domrémy might have been too remote to have immediate access to all
of these tidings, but inevitably echoes of this intelligence seeped down into
the villages. Because later, when Joan had an opportunity to meet the old,
gouty duke of Lorraine, she said to him very specifically "that he should
give me his son [she meant his son-in-law; the duke of Lorraine had no son]
and some men-at-arms for France and that I would pray to God for the
restoration of his health," indicating that she recognized René and was
aware that he in particular could be of use to her. So Joan knew enough
about René to gauge his relationship to the dauphin, and this knowledge
must have come from the regional court. And if Joan from the tiny village
of Domrémy knew it, this information must also have been well dissemi-
nated throughout the rest of the duchy.

In the end, the queen of Sicily's decision to hold Bar for Charles was
perhaps even more far-reaching than she herself might have realized. For if
the English duke of Bedford or some other ally of the duke of Burgundy had
succeeded in marrying Isabelle of Lorraine, local sentiment in favor of the
dauphin and the Armagnac side in the civil war would likely have been
stamped out and Joan's own political leanings affected. Certainly there was
no possibility that she would have been aided in her design by an officer of
the court. As it was, the introduction of René into the duchy during Joan's

early childhood served instead to nurture and fan the loyalties of this singular girl and those who lived near her. So when her inquisitors later asked, "In your extreme youth had you great wish to go out against the Burgundians?" Joan answered as Yolande or any of her family would have hoped one of their subjects would answer. "I had a great will and desire that my King have his kingdom," she said.

BUT IN THE EARLY 1420s, Charles was very far from doing that. The assassination of John the Fearless, meant to eliminate the principal threat to his rule, served only to unite his enemies against him. John's widow screamed her fury and dispatched dozens of letters and embassies to the various heads of state, including the king and queen of France, the Holy Roman Emperor, and the pope, demanding that justice be done. In December 1420 she managed to have the murderers tried in absentia in Paris and then used the subsequent guilty verdict as justification for the savage torture and death of one of the suspected assailants whom her agents had managed to capture. Her twenty-three-year-old son, Philip, the new duke of Burgundy, was so tormented by the news of his father's death that he writhed around on his bed in a fit of incoherent rage, swearing revenge, and was unable to compose himself sufficiently to assume his new duties for nearly two weeks. When he finally did emerge, he sent ambassadors to treat with Henry V, who coolly laid out the terms of an English-Burgundian alliance far more advantageous to England than to Burgundy. Henry was to have the princess Catherine in marriage, and to govern the kingdom as regent until the death of Charles VI, after which Henry and his heirs would rule France. If Philip was willing to put aside his own political aspirations with regard to the throne of France and agreed to support this plan, the English king promised to aid him by pursuing and punishing his father's murderers, and he further offered to marry one of his own brothers to one of Philip's sisters.

These were markedly weak incentives, but Philip, who lacked his father's fierce ambition and homicidal ruthlessness (and for this reason was known as "Philip the Good"), felt he had no choice but to take them. The English king did not really need Philip the Good's military support in order to take Paris; with his enemies in such disarray, his army was sufficiently intimidating to do that on its own. Besides, Isabeau, lured by Henry's pledge that she could continue to live in queenly splendor during the English occupation, had already convinced Charles VI to accept Henry's conditions. Philip gritted his teeth, signed the treaty of alliance, and sent troops from Burgundy to aid England in the conquest of France.

In the spring of 1420, Henry V and his army, having been joined by Philip the Good's men-at-arms, swept easily through northeastern France and took the cities of Laon, Reims, and Châlons, very close to the duchy of Bar. On March 23, Henry triumphantly entered Troyes, where he was met with great ceremony by Isabeau and Charles VI, who treated him like a long-lost and much-beloved member of the family. The final details of the French surrender were hammered out; Henry promised to bring all of France under his rule; and the dauphin Charles was officially disinherited. Not a man to waste time, Henry married Princess Catherine on June 2, 1420, at the cathedral of Troyes, and by June 4 was on the road again with his army, with the intention of attacking Montereau and Melun, whose citizens were still loyal to the dauphin. Melun in particular was strongly defended and held out as long as it could, but by November hunger forced its garrison to open the gates of the city to its besiegers.

On December 1, 1420, Henry V rode into Paris and took possession of the capital and the government of France. A month later, on January 17, 1421, Charles VI issued a formal letter to his Parisian subjects in which he in effect reiterated the clause in the Treaty of Troyes disinheriting his son. ("*Item,* In view of the horrific and enormous crimes perpetrated in the said kingdom of France by Charles, so-called dauphin of Vienne, it is agreed that neither we, nor our son Henry, nor our very-dear son of the duke of Burgundy, shall negotiate any peace or agreement with the aforesaid Charles.") In his letter, the king warned his subjects against remaining loyal to the dauphin. "One should not take account of the youth of the said Charles," the mad king wrote, "because he is quite old enough to tell good from evil."

But the "so-called dauphin" was not ready to give up. On March 22, 1421, Charles fought back at the battle of Baugé, in Yolande's duchy of Anjou, between Angers and Tours. A thousand knights and men-at-arms from Angers in service to the queen of Sicily were mustered under the command of one of her leading vassals, the lord of Fontaines, and these, in combination with a seasoned force of four thousand archers sent from Scotland to fight on the side of the dauphin (the Scots hated the English and could always be counted upon to fight against them) and a third troop of loyalists from La Rochelle, met an army of approximately sixty-five hundred

English soldiers led by Henry V's younger brother, the duke of Clarence. (Henry had returned to England for a short visit to drum up additional money and troops for his French occupation.) Combat lasted into the darkness, but at midnight the Scottish commanders, the earls of Douglas and Buchan, were able to send a messenger to the dauphin, who had remained behind at Poitiers, with the glad tidings that the battle was won, the enemy vanquished or taken prisoner, and the English duke of Clarence killed.

But this victory, while protecting Yolande's all-important duchy of Anjou and effectively preventing the English from making further inroads into the dauphin's territories south of the Loire, represented Charles's one bright moment in a time line of otherwise increasingly bleak episodes. No matter how hard the dauphin tried, Henry always seemed to have the upper hand. Never much of a soldier—"He didn't willingly arm himself, and he didn't love war at all, if he could avoid it," wrote a chronicler of the period—Charles nonetheless managed to muster an army of some eighteen thousand men and made an attempt to take back Chartres in the summer of 1421, only to retreat in the face of the English king's superior numbers. (Henry had returned from England accompanied by an alarming contingent of men-at-arms, some twenty-eight thousand in all.) On December 6, 1421, Charles's sister Catherine launched a further attack on his fortunes by giving birth to her first child, a son, thereby providing her husband Henry V and the crown of France with a male heir. Charles countered feebly by finally marrying his longtime fiancée, Yolande's daughter Marie (a commitment he had clearly been putting off for as long as he could), at a ceremony in out-of-the-way Tours on June 2, 1422. So limited were his funds and so great his military expenses that he had to sell the tapestries off the walls of one of his castles to pay for the wedding.

Even in death, the English king seemed to triumph. When Henry V was cut down by dysentery at the age of thirty-five on August 31, 1422, and Charles's own father, the poor insane king of France, finally made peace with his demons and followed his adopted English heir to the grave on October 21 of the same year, it was not the dauphin who was recognized publicly in Paris to succeed to the throne, but Henry's infant son, Henry VI, with Henry V's brother, the duke of Bedford, acting as regent. Charles could not even attend the funeral of his father, which was held in grand manner, first at Notre Dame, before an audience consisting of the masters of the university, the mendicants, and the Parlement of Paris, and then at Saint-Denis, where he was buried by some estimates before a crowd of eighteen thousand. The common people were bereft; Charles VI had ruled for over forty years, and although his terrible illness had made possible the turmoil in which the kingdom found itself, the king himself had ever held the loyalty, compassion, and goodwill of his subjects, some of whom could still remember the golden promise of his youth. "All the people in the streets and at the windows sobbed and cried as if every one of them were watching his own heart's darling die," wrote an eyewitness. "In front were two hundred and fifty torches carried by the poor servants, all dressed in black and weeping bitterly; just ahead were eighteen funeral bell-men. There were also thirty-four crosses of religious orders, and others who went before him sounding their bells."

Yet eerily, for all of the outpouring of grief among the populace, not a single member of the royal family was in attendance. Catherine was in England with her child, and Isabeau, although living in Paris at the time, did not put in an appearance. The queen was no doubt aware that she was not held in the same high regard by the citizens of Paris as her husband had been and might have been afraid to show herself publicly. "Thus his body was borne along and after it came the Duke of Bedford, brother of the late King of England, all alone, the only mourner; there was not one French prince there." At the burial site, the chief of the gendarmes shouted, "'God grant life to Henry, by the grace of God, king of France and of England, our Sovereign Lord,' to which the masses cried out in a single voice, 'Vive le roi! Vive le roi! Long live the king! Long live the king!'"

By contrast, Charles was forced to hold his own induction ceremony a few days later. It was reported by chroniclers that he wept when informed of the death of his father, and wore black, but for only one day; the next morning he appeared in church in a majestic crimson robe, "and there were many heralds clothed in coats fashioned with the arms and blazons of their lords and masters." Charles was in Auvergne, in southern France, when he heard the news, so the inaugural, such as it was, took place at a local church near Le Puy. "Then there was raised a banner of France within the chapel, and those officers of the arms began to cry many times loudly and clearly, 'Long live the king,'" the chronicler reported. "After the cry had ceased, Divine Service began in the church, and no other solemnity was then performed, and from that day forward those adhering to his party began to call him king of France."

LE TRESVETORIEVX ROY TE FRANCE

CHARLES SEPTIESME TE CE NOM

Portrait of the man Joan of Arc called the dauphin, the future Charles VII.

Altogether, this convocation was a decidedly depressing affair that only served to highlight Charles's impotence; no French king in living memory had assumed the throne so ignominiously, and with such a paltry display of pomp and ritual. "French historians have speculated that he would not even have made the gesture if it had not been for the promptings of his mother-in-law, Yolande, who . . . enlisted Regnauld of Chartres's [the arch-bishop of Reims] help in badgering Charles into speaking up for himself," observed one of Joan of Arc's biographers. Worse, this self-administered investiture only added to the humiliation heaped on Charles by his enemies, the English and the Burgundians, who thereafter derisively referred to him as "the king of Bourges."

DURING THIS PERIOD, passions in Domrémy mirrored those in the king-dom at large. With the inhabitants of the duchy of Bar loyal to the dauphin, and those of Lorraine partisan to Philip the Good, conflict broke out regu-larly, as if the war were being fought in miniature. In May 1422, while Henry V was still alive, René's father-in-law, the gouty duke of Lorraine, observing that Charles's fortunes were not very promising, made a special visit to the Burgundian city of Dijon in order to pledge his alliance and goodwill to Philip the Good; at the same time he recognized Henry V as the legitimate sovereign of France. René, only thirteen at the time, was in no position to stop him. Encouraged by their duke's action, Joan's neighbors on the east bank of the river—the Burgundians—began conducting raids against those of the dauphin's loyal subjects living on the west bank. When an inquisitor later asked Joan, "In the town of Maxey, were they Burgundians or enemies of the Burgundians?" she answered, "They were Burgundians." When he pressed her further—"Were you ever with little children who fought for the side which is yours?"—she responded, "No, I have no memory of that; but I did see that certain people of the town of Domrémy had fought against those of Maxey, whence they came back sometimes much wounded and bleeding." Joan also volunteered that during these years of her childhood she frequently had to help take her father's cattle "to a fortified place which was called the Isle, for fear of men-at-arms."

It was in late childhood, with a dangerous conflict swirling around her, and the tacit presence of soldiers ever in the background, that Joan began to display a deep spirituality. She attended church regularly and her obvious devotion to religion was remarked on by her friends and neighbors. "Jean-nette would go often and of her own will to church and to the hermitage of Notre Dame de Bermont near to the town of Domrémy, when her parents thought that she was ploughing or working elsewhere out in the fields," said a farmer from nearby Greux who knew her in childhood. "When she heard the bell toll for Mass while she was out in the fields, she came away to the town and to the church to hear the Mass, as I have seen her do." "She was brought up in the Christian religion and full of good ways, as it seemed," said her next-door neighbor, Marguerite. "She went of her own will and often to church and gave alms out of her father's property and was so good, simple and pious that I and the other young girls would tell her that she was too pious." Joan confessed regularly to her parish priest and was so reverent that her overt displays of devotion provoked some teasing, particularly by the boys of the village. She was particularly drawn to the peaceful quiet of her local church, which might have contained images of the virgin martyrs Saint Catherine of Alexandria and Saint Margaret of Antioch, or perhaps a statue of Saint Michael the Archangel, "the captain-general of the armies of heaven"; in any event, she would have learned about the lives of these saints from the sermons given on their annual feast days.

Saints, soldiers, God, devotion, the dauphin, and the Burgundians— these were the disparate influences that contrived to weave their pattern on Joan's soul as she grew into adolescence. She did not, as so many believe, become who she was *despite* having been born in provincial, out-of-the-way Domrémy, but *because* of it.

THEN, IN THE SUMMER of 1423, Yolande of Aragon finally returned from Provence.

The queen of Sicily had been extremely productive during her four-year absence from Anjou. She had installed her eldest son, Louis III, as count of Provence in her deceased husband's place, and seen to it that he received the homage of all of the most important barons in the county. In keeping with the hopeless Angevin tradition of trying to reclaim the family's Italian inheritance, she had then sent seventeen-year-old Louis III to Rome in 1420 to obtain the consent of the pope for his enterprise, convinced the general assembly in Aix to contribute 100,000 florins toward his war effort, used the money to purchase an army and a fleet of Provençal ships, and then sent this force to Naples to aid her son in his conquest. Southern Italy, plagued by political factions, folded in the face of such competent management. By June 1423, Louis III had been officially accepted as the heir to the throne by the then reigning queen of Naples, Joanna II, and was ensconced at her court, learning the ways of his future kingdom and waiting for her to die so he could come into his inheritance. Her eldest son's future being thus assured, Yolande turned her attention once again to the fortunes of her daughter and son-in-law in France.

She found Charles's campaign to be a disaster on nearly every front. If he had been trying to lose the monarchy he could not have done a more efficient job of it. On April 17 of that year, the duke of Brittany, whose friendship Yolande had so carefully cultivated before she left for Provence, had abandoned Charles's cause as unsalvageable and signed a treaty with the duke of Bedford and Philip the Good, which became known as the Triple Alliance. This diplomatic disappointment had been followed almost immediately by a further military setback when on July 30 Philip's forces had trounced Charles's at the town of Cravant in Champagne. The English were again advancing into Yolande's dominions of Maine and Anjou; an army led by the duke of Suffolk was within ten leagues (about thirty miles) of her home castle of Angers; and Charles himself was demoralized, profligate, and surrounded by a staff of bickering counselors who jostled for money and influence. About the only positive development at court for which Charles could take some credit had occurred on July 3 when Yolande's daughter Marie had given birth to the couple's first child, a son, Louis, thereby establishing a line of succession, although even here Charles could not really be said to have done the heavy lifting.

Yolande wasn't at Bourges with her daughter and son-in-law a week before she realized that if anything was going to be done to remedy this situation she was going to have to do it herself. Her first and most pressing problem was the English invasion of Anjou. The castle at Angers, which Yolande as regent was responsible for maintaining in the absence of Louis III, was one of the most important fortresses in France. If the enemy occupied that great stronghold they would be almost impossible to dislodge; Angers simply could not afford to be lost. Yet Charles's army had been decimated by the Burgundians at the recent battle at Cravant—more than six thousand of his men-at-arms had been killed, with another two thousand taken prisoner—and he had neither the will nor the resources to launch another counteroffensive so soon. Some other means of defense would have to be arranged.

So Yolande left the safety of Bourges and traveled to her threatened castle in Angers to mobilize and prepare for an assault. She arrived on August 19, 1423, and immediately summoned her vassals from Anjou and Maine as was her legal right as duchess, ordering them to present themselves and their required men-at-arms for battle. Her call was heeded by both the nobility and the peasantry, and a strong force—one chronicler put it at as large as six thousand armed men—was quickly organized under the banner of the count of Aumale, an experienced Angevin commander. The English, under the earl of Suffolk, thinking the territory undefended, were at this point ravaging the countryside. "In this same year [1423] there assembled in Normandy about two thousand five hundred English combatants, under the lead of lord de la Pole [the earl of Suffolk] . . . and [these] passed in good order the country of Maine, and from thence, laying waste the country, they went as far as Angers, where they did great damage, and took in the said country a great spoil of prisoners, cattle, and other goods," wrote an English chronicler.

But the count of Aumale, who was far more familiar with the terrain than his opponents, crept up with his army from behind Suffolk's men, cut them off, and on September 26 launched a sneak attack. "The said English, not knowing of the approach of their enemies, were so taken by surprise, that . . . at length they were forced to yield the victory to their said enemies; and they lost upon the spot about eight hundred men. . . . And there were taken prisoners the said lord de la Pole, and with him thirty gentlemen of his party." Those English who were not killed or captured were forced to retreat out of Anjou and Maine. This was not a decisive battle—Suffolk's troops represented only a fraction of the overall English force—but the initiative at least gave Charles's adversaries pause; more important, the castle of Angers remained safely in Yolande's hands.

Having bought herself some breathing room, she was able to focus on diplomacy, an art at which, after so many years of practice, she excelled. In November, the queen of Sicily traveled to Nantes to confer with her old friend, the duke of Brittany. The upshot of this parley was that the duke of Brittany's brother, Arthur of Richemont, although married to one of Philip the Good's sisters, nonetheless deserted the Burgundians and instead agreed to be Charles's constable. "There can be little doubt that [this] . . . was a result of the mediation of Yolande of Aragon, who used her influence with [the duke] of Brittany to win him over," observed medievalist M. G. A. Vale.

However, as promising as these negotiations were, they were not in themselves enough to resuscitate Charles's political and military fortunes. Because the next year, 1424, he lost another terrible battle, this time to the English at Verneuil.

The French defeat at Verneuil was devastating. By some accounts as many as fifteen thousand of Charles's men-at-arms were killed. Yolande saw Le Mans, the most important city in her home duchy of Maine, fall to England and the regency government. Charles's Scottish generals, the earls of Douglas and Buchan, and almost all of their army of six thousand also perished, as did Yolande's most experienced commander, the count of Aumale, and many of her troops. Charles despaired at the news; his soldiers had significantly outnumbered the English and yet they had lost again.

The destruction of the French army at Verneuil was so crushing, the human slaughter so profound, that it triggered a spiritual crisis within Charles. He began to fear that he could not win—that for some reason God looked unfavorably upon him. Perhaps his cause was not just. His trepidation and uncertainty were obvious to those around him. Yolande in particular understood that in the wake of these losses, the issue became one of faith. The queen of Sicily had already given Charles military and diplomatic aid; now she sought intervention of a higher order.

Sometime after the battle of Verneuil, an unusual prophecy, attributed to a seer from Provence named Marie of Avignon, began circulating throughout southern France. There were wise men and women all over medieval Europe who purported to be able to foretell the future; Marie of Avignon was one of the better known of these mystics. She had even taken the trouble to write down her revelations in a book, although, strangely, this particular prediction did not appear with the others. It just seems to have surfaced one day at Charles's court at Bourges and was attributed to her, and since Marie of Avignon was already famous for her prophecies, no one questioned that she had said it.

Because it was not among those previously published, but was passed along verbally, the prognostication took different forms as it made its way from person to person; however, two principal versions were eventually written down. The first of these was that "France, ruined by a woman [a reference to Isabeau of Bavaria], would be restored by a virgin from the marches [border region] of Lorraine." The second was that "a Maid [a virgin] would come . . . who would carry arms and would free the kingdom of France from its enemies."

That the divination singled out Isabeau as the principal culprit in the conflict is interesting. After all, the queen of France had been only one of a group of seditionists whose actions had led to the current strife. Certainly the duke of Burgundy (not to mention the English!) had as much to do with provoking the civil war as Isabeau, if not more. Yet to her alone was attributed the evils that had befallen France. This sentiment seems more in the nature of a private grievance than a political manifesto, and is consistent with Yolande of Aragon's position that she had been personally betrayed when Isabeau had renounced her original contract with the queen of Sicily and her family by helping to convince Charles's father to disinherit him and, by extension, Yolande's daughter Marie.

Similarly, the focus on a female savior was unusual. There was no precedent for it in French history—unless the parallels to *The Romance of Melusine* are considered.

The dissemination of this prophecy, which was purported to have emanated from that part of the country of which Yolande was countess, and which referred specifically to the duchy of which her son René was heir, was so widespread that it was astonishing. People over a hundred miles away repeated it. It was almost as if the divination was some sort of code or message—or perhaps, more accurately, a prayer—that was being broadcast purposely to the outermost reaches of the kingdom in the faint but desperate hope of an answer.

In nearly every hamlet, town, or village in fifteenth-century France there lived someone who claimed to have visions, or who could interpret dreams, or who was otherwise believed to have been somehow touched by God. These were the likely targets of the prophecy, and it acted upon them like a recruitment slogan.

And just at this time, Joan began to hear voices.

CHAPTER 7

The Angels Speak
to Joan

⚜

The first time that I heard the voice, I promised to
keep my virginity for as long as it should please
God, and that was at the age of thirteen or there-
abouts.

*—Joan of Arc, in response to an inquisitor's question
at her Trial of Condemnation, 1431*

HIRTEEN, THE AGE OF PUBERTY: a rush of hor-
mones accompanied by new and confusing emotions, turbulent mood swings, and a heightened
sensitivity to the often conflicting demands of
responsibility and desire. The difficult and complex
entry into adolescence was made even more chal-
lenging in the fifteenth century since thirteen was
the legal age at which a girl could be married. Partly, this was a function of
economics—for a poor family, an early wedding meant one less mouth to
feed. But there was also an element of control involved, as a thirteen-year-
old could on the whole be cajoled or bullied into an undesired marriage
much more easily than an older girl.

Joan clearly felt this pressure as, by her own admission, her first experience with what she would later identify as the voice of an angel had nothing
to do with politics but rather focused on her personal life. In addition to
eliciting a promise that she keep her virginity, the voice instructed her in
how to behave, which included regular attendance at church. Joan later

described the occasion of this first heavenly encounter in detail to her inquisitors. "When I was thirteen years old, I had a voice from God to help me govern my conduct," she said. "And the first time I was very fearful. And came this voice, about the hour of noon, in the summer-time, in my father's garden; I had not fasted on the eve preceding that day. I heard the voice on the right-hand side, towards the church; and rarely do I hear it without a brightness. This brightness comes from the same side as the voice is heard. It is usually a great light. . . . After I had thrice heard this voice, I knew that it was the voice of an angel."

The voice seems to have first come to Joan when she was feeling guilty about her behavior. "I had not fasted on the eve preceding that day" implies that this was something she thought she ought to have done; perhaps it was a fast day and she had forgotten or been too hungry to comply.* This transgression would have weighed heavily on a girl as pious as Joan; interestingly, the voice takes the responsibility for not fasting away from her by promising to help her better govern her conduct in the future. Similarly, by vowing to keep her virginity "for as long as it should please God"—that is, until the voice tells her not to—Joan also relieved herself of the burden of having to judge the merits of an early marriage, or to be answerable for the disobedience to her family that would be involved in rejecting one. God or the angel acting for God would now make that decision for her.

And her family was, in fact, arranging such an alliance with a man from the nearby city of Toul. Later, when Joan's inquisitors asked, "What made you cause a certain man at the city of Toul to be summoned for [breach of promise of] marriage?" she answered, "I did not have him summoned, it was he who had me summoned. And there I swore before the judge to speak the truth and in the end he roundly said that I had made the man no promise whatever." To be called before a judge in this fashion was tantamount to an indictment; Joan might not have promised the man from Toul anything, but *someone* did, and this someone was surely one of her parents, as Joan also stated at this time that "I obeyed them [her parents] in all things save only in that lawsuit I had in the city of Toul in the matter of marriage."

By the third time the voice spoke, Joan had identified it as belonging to Saint Michael. "The first time I had great doubt if it was Saint Michael who

---

*Later when she was older and wished to consult her voices, Joan would often fast as a way of calling them.

came to me, and that first time I was very much afraid; and I saw him afterwards several times before knowing that it was Saint Michael," she said. When her inquisitors pressed her: "How was it that you recognized Saint Michael rather on that occasion when you did believe [it to be him], than the first time he appeared to you?" Joan answered, "The first time I was a child and was afraid, and afterwards Saint Michael taught me and showed me and proved to me that I must believe firmly that it was him."

Saint Michael the Archangel occupies a high place in the hierarchy of heaven. He is the princely leader of the angels and their commanding general in the struggle against Satan; his name is synonymous with the war of good against evil. The feats of Saint Michael, who disputed with the devil and battled a dragon, were sure to be repeated, and his aid prayed for, wherever Christian soldiers and men-at-arms were stationed, and there were quite a number of these stationed in the region surrounding Domrémy. In her early teenage years, these soldiers seemed to have exercised some sort of fascination for Joan, because her family remarked on it and worried about it. "When I was still in the house of my father and mother, I was several times told by my mother that my father had told her that he had dreamt that I, Joan, his daughter, would go away with some men-at-arms," Joan remembered. "And much care did my father and mother have about it and they kept me close and in great subjection. . . . And I have heard my mother say that my father told my brothers, 'Truly, if I knew that that must happen which I fear in the matter of my daughter, I had rather you drowned her. And if you did not do it, I would drown her myself.'"

The implication here is that Joan's father was not afraid that his daughter would go away with men-at-arms in order that she might lead an army to expel the English from France—there would be no reason to drown her for that (not to mention that such a possibility was beyond comprehension)—but rather that she would run away with soldiers in the more conventionally immoral sense of engaging in relations outside the bonds of marriage. Although it is clear that he did not understand his daughter's character, parental concerns of this sort are generally based on some degree of observed evidence, which means that Joan's growing preoccupation with the military during this period was sufficiently obvious that it was heeded by her family.

Between the ages of thirteen and sixteen, when events began to move rapidly, the voice continued to speak to Joan. Once she was no longer "a child and . . . afraid," as she had been when the voice first appeared—in other words, as she got older and identified herself as an adult, probably around the age of sixteen—Joan came to trust that she was hearing the words of an angel. "I believed it quite quickly and I had the will to believe it," she testified. It seems that over this transitional period, the voice of Saint Michael became more insistently political. "What doctrines did he teach you?" her inquisitors asked. "Before all things he told me to be a good child and that God would help me," Joan replied. "And, among other things he told me to come to the help of the King of France. . . . And the Angel told me the pity [pitiful state] that was in the Kingdom of France."

THE VOICE that Joan identified as Saint Michael's conveyed an all too accurate assessment of Charles's woeful campaign against the English. From a timid, lonely, insecure boy, Charles had grown into a conflicted, anxious, and insecure adult, easily manipulated by those around him, and hopelessly, almost comically inconstant and indecisive.

For example, in the summer of 1425, Yolande finally succeeded in bringing the duke of Brittany's brother, Arthur of Richemont, to Charles's side as constable. However, no sooner had she achieved this diplomatic coup than Jean Louvet, an adviser of long standing jealous of Arthur's promotion, convinced Charles to turn against his new constable. Arthur, who was in Brittany raising troops, found out about the intrigue against him and, furious, marched back with an army to occupy the royal court at Bourges, a discouragingly predictable reaction that led to Charles and Louvet's raising an army of their own to fight against him.

As it was hardly useful for Charles's troops to fight each other rather than the English, Yolande took over. When Charles's army took a route that required them to travel through Tours, Yolande made sure that the doors of the city were closed to him. "We should not let any men of arms enter who are stronger than the people of [the] town, be he the King our sire, or the president in his attendance, who directs his government, nor other governors who disrupt and prevent the said peace, and whom the lord of Richemont, constable of France, and the said Queen intend to oust shortly from the attendance and government of the King," she wrote coolly to the captain of the city. Charles, incredulous, halted outside Tours, giving Yolande a chance to intercept him; she arrived on June 8 and with her usual dispatch within two days had delivered on her promise to reorganize the king's government along lines more to her liking. Louvet was exiled to Provence, Charles was reconciled with Arthur, and the queen of Sicily even used this occasion to send a conciliatory signal to Philip the Good by dismissing Tanneguy du Chastel, whose role in the murder of John the Fearless could not be ignored.

After this incident, to avoid further unpleasantness, Yolande regularly chaired Charles's council, and the political situation continued to improve. The duke of Brittany abandoned the Triple Alliance and began cautiously to support Charles; even better, the banishment of Tanneguy du Chastel prompted Philip the Good to send emissaries to begin talks with members of Charles's circle that everyone hoped would lead to reconciliation.

But she could not get her son-in-law to fight the English, and this had to be done, and done quickly, lest the duke of Bedford's forces succeed in conquering more of the portion of the kingdom that included Yolande's own territories. Charles, however, was still so unnerved by his defeat at Verneuil that he refused to mount another offensive. Worse, in his impulsive, erratic way, he had formed an attachment to a new counselor, Georges de la Trémoïlle, who was introduced at court by Arthur of Richemont in the summer of 1427. Although Yolande at first approved this appointment—La Trémoïlle had a brother who served the duke of Burgundy, whom the queen of Sicily hoped to use to further a negotiated peace with Philip the Good—she soon came to regret this decision. Corrupt, cunning, and enthusiastically self-serving, La Trémoïlle, described as "a fat man of about forty," flattered Charles and played upon his vices and insecurities, encouraging inaction. He was especially masterful at detecting weakness in others and exploiting conflict to his own advantage. Charles knew it. "Dear cousin," he said to Arthur of Richemont when he first introduced La Trémoïlle at court, "you give him to me, but you'll repent of it, because I know him better than you do."

And suddenly, with the accession of La Trémoïlle, Yolande, who had been Charles's primary support and mentor from the age of ten, felt her mastery over her son-in-law recede. This must have been something of a shock, not to mention irritating after all she had done for him. They must have quarreled, as Yolande abruptly quit the royal court and retired to her castle in Saumur in June 1427. She was not the only adviser to feel the chilling effects of Charles's fickleness; three months later, she was followed by her protégé, Arthur of Richemont, who was also evicted from his position as constable by La Trémoïlle's influence. With the loss of these two key players, the kingdom was left entirely at the mercy of a councillor whose principal interests lay in undermining the king's confidence as a means of controlling him and enriching himself as much as possible at the public expense.

This period of Georges de la Trémoïlle's greatest power—he almost single-handedly ran Charles's court from September 1427 until the following September—unquestionably marked the low point in Charles's already none-too-stellar career, and the English were quick to capitalize on it. By the spring of 1428, word reached France that substantial troop reinforcements under the direction of an accomplished general, the earl of Salisbury, were due to arrive that summer in preparation for a major new offensive. On April 28, 1428, the duke of Bedford very publicly summoned a war council to Paris to debate military options and chart the future course of hostilities in preparation for the earl's arrival. Philip the Good made a special trip to the capital at this time to participate in the conclave. News of these talks, and the impending embarkation of fresh troops from England, were grimly reported to Charles's court and from there leaked to his supporters; the atmosphere was tense as those who resisted the English-Burgundian alliance on his behalf braced themselves for a new onslaught.

Against this ominous background, Joan made her first attempt to reach Charles.

THE TIMING OF THIS, Joan's initial foray into the world outside of Domrémy, was no coincidence. Her voices—by now Saint Catherine and Saint Margaret were also speaking to Joan—became exceedingly urgent in May 1428, clearly in reaction to the English war council in Paris and the anticipated arrival of the earl of Salisbury and his troops. "The voice told me that I should go to France and I could not bear to stay where I was," she said. "The voice told me also that I should make my way to Robert de Baudricourt in the fortress of Vaucouleurs, the Captain of that place, that he would give me people to go with me."

Unwilling to let her parents know her true intention—"As for my father and my mother, my voices would have been satisfied that I tell them. . . . As for me, I would not have told them for anything in the world," she admitted—Joan feigned a simple social visit to her aunt and uncle, who lived about halfway between Domrémy and Vaucouleurs. "I went to my uncle's and I told him that I wanted to stay with him for a time and there I stayed about eight days," Joan reported. "And I then told my uncle that I must go to the town of Vaucouleurs and my uncle took me there. And when I came to this town of Vaucouleurs I recognized Robert de Baudricourt, whereas never before had I seen him and by my voice I knew this Robert, for the voice told me that it was him. And I told this same Robert that I must go into France."

Joan's uncle—actually, he was her mother's cousin's husband, she just called him uncle—was named Durand Laxart, and he later confirmed Joan's account of this episode, detailing the arguments she used to convince him to help her. "I went myself to fetch Joan at her father's house and I took her to my house," he reported. "And she told me that she wanted to go to France, to the Dauphin, to have him crowned saying, 'Has it not been said that France will be lost by a woman and shall thereafter be restored by a virgin?' And she told me also that I was to go to Robert de Baudricourt that he might have her taken to the place where the lord Dauphin was to be found."

Accompanied by her relative, Joan reached Vaucouleurs safely. The distinguishing feature of the town was its fortified castle, a twenty-three-stone-tower edifice on the bank of the Meuse supported by an escarpment, at which was stationed a garrison loyal to Charles. The soldiers of this unit were responsible for defending the territory surrounding Vaucouleurs against the Burgundians. Joan and her cousin went searching for Robert de Baudricourt and eventually found him. There followed a conversation that was overheard by a number of bystanders. The event was sufficiently unusual to be remembered long afterward: an unknown sixteen-year-old girl, attired in a shabby red dress or surcoat, loudly declaiming to a seasoned military commander while her adult male cousin looked on uncomfortably. This sort of thing did not occur every day in Vaucouleurs. An eyewitness reported, "Joan the Maid came to Vaucouleurs at the time of the Ascension of Our Lord [approximately May 14], as I recall it, and there I saw her speak with Robert de Baudricourt who was then captain of the town. She told him that she was come to him, Robert, sent by her Lord to bring word to the Dauphin that . . . the Lord wanted the Dauphin to be made King and he was to place his kingdom at her command, saying that despite his enemies the Dauphin would be made King and that she would lead him to his coronation." The outcome of this first parley was not successful. "This Robert several times told me that I should return her to her father's house after having cuffed her soundly," Joan's hapless cousin Durand Laxart reported.

Durand took the captain's advice and returned Joan to Domrémy, but the war intervened and she didn't remain there long. On June 22, taking the recommendation of the military council in Paris, the duke of Bedford ordered the governor of the nearby county of Champagne, Antoine de Vergy, a Burgundian ally who was on the English payroll, to attack the fortress of Vaucouleurs. In July, Antoine invaded the Bar-Lorraine region with an army of some twenty-five hundred soldiers, frightening the inhabitants of all of the villages in the area, including Domrémy. Gathering their possessions and livestock, Joan and her family followed their neighbors and fled to Neufchâteau, the nearest walled city, which was located only about ten miles south of Vaucouleurs.

Neufchâteau was large enough to boast an inn, owned by a woman known as La Rousse (the Redhead), and here Joan lodged, helping out in the kitchen to help pay for her stay. Both the inn and the city were crowded with people and men-at-arms similarly displaced by the war, and as might be imagined, there was much talk about the political situation and the need for Charles's government to take action against the enemy, particularly when the Burgundians began burning everyone's fields, an infuriating measure that could be witnessed simply by climbing onto the city's walls. There was much fear that Vaucouleurs would surrender, but Robert de Baudricourt and his men stubbornly resisted, and by the end of July the enemy, finding the fortress more difficult to conquer than they had expected, lifted the siege and retreated to their home base in Champagne.

FROM HER EXILE in Saumur, Yolande monitored the renewed English military offensive, and Charles's pathetic response to it, with increasing concern. Ordinarily, as a diplomat, she would have preferred to work quietly behind the scenes in order to regain her former influence at court. But conditions were deteriorating so rapidly that she didn't have the time. So she effectively staged a coup.

In February 1428, she hosted a small but select conclave at her castle to discuss what could be done to redeem the political and military situation. Attending this private conference were three former members of Charles's council—Arthur of Richemont (the constable), the duke of Clermont, and the count of Pardiac—all persons of high birth who, like Yolande herself, had left the king's court the year before. An understanding was reached, an army was mobilized, and by summer a plan of action was in motion.

On June 15, 1428, just after Joan's first unsatisfactory conversation with Robert de Baudricourt, Charles received a written communication signed by the constable and the two noblemen who had been called by Yolande to Saumur. In their letter, the three called for a meeting between the "États généraux" (a representative assembly from all the territories loyal to Charles) and the king and his councillors, for the purpose of determining the direction of the war. The three "princes of blood" noted that they wished to be reconciled with the king but only if the policies drawn from these deliberations were actually put into effect (a reference to La Trémoïlle's influence over Charles, which was generally recognized as inhibiting the king's will to act). To see that this condition was met, they demanded that "the queen of Sicily and those whom she was pleased to designate for this task, be responsible for ensuring the execution" of whatever resolutions came out of these discussions, evidence of Yolande's guiding influence over these events. That these three princes, with the queen of Sicily's aid, had managed to raise a substantial army capable of taking over the government with or without Charles's permission was well known at the royal court, and added greatly to the persuasiveness of their argument.

Charles was in no position to refuse this ultimatum. The prospect of a new offensive by the English frightened him; if the enemy broke through to the south of France he could be captured or killed. He needed allies and troops, and he recognized that the three princes, once reconciled, could bring the forces they were now using to threaten him to his defense. Accordingly, he acceded to all of their demands, and on September 15 a meeting of the États généraux was convened at Chinon. Yolande was back in power.

Having once again organized events to her satisfaction, the queen of Sicily returned to Charles's court. Mindful of the lessons of her own mother-in-law, Marie of Blois, to ease the process of mediation and smooth over any lingering hurt feelings, Yolande thoughtfully remembered to pack 500,000 francs, which she immediately donated to Charles's war effort. Even more important, she brought with her two new influential allies, the duke of Alençon and the count of Vendôme, high-ranking noblemen who, with Richemont, Clermont, and Pardiac, now formed the core of her political party.

Reconciliation was effected, and the queen of Sicily resumed her former position of authority within the royal council. At the September meeting, the États généraux, in combination with the councillors of the court, recommended that a new battalion be raised to meet the English threat, and, as previously agreed, Yolande was put in charge of organizing and supplying this army. She now had the policy she wanted—to meet the English with force—and the authority to implement it. She worked feverishly over the next few months to assemble the best and most experienced military commanders and soldiers available from within Charles's dominion and to gather the necessary provisions and equipment. By winter, all was in readiness, awaiting only the king's command to attack.

But despite all of her efforts, she was unable to convince Charles to act militarily, and only the king could order the army to advance. Subtler methods would be necessary to effect that transition.

BY SEPTEMBER, the reinforcements under the command of the earl of Salisbury had arrived in Paris and the English once more made plans to launch an offensive. Against the orders of the duke of Bedford, who wanted to attack and hold Anjou, the earl of Salisbury instead chose the city of Orléans, about halfway between Paris and Bourges, as his primary target. Orléans, on the north bank of the Loire, was protected by a number of walls and moats but was vulnerable to a blockade. In October, the earl of Salisbury had seized a number of towns in the surrounding area, including an important fort on the south side of the river, effectively isolating the city. Although Salisbury died from wounds incurred in the attack, he was immediately replaced by the earl of Suffolk, whose plan was simply to starve the inhabitants into submission. The English forces encircled the city and dug in for the winter, and so began the siege of Orléans.

Charles, despite having earlier agreed to implement the war policies recommended by his councillors and the general assembly, hesitated. He was terrified of losing, and this fear manifested itself in the form of an obsession with the possibility that he might be illegitimate. As part of a propaganda campaign to win the allegiance of their French subjects, the English had circulated a poster depicting in verse and images Henry VI's lineage, tracing the child's genealogy back to the great French king Louis IX. (Louis IX had later been deified Saint Louis; everyone in France, from the lowest peasant to the most exalted aristocrat, knew and revered Saint Louis.) The poem that accompanied this exceedingly clever and persuasive pictorial representation stressed the legitimacy of Henry V's son to the French crown. "How this Herry in the eight degree / Is to seint Lowrys sone and very heire / . . . For to possede by enheritaunce / Crownes two of englond and of Fraunce," the poet charged with this task wrote. The implication, of course, was that Charles was *not* legitimate—that he was instead the bastard son of Louis, duke of Orléans, by Isabeau of Bavaria, an accusation that Isabeau herself strenuously denied, and that the chronicler Jean Chartier accused the English of spreading deliberately, after which, he wrote, the queen "never again had joy in her heart."

Although the taint of Charles VII's illegitimacy would follow him throughout the centuries, the bulk of the evidence sustains the theory that he was in fact the son of the king of France. Disapproval of Isabeau's relationship with the duke of Orléans was not even hinted at by any chronicler until 1405, and Charles was conceived in 1402, when Isabeau's fidelity to her husband was never questioned. Moreover, based upon the date of his birth, February 22, 1403, modern science is able to pinpoint the period of Charles's conception as occurring between May 30 and June 1, 1402. The Monk of Saint-Denis specifically stated that "at the beginning of the month of June [1402]" the duke of Burgundy was apprised of the recovery of the king from one of his psychotic episodes. However, the duke of Burgundy was at this time in his northern territories, which meant that it would have taken a messenger at least a few days, if not a week, to transmit this information to him, so Charles VI had likely recovered by the last week in May. To prove that he was healthy again, the king would have once more begun sleeping with his wife, an action that resulted in Charles VII.

But no matter how many times Yolande assured him that he was legitimate—"you are the son of a king," she had told him repeatedly over the years—Charles continued to be racked by the fear that he was not legally heir to the kingdom, and so was fated to have his armies lose to the English. Even worse, egged on by Georges de la Trémoïlle, who was at his most influential when the king was faltering, instead of launching a counterattack, Charles instead began to toy with the idea of fleeing the kingdom as a means of avoiding disgrace or capture. One of Charles's chamberlains later reported that in 1428, Charles went into his private chapel and silently prayed, "saying nothing, but begging God in his heart that if he were indeed the true heir of the blood and noble house of France, and the kingdom lawfully his, God would protect and defend him; or at least grant him grace to be spared death or captivity, and escape to Spain or Scotland, whose kings had long been brothers in arms and allies of the kings of France; hence he had chosen them as his last refuge."

To have her son-in-law abandon the kingdom was the worst possible scenario, not simply for her daughter Marie but for Yolande herself. If the king fled, the English army would march uncontested into his territory and the queen of Sicily would lose all her lands and castles and estates in Anjou and Saumur. This was unacceptable. And she knew all about his plan. Charles might have thought that he was keeping his prayers to himself, but the sentiments he professed to express only to God would hardly have been mysterious to those around him, particularly his wife and mother-in-law. Yolande had eyes and ears all over the court; many of the domestics who waited upon the king had initially been in service with the queen of Sicily or a member of her family and remained loyal to her. Not that spies were particularly necessary in this instance; the idea of escaping to Scotland, for example, was one that had already been openly broached by Charles's advisers. As early as April 1428, Charles had sent ambassadors to try to arrange a marriage between his young son Louis and the daughter of the Scottish king as a means of further enabling this option. So widespread were the reports of Charles's Scottish project that Joan herself mentioned Scotland in a chance conversation with a man who was at the time a complete stranger to her. "I must be at the King's side, though I wear my feet to the knees. For indeed there is nobody in all the world, neither king nor duke, or daughter of the King of Scotland, nor any other who can recover the kingdom of France," she said.

Well indeed should Charles seek an alliance with the king of Scotland and get on his knees and beg God for assistance. The assault on Orléans was a blow meant to wound emotionally as much as militarily, a symbol of the futility of his efforts. Apprehensive that the return of the popular duke of Orléans might lead to further uprisings in France, the regency government had refused to set a ransom figure on him, and so thirteen years after Agincourt, the duke was still a prisoner of the English. To have a royal prince of once-mighty France held in captivity for so long was disgraceful enough, but for his captors to take advantage of his absence to seize and perhaps occupy his birthright was, at least to the common people, unthinkable. And yet throughout the winter of 1428 and into the early months of 1429, the king remained completely immobilized. It was as though Charles was waiting, yearning—begging—for a sign from God to tell him who he was and what to do.

The frustration Yolande of Aragon experienced at the king's obstinacy must have been overpowering. She had struggled to raise and supply a strong army and Charles refused to use it! And the English were within months, or perhaps even weeks, of taking Orléans! Desperate to shake him from his lethargy, the queen of Sicily was forced to intervene once again.

Around this time—the date was not specifically recorded—a royal messenger named Colet de Vienne was quietly dispatched to the court of Lorraine. Subsequent events would prove that he was not ordered away by the king, as Charles was unaware of his whereabouts or his role in the drama that would later unfold. Most likely, then, the messenger was sent under the guise of a routine family communication between Yolande (or Queen Marie, acting for her mother) and her son, as no one else of note at court would have had business in Lorraine. But Colet de Vienne's errand was anything but ordinary.

The king needed the confidence that God was with him in order to pursue the military policy she favored? Very well, Yolande of Aragon would arrange to have his prayers answered.

BY THE WINTER of 1428, the crisis was so acute that the French clergy was enlisted to organize regular weekly processions in the hopes that a public display of piety would find favor with God and lead to "the prosperity of the king's arms." In response, Joan's voices became even more urgent and they again told her to approach Robert de Baudricourt, this time with a new mission. "The voice told me, twice or thrice a week, that I, Joan, must go away and that I must come to France and . . . that I should raise the siege laid to the city of Orléans," she later told her inquisitors. "And me, I answered it that I was a poor girl who knew not how to ride nor lead in war." Sometime in either December 1428 or early January 1429, Joan again enlisted the aid of her cousin and went to Vaucouleurs. She did not try to approach Robert de Baudricourt immediately as she had done previously, but instead took up residence at the home of a husband and wife, Henri and Catherine Le Royer, who owned a house in the town. By this time, Joan was convinced that she was the virgin referred to in the prophecy and made no secret of her belief or the reason for her visit. "At the time when Joan sought to leave the town she had been in my house for a period of three weeks," Catherine Le Royer later testified. "And it was then that she sent to have speech with the lord

Robert de Baudricourt that he take her to that place where the Dauphin was. But the lord Robert would not. And when Joan saw that Robert would not take her, she said—I heard her—that she must go to the place where the Dauphin was: 'Have you not heard it said that it has been prophesied that France shall be lost by a woman and restored by a virgin from the Lorraine marshes?' I remembered having heard that and I was stupefied . . . and after that I believed in her words and with me many others," Catherine said.

This was Robert's second refusal to take Joan, but it was not nearly as scornful or vehement as his first rejection. During the three weeks she spent in Vaucouleurs, Joan had begun gathering support for her mission. Those she lived with were so impressed by her speech, her piety, and her passion—and so in agreement with her views that the siege of Orléans ought to be lifted and Charles crowned at Reims and restored to his hereditary position as king of France—that they offered to take her themselves. Together with Durand Laxart and another man from Vaucouleurs, Jacques Alain, Joan started out on her own to reach Charles's court. But she soon thought better of it and returned to Vaucouleurs, telling her companions that it was "not thus that they should depart." Still, the attempt was an indication that public opinion in the town had shifted enough in her favor to give Robert de Baudricourt pause.

Robert might have been the reigning power in Vaucouleurs, but like any knight he was also the vassal of a great lord, with whom he kept in regular contact and from whom he received military instructions. Robert was particularly close to his seigneur, and would later become his chamberlain and valued counselor. Robert de Baudricourt's great lord was—Yolande of Aragon's son René, the future duke of Bar and Lorraine.

René was now twenty years old, the father of two sons and a daughter. Both his uncle and his father-in-law were ailing—each would die within the next two years—and René was shouldering the brunt of the work associated with the administration of Bar and Lorraine. René had maintained his love of art and was still a devoted reader of romances and a loyal follower of the chivalric tradition, but he was also keenly aware of the conflict with England and the need to protect his duchies from encroachment. Robert de Baudricourt was one of his best men; he had been instrumental in holding the important fortress at Vaucouleurs. The two were in frequent communication. "The register of the Archives of La Meuse . . . bears trace of a regular correspondence between the Duke of Bar [René] and Baudricourt," wrote the great French scholar Anatole France.

Robert, uncertain of what to do about Joan, who was rapidly developing a following as a seer or holy woman, must have apprised the court of Lorraine of her existence. Because on January 29, 1429, after receiving a dispatch from René, he suddenly subjected Joan to the first in a series of tests. To the great surprise of her hostess, Catherine Le Royer, the captain, accompanied by a priest, appeared at the Le Royers' door one day—clearly something that had never happened before—and asked for Joan. "I saw Robert de Baudricourt, then Town Captain at Vaucouleurs, come into my house with Messire Jean Fournier," Catherine later testified. "I heard him telling Joan that the latter, a priest, was wearing a stole, and that he had exorcised it in the Captain's presence, saying that if there was any evil thing in her, she would draw back from them, and if there was something good, she would approach them. And Joan approached the priest, and gone onto her knees."

The precaution of exorcism having been satisfied, a messenger from the court of Lorraine next appeared in Vaucouleurs seeking Joan. She was informed that the old duke—René's father-in-law—was sick and wished to consult her about his illness; the messenger had brought with him a letter of safe conduct for her to the town of Nancy, where the duke was staying. This invitation must have been a cause for excitement among the townspeople, for Joan was suddenly the beneficiary of an outpouring of generosity. Especially, there was concern that her clothes were too shabby to appear before the duke or to protect her adequately from the rigors of a long journey in winter. "When Joan the Maid came to the place and town of Vaucouleurs, in the diocese of Toul, I saw her, dressed in poor clothes, women's clothes, red," reported Jean de Novellompont, another resident of the town. After Joan received the summons from the duke of Lorraine, "I asked her if she wanted to go in her own clothes," Jean continued. "She replied that she would rather have men's clothes. Then I gave her clothes and hose of my servants that she might don them. And that done, the inhabitants of Vaucouleurs had men's clothes made for her and shoes and all things necessary to her and they delivered to her a horse which cost about sixteen francs. When she was dressed and had a horse, with a safe conduct from the Duke of Lorraine, the Maid went to speak with that lord and I went with her to the city of Toul."

So the impetus to change her dress came not from Joan herself but from a kind supporter who was worried about the impression she would make if she went in her own garments. Nor did he find it strange that she chose to clothe herself in men's attire. Joan was going on a journey where, despite the safe conduct, she would be vulnerable to men-at-arms and other bandits; she would also be accompanied by men for the entire trip and would be forced to live and sleep beside them. Joan was a virgin and it was important that she remain so; the less temptation the better. Male apparel in this instance served as a practical form of protection.

Interesting too was the purchase of the horse. Since Joan did not protest when the people of Vaucouleurs provided her with a mount but simply thanked them and set off for Nancy, it must be presumed that by this time she had learned to ride. Her neighbors may even have helped her to master this skill, knowing that she would need it in the future to complete her mission. This may also perhaps explain why Joan waited three weeks or so before approaching Robert de Baudricourt the second time. She was already fascinated by soldiers and might have been using this interlude to observe the men in their military exercises so as to be able to emulate them. Certainly, if she had wished to acquaint herself with army behavior and tactics she could not have chosen a better venue than the fortress of Vaucouleurs.

Suitably outfitted, Joan obeyed the duke's summons and left for Nancy, probably at the beginning of February 1429. "The Duke of Lorraine required that I be taken to him," Joan reported. "I went and I told him that I wanted to go to France, and the duke questioned me about the restoration of his health and I told him that of that I knew nothing; I said little to him about my journey, but I said to the duke that he [should] give me his son and some men to take me into France and that I would pray to God for his health; I went to him by means of a safe-conduct and I returned afterwards to the town of Vaucouleurs." Joan's reference to the duke's "son" indicates that René sat in on this audience.

René was thus given a chance to observe Joan's behavior and assess her character. He already knew from Robert that she claimed to be the virgin of the prophecies, and was believed to be such by the townspeople of Vaucouleurs, and what René saw of Joan in her interview with his father-in-law would only have confirmed that picture. Despite the male attire, here was a modest, obviously pious, extremely articulate young woman, purporting to come from God, who showed immense confidence and self-possession in the presence of a high aristocrat. In addition to asking the duke to aid in her quest, Joan had apparently gently admonished him for having left his wife for another woman. According to a witness, Joan "had told him [the duke] that he was behaving badly and that never would he recover his health if he did not mend his ways, and she exhorted him to take back his good spouse," another indication that news originating with the duke of Lorraine's entourage reached as far as Domrémy, for Joan was very specific about the intelligence she received from her angels, and nowhere in her testimony did she mention that they had supplied her with this bit of gossip.

René would also already have been familiar from Robert de Baudricourt with everything Joan had said about Charles being the true king of France and the need to lift the siege of Orléans, and these would have reflected René's own views (which was hardly unusual, as Joan's opinions had been shaped over the years by information emanating from his court). "Precisely because her assumptions accorded so well with the prophecies then current among Charles' supporters, she was almost guaranteed a warm reception, at least from those whose own views coincided with hers," observed renowned medievalist Charles T. Wood. If Joan was not some incarnation of Melusine, she gave a very good impersonation of her; she had been vetted by a priest; she was obviously holy; she was worth a chance.

René must have informed his mother of Joan's existence prior to this interview, because Colet de Vienne, the royal messenger sent by Yolande, was already in Nancy awaiting instructions when Joan made her appearance there. And immediately following this audience, Colet de Vienne was dispatched to Vaucouleurs with a communication for Robert de Baudricourt from René. Colet rode quickly and arrived before Joan, who stopped along the way to make a pilgrimage to a local shrine.

So it was that upon her return, Joan found that Robert de Baudricourt had for no apparent reason reconsidered her request; more than this, he was now suddenly prepared to accede to her wishes and provide her with an escort to the royal court at Chinon, where Charles was currently in residence.* Colet de Vienne, who had made the journey previously and knew the back ways, would lead her party. "Robert twice refused and repulsed me, and the third time he received me and gave me men," Joan later recalled. "The voice had told me that it would happen so."

Joan left Vaucouleurs for Chinon on February 12, 1429. Robert de

---

*Prevailing wisdom states that Robert de Baudricourt simply changed his mind about Joan and sent her to Charles on his own authority. This is highly unlikely. Robert was not of sufficient rank to make that decision. The participation of the royal messenger is further evidence that the order to send Joan to Charles originated with René.

Baudricourt was at Joan's leave-taking; he had given her a sword for protection on the journey, which she held in her hand. "Robert de Baudricourt caused those who escorted me to swear that they would lead me truly and surely," Joan later recounted. "And Robert said to me, 'Go' as I set off, 'Go and let what is to be come to pass.'"

CHAPTER 8

Joan Meets
the
Dauphin

⚜

When I arrived at the town of Sainte-Catherine-
de-Fierbois, I sent [a letter] to my king; then I went
to the town of Chinon, where my king was; I
arrived there about the hour of noon and found
lodging at a hostelry.

*—Joan of Arc, in response to an inquisitor
at her Trial of Condemnation, 1431*

HE JOURNEY FROM VAUCOULEURS lasted eleven
days. To get to Chinon, Joan and her companions
were forced to cross territory controlled by the English and the Burgundians. If they betrayed their
political affiliation in the slightest way, or were challenged for traveling without a safe conduct, they
would be taken captive or perhaps killed. Although
Colet de Vienne knew from past expeditions which roads and towns to avoid,
they were a large enough party to attract attention, and so to reduce the risk
of exposure they often traveled by night. Darkness carried its own perils; in
the nocturnal hours they were vulnerable to roving gangs of bandits or mercenaries who preyed on travelers too poor or lost to find shelter. Long afterward, members of Joan's party vividly remembered the need for secrecy and
the fear that haunted them "because of the Burgundian and English soldiers
who were masters of the roads."

Perhaps because they were afraid, in the beginning there was resentment against Joan. Despite the admonition from Robert de Baudricourt to lead her "truly and surely," at least a few of the men felt they were risking their lives on a fool's errand and sought to punish her. "Afterwards I heard those who took her to the King speak of it and heard them say that, to begin with, they thought her presumptuous and their intention was to put her to the proof. . . . They wanted to require her to lie with them carnally," recalled Marguerite la Touroulde, a witness. "But when the moment came to speak to her of this they were so much ashamed that they dared not speak of it to her nor say a word of it." Bertrand de Poulengy, one of Joan's original sponsors from Vaucouleurs, recalled that "every night she lay down with Jean de Metz and me, keeping upon her her surcoat and hose, tied and tight. I was young then and yet I had neither desire nor carnal movement to touch [her] . . . because of the abundance of goodness which I saw in her." The precaution Joan had taken of donning male attire was thus immediately justified. The clothing helped the other members of her group to separate Joan's femininity from her spirituality, and her modesty and piety were soon noted. By the end of the trip, her exemplary courage and irreproachable behavior had completely won over every member of her entourage. "She never swore, and I myself was much stimulated by her voices, for it seemed to me that she was sent by God, and I never saw in her any evil, but always was she so virtuous a girl that she seemed a saint," Bertrand testified. Jean de Novellompont agreed. "The Maid always told us to have no fear and that she had a mandate to do this thing. . . . I believe that she was sent by God. . . . She liked to hear mass and she crossed herself with the sign of the Cross," he said. "And thus we took her to the King, to the place of Chinon, as secretly as we could."

They arrived at around noon on February 23, 1429, and found lodging at a local inn. "I sent letters to my King in which it was contained that I sent them to know if I could enter the town where my King was, and that I had made my way one hundred and fifty leagues to come to him and bring him succour, and that I knew many things [to the] good touching him, and I believe that in the same letters it was contained that I should know the King well [from] all others," said Joan.

But merely surviving this frightening journey and announcing her arrival was not enough to ensure the success of Joan's mission. She still faced the burden of convincing Charles to admit her into his presence, an event that Joan serenely believed would occur, but of which the other members of her escort were by no means as confident. They were right to worry, for the royal court was bitterly divided over whether Charles ought to receive her. In particular, Georges de la Trémoïlle was strongly opposed to the idea of allowing Joan access to the king, and argued strenuously against it. When Joan's letter was delivered announcing her arrival, La Trémoïlle was at the head of the faction that convinced Charles to send emissaries not to receive her but to interrogate her. According to Simon Charles, a member of the king's administration, "I know that, when Joan arrived in Chinon, there was deliberation in counsel to decide whether the King should hear her or not. To start with they sent to ask her why she was come and what she was asking for. . . . She said that she had two [reasons] for which she had a mandate from the King of Heaven; one, to raise the siege of Orleans, the other to lead the King to Rheims for his sacring [coronation]. Which being heard, some of the King's counselors said that the King should on no account have faith in Joan [believe her], and the others that since she said that she was sent by God, and that she had something to say to the King, the King should at least hear her."

These "others" were those members of the council allied with Yolande of Aragon. "There is no evidence of opposition to Joan's 'mission' from any member of the house of Anjou," observed medievalist M. G. A. Vale. This is an understatement; in fact, it is clear that Yolande and her supporters within the council were the advisers urging Charles to see Joan for himself and to listen to what she had to say. "Orliac [a noted French historian] assigns a major role to the Angevins, and especially to Yolande of Aragon, in fostering the career of the Maid," wrote medievalist Margaret Kekewich. "She was sheltered, supplied and encouraged by a number of Angevin servants as she made her way to Chinon and whilst she remained in the Loire Valley."

Charles, ever the equivocator, took all day to make up his mind, but at last his craving for spiritual reassurance prevailed and Joan was invited to the castle. She arrived late in the evening. The opposition, recognizing this peasant girl's visit for what it was—a play by Yolande of Aragon and her faction for political supremacy at court—fought desperately against Charles's meeting her until the very last moment. La Trémoïlle used every persuasion he could think of to unsettle the king and make him reverse his decision, a stratagem that he had employed to keep himself in power with

notable success for many months. But Yolande and her family understood
Charles, and especially his superstitions and fears, better than any of their
rivals; and they employed those arguments to which they knew he would
be most susceptible. "When she [Joan] entered the castle of Chinon to come
into his presence, the King, on the advice of the principal courtiers, hesitated
to speak to her until the moment when it was reported that Robert de Baudricourt had written to him that he was sending him a woman and that she
had been conducted through the territory of the King's enemies; and that,
in a manner quasi-miraculous, she had crossed many rivers by their fords, to
reach the King," reported Simon Charles. "Because of this the King was
pressed to hear her and Joan was granted an audience." Since Robert de
Baudricourt, being still in Vaucouleurs, had no way of knowing what had
occurred on Joan's journey, or even whether at this point she had arrived
safely, it must be presumed that this letter was an invention by the members
of Yolande's faction who knew to stress the mystical aspects of the case.*
Georges de la Trémoïlle was overruled, and Joan was invited to enter the
great hall.

This was Joan's first experience of a royal court, and although the surroundings were far less magnificent than those of Paris, the splendor of
Charles's retinue was more than enough to dazzle her: "There were more
than three hundred knights and fifty torches," Joan later recounted in awe.
She must have looked as foreign to that great company as they did to her: a
slim young woman, obviously provincial, attired in the clothes of a man; by
this time she had cut her hair as male pages did in the shape of a bowl, which
only enhanced the quaint, otherworldly nature of her appearance. Even
now, so close to achieving her goal, she faced one last obstacle: Charles's fear
of meeting her caused him to try to camouflage himself by retreating behind
his courtiers. Much has been made of Joan's ability to recognize Charles,
whom she had never seen before, despite this subterfuge; it added greatly to
the miraculous nature of her visit. "When the King knew that she was coming, he withdrew apart from the others," Simon Charles reported. "Joan,

---

*It was vital that Charles not see the connection between René and Joan to preserve the illusion
that Yolande of Aragon had nothing to do with Joan's arrival at court; that was the reason that
Robert de Baudricourt always appeared to have acted upon his own authority when it came to
the Maid. "It was essential for Joan to seem as if she had come to Charles unaided by anything
except the will of God and a letter of recommendation from Robert de Baudricourt, the loyal
captain of Vaucouleurs," noted M. G. A. Vale. "If she had come from one of Yolande's son's fiefs,
a display of patronage was not politic."

however, knew him at once and made him a reverence and spoke to him for some time." Joan herself confirmed this observation. "When I entered my King's room, I knew him among the others by the counsel of my voice which revealed him to me," she said simply.

This episode has naturally been attributed to divine revelation; however, there was perhaps another explanation for Joan's perspicacity. She did not in fact discover Charles by wandering alone into the main hall and through a body of three hundred knights as is implied; rather, she was *escorted* into Charles's presence by the count of Vendôme. The count of Vendôme was among those who had conspicuously accompanied Yolande of Aragon when she returned to the royal court the previous September, and was one of the lords who formed the nucleus of her political party. He understood precisely what was at stake and how important it was that this young woman see Charles and convince him to stay in France and fight the English. The count of Vendôme, not finding the king precisely where he had left him, would naturally have looked around for him, and the count of Vendôme knew what Charles looked like. Since her escort both wanted and needed Joan to detect the king, it is hardly surprising that she did so. It also helped that Charles was distinctive-looking. He had inherited his father's and uncle's extremely large nose, and this would have been known even in Domrémy.

However Joan managed to recognize him, from the moment she approached Charles, she demonstrated the same piety, passion, and strength of purpose that had so impressed all who had met her previously. With a deep reverence that must have put the timorous king immediately at his ease, she curtsied before him. "I was myself present at the castle and the city of Chinon when the Maid arrived, and I saw her when she presented herself to his royal majesty," said Raoul de Gaucourt, a member of Charles's entourage. "She showed great humility and simplicity of manner, this poor little shepherdess. . . . I heard her say the following words to the king: 'Very noble lord dauphin, I have come and I have been sent from God to bring aid to you and to the kingdom.'" The duke of Alençon, who was out hunting quail, was called back to Chinon in a hurry "when a messenger came to tell me that a maiden had arrived at the king's court who declared herself to have been sent by God to chase out the English and raise the siege the English had set around Orléans." Joan later described her meeting with Charles to Friar Jean Pasquerel, her confessor, in greater detail: "When [the king] saw her, he asked Joan her name and she answered: 'Gentle dauphin, I am Joan the

Maid, and the King of Heaven commands that through me you be anointed and crowned in the city of Reims as a lieutenant of the King of Heaven, who is king of France. . . . I say to you, on behalf of the Lord, that you are the true heir of France, and a king's son, and He has sent me to you to lead you to Reims, so that you can receive your coronation and consecration if you wish it.' This being understood, the king said to his courtiers that Joan had told him a certain secret that no one knew or could know except God; and that is why he had great confidence in her. All of that I learned from the mouth of Joan, because I was not present," reported Friar Pasquerel.

The mystery of what secret Joan told Charles in order to win his confidence has remained a matter of speculation for six centuries. Some people believe she passed the king a ring verifying his royal birth; others aver that Joan revealed herself at this time to have been Charles's half sister, the product of a liaison between Isabeau of Bavaria and the duke of Orléans, who had been spirited away from the Hôtel Saint-Pol at birth to be raised by peasants in Domrémy. Both of these hypotheses, and many others like them, were long ago refuted by the historical evidence and have been rejected as a matter of record; they persist only in fiction.

The truth was there was no "sign" as such. Joan herself expressed frustration when later questioned about this by Charles's advisers. "In God's name, I am not come to Poitiers to make signs; but take me to Orléans, I will show you the signs for which I have been sent!" What Joan did was speak in her convincingly passionate manner directly to Charles's innermost fears and especially to his obsession with his possible illegitimacy. At the very end of his life, in confession—not a place where people ordinarily prevaricate— Charles confirmed that he had believed in Joan because she had known "the secret prayer" he had made to God. This prayer consisted of three "requests," the principal entreaty being that Charles's questions concerning his own parentage be answered by God, and he himself established, both within his own mind and that of the kingdom at large, as the legitimate son of Charles VI, king of France, and thus the true heir to the throne.*

A three-part heartfelt supplication to God to give him some sign that he

*That Charles had in fact prayed silently, if not exactly secretly, to God on this subject in 1428 was confirmed by Guillaume Gouffier, later one of Charles's chamberlains. Guillaume, who slept in Charles's bedroom as part of his duties, claimed that Charles volunteered this information to him one night. The prayer can hardly have been that much of a secret if Charles told one of his servants. By coincidence, Guillaume Gouffier was also a former member of Yolande of Aragon's household.

was who he was supposed to be, to silence the doubts that had been raised by the opposition and that nagged at his soul and tormented his reason, to give him aid and succor in his struggle with the English, to protect him from harm by showing him which path was best to take—and then, suddenly, Joan, an obviously devout peasant girl reputed to be a holy woman, materializes out of the farthest reaches of the kingdom promising to lift the siege of Orléans and drive out the English in words that echo in the strongest possible tones the terms of that prayer: "I say to you, on behalf of the Lord, that you are the true heir of France, and a king's son, and He has sent me to lead you to Reims." In his darkest hour, Charles had cried out to God for a sign of divine favor, and God had answered his prayer and sent a messenger to reassure him of the truth. History and literature were full of accounts of similarly miraculous events; why should this not be one of them? What other explanation could there be for Joan's presence at court? How else could she, a poor ignorant peasant girl from so far away, possibly have known what was in a king's heart? What else but a divine command could have compelled her to attempt such a dangerous journey, one that had so little prospect of success? Charles had asked for a talisman, and God had sent one. Joan did not have to produce a sign, *she was herself the sign.*

After their conversation, "the king seemed radiant," reported Simon Charles. No longer unsure, Charles began to act with energy, and to believe once more in himself and his cause. It was a turning point in his career and the war, and it all came from this meeting. "To introduce a prophetess to the impressionable Charles could have been a stroke of something approaching political genius," admitted his biographer M. G. A. Vale.

CHARLES ORDERED that Joan be treated as a guest of the court for a week while he made up his mind exactly what to do with her. She was given rooms in the tower of one of his castles and assigned a page to accompany her during the day and a small household of women to stay with her at night. According to the duke of Alençon, the next day, "Joan came to the king's mass, and when she saw the king, she bowed deeply; and he led Joan into a chamber," recalled the duke. "The king kept the lord of La Trémoïlle and myself with him, saying to everyone else that they could retire. And then Joan made several requests of the king. . . . Many other things that I do not remember were said until it was time for dinner." After the meal, they

Joan addresses Charles at the royal court.

took Joan into a nearby field where she demonstrated her martial abilities. "Joan ran about charging with a lance, and I, seeing Joan behave like this, carrying and running with the lance, gave her the gift of a horse," the duke of Alençon continued.

The presence of Georges de la Trémoïlle at these meetings ensured that Joan's influence on Charles would not go uncontested. For all of her passion and piety, which had in the past won her so many followers, Joan never succeeded in convincing this particular councillor that she had come from God and not the opposition. La Trémoïlle, shrewd and practiced, knew better than to attack Joan openly while the king was so obviously taken with her. Instead, he merely planted doubts, and the upshot of these was that Charles decided that Joan should be examined by members of the Church to verify that she was genuinely an agent of God and not a trick played by the devil.

A small group of regional clerics, led by a couple of bishops in company with some lesser local Church officials, were accordingly rounded up and commanded to investigate Joan and render an opinion on her authenticity. The reluctance of this group to take responsibility for a definitive verdict is not difficult to imagine. After questioning Joan and deliberating for a week, they prudently recommended that she be interrogated by more learned authorities, and Charles arranged for her go to Poitiers, where she could be scrutinized by established specialists in scripture and theology.

The subsequent investigation of Joan at Poitiers, by a tribunal that boasted a number of masters from the University of Paris who had been exiled from the school for maintaining their political allegiance to Charles, was an extremely odd affair. Hurriedly conducting the inquiry in three weeks, this group made no attempt to appeal to the pope for guidance, as similar panels had done in the past with other holy women such as Elizabeth of Hungary, Catherine of Siena, or Bridget of Sweden. Nor was any real effort made to challenge Joan's view of herself or her mission. Her interrogators did not even mind when she answered rudely or evasively. For example, Friar Pierre Seguin reported, "I asked her what language her voice spoke. She answered, 'Better than yours.' Me, I spoke the dialect of Limoges; and then I asked her if she believed in God; she answered 'Yes, better than you.' And I then said to her that God wouldn't want us to believe in her unless something made us think that we should do so. I could not advise the king simply on her assertion that he should entrust men-at-arms to her so that she might lead them into peril, unless she could at least tell him something further. And she answered, 'In God's name, I did not come to Poitiers to produce signs. . . . But lead me to Orléans, and I will show you the sign for which I was sent.'" Rarely in history have members of the Church shown such patience and forbearance in their investigation of a young woman purporting to know the will of God better than they did.

An account of the proceedings hints at the explanation for this uncharacteristic deference, which clearly had far more to do with politics than theology. "Finally, it was concluded by the clerks after their interrogations . . . that given the great need in which both the king and the kingdom found themselves—since the king and his subjects were at that moment in despair and had no other hope of aid if it came not from God—the king should make use of her assistance." The wording of their final decision—"In her, Joan, we find no evil but only good, humility, virginity, devotion, honesty, and simplicity"—was a masterful display of the art of appearing to authenticate Joan and her mission without actually saying so, a necessary precaution in case she should turn out to be under the influence of an evil spirit or a heretic after all.

The tribunal's reference to Joan's virginity provides the final clue to the motivating force behind this verdict. According to the prophecies, the woman destined to save France would be a virgin, and although Joan claimed to be such, it was necessary to offer more substantive proof. As this evidence obviously could not be obtained through scriptural questioning, a physical examination was required. It was not appropriate that she be inspected by men, so two noblewomen were instead enlisted in the effort. "I heard it said that Joan, when she came to the king's court, was examined by women to know what was in her, if she was a man or a woman, and if she was a virgin or corrupted," recalled Joan's confessor, Jean Pasquerel. "Those who visited her for this purpose were, from what I heard, the lady of Gaucourt and the lady of Trèves."

It should come as no surprise that the lady of Gaucourt and the lady of Trèves were both devoted and long-standing members of Yolande of Aragon's household. The lady of Trèves was in fact the wife of Robert Le Maçon, who had been Charles's counselor since he was fourteen, and who had helped him to escape Paris by giving up his own horse to the boy when the Burgundians overran the city in 1418. To add the authority and prestige of rank to these proceedings, Yolande herself oversaw the manner of Joan's physical examination and presented the findings to Charles. "The Master's report having been made to the King, this Maid was put into the hands of the Queen of Sicily, mother of the Queen our sovereign lady, and to certain ladies being with her, by whom this maid was seen, visited and secretly regarded and examined in the secret parts of her body," reported Jean d'Aulon, Joan's steward. "But after they had seen and looked at all there was to look at in this case, the lady [Yolande] said and related to the King that she and her ladies found with certainty that she [Joan] was a true and entire maid in whom appeared no corruption or violence. I was present when the lady made her report.

"After having heard these things, the King, considering the great goodness which was in this maid and what she had said to him, that by God was she sent to him, concluded in his Council that, henceforth, he would use her aid for the war," Jean concluded.

Joan was going to Orléans.

BUT FIRST she had to be outfitted as befit her new position as a knight in the king's army. She was sent to Tours for her equipment. Charles paid 100 livres tournois to have a suit of armor and a banner made especially for her; she chose her own standard, "on which was painted the image of Our Savior seated in judgment in the clouds of the sky, and there was an angel painted holding in his hand a *fleur-de-lys* which the image was blessing," noted her confessor. To round out her military entourage she was given, in addition to her squire, two pages and two heralds. Two of her brothers, sent by the family to search for her, apparently also joined her at this time as part of her retinue. Although Robert de Baudricourt had already given her a sword, Joan wanted one with a religious provenance and wrote to the clerics of the church of Sainte-Catherine-de-Fierbois, a town she had stopped in on her way to Chinon, asking them to unearth a blade that had been brought back from a crusade and buried as a relic behind the altar. Word that a young woman purporting to be an emissary from God had promised to lift the siege of Orléans had already spread throughout the vicinity. The officials of Sainte-Catherine-de-Fierbois, sensible of the miraculous nature of the undertaking, hurriedly exhumed the sword and had it cleaned. "An arms merchant of Tours went to seek it, and the prelates of that place gave me a sheath, and those of Tours also, with them, had two sheaths made for me: one of red velvet and the other of cloth-of-gold, and I myself had another made of right strong leather," Joan noted.

Finally all was in place, and Joan left Tours for nearby Blois, where Charles's army was massing and a convoy was being readied with food and other provisions to relieve the siege of Orléans. This was the force that Yolande of Aragon had fought and pushed and schemed for, the goal to which she had devoted all her diplomatic and political energies. To ensure that this critical military effort was given the optimum chance for success she had assumed the responsibility for financing the operation herself. So committed was she to this mission that she donated her own tableware to the expedition. By April, she had accumulated a great store of foodstuffs: "Laden in the town of Blois [were] many carts and small carts of wheat and were taken great plenty of beeves, sheep, cows, swine and other victuals," wrote the chronicler Jean Chartier. But even more important than the provisions was the number of skilled and experienced captains—including Étienne de Vignolles, known as "La Hire," a seasoned commander of great renown, who brought with him a company of war-hardened mercenaries— whom Yolande had convinced to participate in this last, desperate attempt against the English.

Like La Hire, it would seem that Joan too was in a strange way recruited by Yolande for this mission. The prophecies had had the desired effect and Joan was by no means the only visionary to heed the call. A French historian reported that in the year 1428 alone, some twenty people, most of them women, publicly claimed to have been chosen by God to deliver a message to the king, and this was just the number of recorded instances. None of these other would-be seers were able to gain an audience with Charles, however, mostly because what they had to say did not conform to what Yolande wanted to hear. Later, Joan would meet one of these competing clairvoyants, a prophetess named Catherine de la Rochelle. Catherine had visions of a woman "dressed in cloth-of-gold, telling her to go to the loyal towns, and that the king would give her heralds and trumpets to make proclamations." Catherine had gone so far as to write to the king promising to unearth a golden treasure with which Charles could pay his soldiers. As Charles was desperately in need of money, this was a large point in Catherine's favor. Like Joan, Catherine had also convinced the people of her town, including a local priest, Brother Richard, of the authenticity of her visions. Catherine's rival prognostications were sufficiently disquieting that Joan made a point of warning Charles against her. "I answered this Catherine that she return to her husband and do her housework and feed her children. . . . And I wrote to my King telling him . . . that it was folly and nullity, this matter of Catherine," said Joan. "They were very ill content with me, Brother Richard and this Catherine," she admitted.

At the same time, despite her role in bringing Joan to Charles's attention, the queen of Sicily, because of her own upbringing, most likely also genuinely believed the girl to be a messenger from God. After all, Yolande's own prayers had been answered as much as Charles's by the discovery of the prophetess—for the king had at last given the order to send the army to the relief of Orléans.

Now, in the final week of April 1429, Yolande witnessed the fruits of her efforts as the convoy of supplies she had assembled, accompanied by a strong contingent of men-at-arms, rolled slowly out of Blois and took the road to Orléans. With Joan's participation, the religious nature of this enterprise was highly visible, giving the procession the ardent air of a crusade. "When Joan left Blois to go to Orléans," reported her confessor, "she had all the priests gather around the standard, and the priests went before the army. They marched out on the side of the Sologne assembled in that fashion; they sang

Veni creator spiritus along with many antiphons, and they camped in the fields that night and the following day as well." Joan forbade swearing and pillaging, and she drove away the prostitutes who inevitably followed in the wake of the soldiers; further, she insisted that the soldiers attend Mass and confess themselves in order to participate. Those who marched out of Blois beside her to do battle against the English felt keenly the difference between this army and those in which they had previously fought, and with this recognition there arose a hope that perhaps, this time, God would be on their side.

CHAPTER 9

The Maid
of Orléans

✤

Jhesus-Maria, King of England, and you, Duke of Bedford, who call yourself regent of the Kingdom of France . . . and you . . . who call yourselves lieutenants of the Duke of Bedford, acknowledge the summons of the King of Heaven. Render to the Maid here sent by God . . . the keys of all the good towns which you have taken and violated in France. She is here come by God's will to reclaim the blood royal. She is very ready to make peace, if you will acknowledge her to be right, provided that France you render, and pay for having held it. . . . And if so be not done, expect news of the Maid who will come to see you shortly, to your very great injury.

—*excerpt from a letter to the English dictated by Joan of Arc,*
March 22, 1429

RLÉANS, A LARGE WALLED CITY, one of the most heavily fortified in France, was situated on the north bank of the Loire about seventy-five miles south of Paris. The siege was in its sixth month by the time the convoy of supplies left Blois, and the situation was indeed dire. Because Orléans was almost completely surrounded by the English, only one of its five gates—the easternmost door, called the Burgundy Gate—could still be accessed by French partisans, which meant that foodstuffs trickled in only sporadically and in far too limited quantity to support the needs of a population that numbered over thirty thousand. On Tuesday, March 8, for example, the town authorities managed to smuggle in a mere nine horses carrying wheat and other victuals. If Orléans was not resupplied quickly, its citizens faced the choice of surrender or starvation.

And yet militarily the situation was not without hope. Although the English had initially committed an army of six thousand men to the effort, in order to encircle Orléans effectively they had been required to subdue the surrounding territory. This meant leaving behind garrisons in a number of towns, thus reducing the size of the force available to conduct the actual siege. Additionally, because living conditions during the winter were so poor—it was difficult to maintain supply lines and the English men-at-arms were often as hungry and cold as those whom they had been assigned to blockade—desertion was a problem. By April 1429, the number of English troops participating in the siege had dwindled to somewhere between twenty-five hundred and four thousand.*

A few thousand soldiers were insufficient to surround a city protected to the south by a large river and that boasted a walled perimeter of two thousand yards supported by a significant number of guns, some of them capable of hurling stone cannonballs weighing nearly two hundred pounds a distance of half a mile. The English commander, the earl of Suffolk, had compensated by erecting a number of bastilles—a series of improvised, detached forts—to encircle the city. There were at least five to the north of Orléans and two on the southern bank of the Loire. Several hundred English soldiers manned each of these bastilles, which were equipped with cannons, although some of the forts had more cannons and soldiers than others.

The problem with this setup was that there was quite a bit of terrain between the bastilles, which meant that the soldiers of one fort could not easily come to the aid of another. Nor could the English fill in these gaps by building more bastilles without a fresh infusion of troops. "Really the *bastilles* were not to blame, but there were not enough of them, because the investing armies were numerically inadequate," observed the eminent

---

*It is very amusing to note that even after all of this time, English historians invariably cite the *lower* of these figures when estimating the size of this force, while French historians consistently maintain that the *larger* number more accurately reflects the level of enemy troops. Similarly, the magnitude of the French force that Joan accompanied from Blois ranged from twenty-four hundred to four thousand men (supplemented by a civilian militia of between fifteen hundred and three thousand Orléans residents), depending on the nationality of the source. In general, it would seem that, including the untrained and poorly armed volunteer citizens' militia, the French force initially maintained a slight superiority in numbers.

historian Andrew Lang. "They [the English] had not soldiers enough to man twice the number of *bastilles*." The success of this strategy was heavily dependent upon the French army and the population of the city itself remaining quiescent. To his credit, the duke of Bedford recognized the siege of Orléans for what it was: a bit of military hubris on the part of the English commanders that he as regent had been unable to prevent. "God knoweth by what advis [advice] the siege of the city of Orleans was taken in hand," Bedford would later write grimly to Henry VI.

THE RESPONSIBILITY for the defense of Orléans would ordinarily have fallen to its duke, but as this gentleman was still detained overseas as a prisoner of the English, the obligation fell to his half brother, Jean. Unlike Charles VII, who many assumed was the illegitimate son of Louis, duke

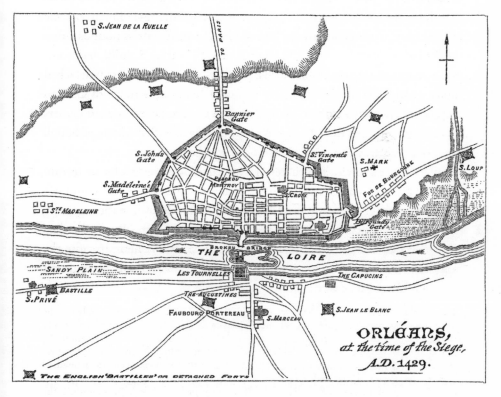

Orléans under siege and surrounded by the English bastilles, 1429

of Orléans, Jean actually *was* Louis's illegitimate son by his acknowledged mistress, Mariette of Enghien. For this reason, Jean was universally referred to as "the Bastard of Orléans," a moniker that carried with it no hint of disparagement, being rather meant only to elucidate, in the most helpful way possible, the specifics of Jean's lineage.

Jean was an experienced and highly skilled captain who had arrived in Orléans very soon after the siege had been laid and so had had ample time over the intervening months to observe the strength and layout of the enemy's forces. It was he, and not Joan, who was in charge of the relief effort. There were only two routes by which to circumvent the English blockade. The first of these was to go north through the forest and around the system of bastilles in a wide, out-of-the-way circle before finally reaching the Burgundy Gate by ducking between the enemy's two easternmost forts, which coincidentally were the least manned and the farthest away from each other. The second was to approach from the south, paralleling the Loire to the town of Chezy, about five miles upstream from Orléans. From Chezy, the supplies could be loaded onto barges and floated downstream to the Burgundy Gate. This second route "was rendered possible owing to the neglect of the earl of Suffolk to stretch a chain across the river—a laxity that would have horrified Henry V," deplored the English military historian Alfred Higgins Burne. The river option was safer but problematic because the barges necessary to load the supplies were in Orléans, which meant that the wind had to be out of the west to get them upstream to Chezy. (It didn't matter which way the wind blew on the way back, as the barges could just float downstream with the current.) The Bastard assessed the situation and ordered the army to come by way of the southern route.

However, as this counsel conflicted with the military policies urged by Joan's voices, which commanded her to take the northern route and engage the enemy at once, it was kept secret from her. Consequently, her first encounter with her commanding officer, as related by Jean himself, who had a keen remembrance of the conversation more than two decades after the fact, was less than auspicious:

"'Are you the Bastard of Orléans?' Joan asked.

"'Yes, I am, and I rejoice in your coming,' Jean replied.

"'Are you the one who gave orders for me to come here, on this side of the river, so that I could not go directly to Talbot [an enemy captain] and the English?'

"'I and others, including the wisest men around me, had given this advice, believing it best and safest.'

"'In God's name, the counsel of Our Lord God is wiser and safer than yours. You thought that you could fool me, and instead you fool yourself; I bring you better help than ever came to you from any soldier to any city: It is the help of the King of Heaven.'"

Luckily for all concerned the breeze, which had previously been unfavorable, shifted direction at that very moment. "Forthwith I had the sails hoisted, and sent in the rafts and vessels," remembered the Bastard. "And we passed beyond the Church of Saint-Loup despite the English. From that moment I had good hope in her, more than before." The Bastard may have credited Joan with the change of the wind, but it was he who had had the foresight to bring the convoy along the southern route to Chezy and to have the boats in place. More important, he had arranged for a diversionary attack—a sortie against the English bastille at Saint-Loup, the fort farthest away from all of the others—just as the barges were being launched for the return trip. This excellent bit of soldiering distracted the enemy forces and allowed the boats to sail through to the city unmolested. And just like that, Orléans was resupplied.

So successful was this venture that the Bastard immediately ordered the royal army that had escorted the convoy to return to Blois to pick up and transport further supplies. Again, this tactic was in opposition to the one urged by Joan's voices, but the Bastard circumvented this problem by convincing Joan to remain behind. "I then implored her to consent to cross the river of Loire and to enter into the town of Orléans where she was greatly wished for," the Bastard later testified. The celebrated French captain La Hire was also invited to stay, presumably to render advice on military strategy, and the three officers—the Bastard, Joan, and La Hire—entered the city in a triumphal procession on the evening of Friday, April 29, 1429, Joan dressed in her armor and riding upon a white horse, with her standard carried before her.

By this time everyone in Orléans knew who she was and the streets were mobbed with jubilant citizens grateful as much for the hope she had brought with her as for the desperately needed grain and livestock. "Came to receive her the other men of war, burgesses and matrons of Orléans, bearing great plenty of torches and making such rejoicing as if they had seen God descend in their midst; and not without cause, for they had many cares, travails and difficulties and great fear lest they be not succoured and lose all, body and goods," reported the *Journal of the Siege,* the official town chronicle of Orléans. "But they felt themselves already comforted and as if no longer besieged, by the divine virtue which they were told was in this simple maid, who looked upon them all right affectionately, whether men, women, or little children. And there was marvelous crowd and press to touch her or the horse upon which she was."

The next day was Saturday, and Joan, of course, wanted immediately to sally forth against the English in battle. But again she was overruled by the Bastard, who, in combination with the other captains, counseled waiting until the army returned from Blois with the additional supplies, so that they could engage the English at full strength. "Joan went to see the Bastard of Orléans and spoke to him, and on her return she was in great anger; for, said she, he had decided that on that day they would not go out against the enemy," remembered Louis de Coutes, one of Joan's pages. Having been prevented from attacking the English militarily, Joan chose instead to confront them verbally. Taking up a position on the street in Orléans closest to the enemy—it was at the intersection of the bridge over the Loire—she shouted across to the English captain, Sir William Glasdale, and those of the enemy troops who were within earshot, telling them to "go away in God's name, otherwise she would drive them out," and later that "they should surrender for God's sake and that their lives would be saved."

Although knowledge of Joan and her mission had spread rapidly among Charles's supporters, and she had previously sent a letter to the duke of Bedford warning him of her approach, it is probable that this shouting match across the Loire was England's first introduction to the Maid. The duke of Bedford, if he had received her letter at all, likely got many such letters from disgruntled French subjects and had disregarded it. Similarly, the English troops surrounding Orléans would hardly have credited the rumors that a French peasant girl had been enlisted to break the siege. Now, in the deepening gloom—Joan had chosen the hour of sunset to acquaint her opponents with her existence—they could just make out the slight figure of a young woman standing on the other side of the bridge hollering at them to surrender to her or else. While the novelty was undeniable, this approach did not have the desired effect on the gruff, war-hardened English soldiers, who were used to winning and had already formed a rather contemptuous opinion of their counterparts in the French military. "Glasdale and those of his company answered basely, insulting her and calling her 'cow-girl,' shouting very loudly that they would have her burned if they could lay hands on her," reported Louis de Coutes.

But the outcome of any particular war or battle does not always rely solely upon such obvious variables as troop size or weaponry or tactics. There is always the possibility that the more elusive concepts of morale and momentum will come into play. Although the English did not yet realize it, merely by breaking the blockade and bringing in that first shipment of supplies, Joan had altered the attitude of the French and caused a shift in the military equation. Many years later, the Bastard, reflecting upon her role in these events, expressed this transformation succinctly: "It seems to me," he said, "that Joan and also what she did in warfare and in battle was rather of God than of men; the change which suddenly happened in the wind, after she had spoken, gave hope of succour, and the introduction of supplies, despite the English, who were in much greater strength than the royal army." Or, as a more modern military scholar observed, "Joan's contribution . . . was that she roused the fighting spirits of the French, which had lain dormant for so long. This contribution was decisive."

IT TOOK THE ROYAL ARMY until Tuesday, May 3, to return to Orléans from Blois. This time, as a ploy, the soldiers came by the northern route but again sent the supplies south to Chezy. To distract the English, they again attacked the easternmost fort of Saint-Loup. ("The fact that Fort St. Loup was so dangerously isolated was evidence of the supreme disdain that the besiegers had for their enemies at this time," noted the same military scholar.) Joan must have heard the noise from the battle, because she accused her page of not having awoken her in time—"Ah, bleeding boy, you told me not that the blood of France was spilling!" he remembered she cried to him. By the time Joan's horse was ready and she was dressed in her armor, wounded French soldiers were already streaming back toward the city. Worse, one of the English officers, Captain Talbot, having been alerted to the attack, had charged out of his headquarters with a regiment and, picking up reinforcements from the various forts along the way, was bearing down on the French army, intending to rout the offensive and vanquish the enemy troops.

At the sight of Talbot and his men, the French soldiers would ordinarily have become disheartened and retreated. But not this time. This time, they had Joan. Undaunted by the bloodied casualties she encountered outside the Burgundy Gate, Joan spurred her horse to the scene of the battle. "The English were preparing their defense when Joan came in haste at them, and as soon as the French saw Joan, they began to shout [cheer]," reported Louis de Coutes, who had followed his mistress to the battlefield.

And then something highly unusual happened. The French soldiers, inspired by the young woman in their midst, renewed their attack rather than quitting it and to their astonishment succeeded in capturing the fort of Saint-Loup and burning it to the ground. Talbot saw the flames and knew the bastille was lost; further, as the bulk of the French army turned to face his troops, he suddenly realized that he did not have a sufficient force to ensure victory. And upon that realization, something even more unexpected and uncommon happened: Talbot abruptly called off his soldiers and retreated to his fort, leaving the French the masters of the field and allowing the supplies to enter the city uncontested a second time.

The following day, the Feast of the Ascension, was given over to rest and prayer. Joan was extremely upset by the number of English dead, fearing they had died without benefit of the sacrament. "She wept much upon them and at once confessed herself to me, and she told me publicly to exhort all the soldiers to confess their sins and to give thanks to God for the victory won; if not she would stay not with them but would leave them," remembered Joan's confessor. The next day, Thursday, May 5, Joan dictated a final letter of warning to the English: "You, Englishmen, who have no right in this Kingdom of France, the King of Heaven orders and commands you through me, Joan the Maid, that you quit your fortresses and return into your own country, or if not I shall make you such *babay* [the precise definition of this word is unclear, perhaps she meant battle] that the memory of it will be perpetual." Then, to ensure they received her warning, she attached the letter to an arrow and had a French archer lob it at the enemy, shouting, "Read, it is news!" at the English soldiers. "News of the Armagnacs' whore!" the English men-at-arms shouted in return, whereupon "Joan began to sigh and to weep copious tears, calling the King of Heaven to her aid. And thereafter was she consoled, as she said, for she had had news of her Lord," Jean Pasquerel later reported. "And that evening, after dinner, she ordered me to rise on the morrow earlier than I had done . . . and that she would confess herself to me very early in the morning, which she did."

And so, finally, on Friday, May 6, the Bastard launched a full-scale attack against the besieging army. Again, the French strategy was well thought out and executed. Instead of building upon the victory against Saint-Loup by confronting Talbot and his troops to the north, the French unexpectedly changed direction and attacked the enemy forces stationed to the south across the Loire. Making use of a small island in the middle of the river called the Isle of Saint-Aignan, a French regiment crossed by boat to this landmass very early in the morning and, taking the enemy by surprise, began immediately to strike at the English fort of Les Tourelles. Under cover of this initiative, more French soldiers crossed by boat to Saint-Aignan and began the construction of a bridge from the island to the southern shore, which their English counterparts in Les Tourelles, busy protecting themselves, were unable to prevent. Upon completion of the bridge, the main body of the French army crossed over to the southern bank of the Loire. Seeing the enemy upon them, the English soldiers stationed in the fort of Les Tourelles abandoned this bulwark in favor of the next closest bastille, called the fort of the Augustins, which was larger and more heavily fortified, and the battle began in earnest.

Although the historical evidence indicates that the French troops significantly outnumbered their English opponents—as many as four thousand French combatants went up against something less than a thousand Englishmen—the English were protected by the stone walls and armaments of the fort of the Augustins, and so the struggle was a desperate, all-day affair with significant casualties. Again, Joan's participation was crucial. She and La Hire crossed the river at the same time and arrived just as the English were mounting a counterattack. "When they perceived that the enemies were coming out of the bastion to charge their men, at once the Maid and La Hire, who were always before them to guard them, couched their lances and were the first to strike among the enemies," reported Jean d'Aulon. "Thereupon the others all followed them and began to strike at the enemy in such fashion that by force they drove them to retire and enter again into the bastion of the Augustins. . . . Very bitterly and with much diligence they assailed it from every side so that in a little while they gained and took it by storm; and there were killed or taken the greater part of the enemies, and those who could escape retired into the bastion of the Tourelles at the foot of the bridge. And thus won the Maid, and those who were with her, victory over the enemies upon that day."

Having gained the fort of the Augustins, Joan, along with the rest of the

French army, took shelter there for the night. But the battle resumed again very early the next morning, Saturday, May 7. By this time the great English knight Sir William Glasdale had arrived with reinforcements from the northern forts to secure the area. Taking cover at the fort of the Tourelles, he put up a valiant defense. Joan herself was wounded by an arrow above the breast at midmorning, and though she "was afraid and wept," she nonetheless fought on to the great inspiration of those around her, just as the young Henry V had in his first battle continued to lead his men after enduring a similar injury. Again, the struggle was an all-day affair; again the spirits of the French soldiers faltered, only to be revived by Joan. "The assault lasted from the morning until eight o'clock of vespers, so that there was hardly hope of victory that day," recalled the Bastard. "So that I was going to break off and wanted the army to withdraw toward the city. Then the Maid came to me and required me to wait yet a while. She herself, at that time, mounted her horse and retired alone into a vineyard, some distance from the crowd of men. And in this vineyard she remained at prayer during one half of a quarter of an hour. Then she came back from that place, at once seized her standard in hand and placed herself on the parapet of the trench, and the moment she was there the English trembled and were terrified. And the king's soldiers regained courage and began to go up, charging against the boulevard [the side of a rampart] without meeting the least resistance."

As the English men-at-arms fell back against this final assault, the drawbridge of the fort of the Tourelles suddenly collapsed under their weight. Soldiers and horses, burdened by heavy equipment, fell into the Loire and drowned; their commanding officer, Sir William, in full armor and waving his banner to the end, was among them. "And Joan, moved by pity, began to weep much for the soul of Classidas [Glasdale] and the others who were there drowned in great numbers. And that day all the English who were beyond the bridge were taken or killed," affirmed her confessor.

The taking of the fort of the Tourelles was a great victory for the French; in addition to vanquishing the formidable Glasdale, it meant that food and other supplies could now be transported into the city without fear of attack. The citizens of Orléans rang the city bells and sang Te Deums throughout the night, "expressing joy in every way, giving wondrous praise to their valiant defenders, and above all others to Joan the Maid." Joan's wound, which appears not to have been serious, was dressed and she took some food.

The next morning, what remained of the English besieging force took stock of the damage. They had lost men, arms, and, most important, their belief in their own invincibility; they were not only outnumbered but demoralized. From mocking and jeering at Joan, the common men-at-arms now actively feared her, believing her to be a witch; and it is likely that their officers agreed with them. There being no real choice of maintaining the siege with any hope of success, the decision was made to abandon it, and the English troops came out of their forts and destroyed them. But they did not retreat. Instead, the English army solemnly arrayed itself in battle formation in front of the walls of Orléans as though daring the French to come out and engage them in open combat.

This action was answered not only by Joan and the royal army but by a large militia of ordinary citizens from Orléans who, arming themselves as best they could, came out from behind the city walls and, joining the soldiers, arranged their forces in a line opposite their former tormentors. But because it was Sunday, Joan forbade anyone on the French side from initiating an attack. According to the official town chronicle, many of the men objected to this prohibition, but she placated them with the assurance that

Joan raises the siege of Orléans.

"if the English assaulted them, they could defend themselves as strongly and bravely as they wished and they should have no fear: They would be the masters of that field." For a solid hour the two opposing armies, whose soldiers were so close in some places that they could look into each other's eyes, faced each other down in this manner, neither force yielding to the other.

At the end of the hour, neither camp having made any movement to renew hostilities, whatever ancient condition of manhood being tested must have been satisfied, because the English army suddenly turned away without further incident and marched off in formation.

The city of Orléans had been rescued from the enemy and recovered for France.

THE ASTOUNDED jubilation with which the news of this victory was greeted at the royal court of Chinon is a matter of record. The king had barely time to learn of the army's departure from Blois before the glad tidings began rolling in. So quickly did the events unfold that a letter Charles was composing to his loyal supporters had to be revised three times between May 9 and May 10 to reflect the current status of the operation. "From the King, dear and well-beloved, we believe that you have been informed of the continual diligence by us exercised to bring all succour possible to the town of Orléans long besieged by the English, ancient enemies of our kingdom," Charles had begun (a trifle disingenuously, since his efforts to aid the city prior to this initiative could hardly be characterized as energetic). "By our Lord's grace from which all proceeds, we have again caused to be revictualled in strength the town of Orléans twice in a single week, well and greatly, in the sight and knowledge of the enemies, without their being able to resist." Then, upon receiving a further update, the king continued, "Since these letters were written, there has come to us a herald about one hour after midnight, who has reported to us on his life that last Friday our aforesaid people crossed the river by boat at Orléans and besieged, on the Sologne side, the bastion at the end of the bridge and the same day won the fort of the Augustins. And on the Saturday likewise assailed the rest of the said bastion . . . where there were at least six hundred English fighting men. . . . And finally, by great prowess and valiance in arms, yet still by means of Our Lord's grace, won all the said bastion and of it were all the English therein killed or taken." And then once more, upon receipt of the final, crowning intelligence, "And since then again, before the completion of these letters, have arrived with us two gentlemen . . . who certify and confirm . . . that after our men had last Saturday taken and demolished the bastion of the bridge end, on the morrow at dawn, the English who were in it, decamped and fled so hastily that they left their bombards, cannons and artilleries, and the best part of their provisions and baggage. Given at Chinon, the tenth day of May. Signed: Charles." Nor did the king neglect to give Joan credit for the miraculous nature of the victory: "For that more than ever before must [we] praise and thank our Creator, that in His divine clemency He has not forgotten us. And [we] cannot sufficiently honor the virtuous acts and things marvelous which this herald who was present has reported to us and likewise the Maid who was always present in person at the doing of all these things," he wrote.

The obvious next step was to follow up this unexpected achievement by a continued pursuit of the enemy forces. The Bastard, taking no chances, himself escorted Joan to the royal court in order to urge the adoption of a new offensive. The more experienced military men among the king's command argued in favor of building upon the victory at Orléans by striking out against the English occupation of Normandy. But this advice ran contrary to Joan's voices, which demanded that Charles be crowned at Reims as soon as possible. Bursting in on a council meeting—Joan was still not included in these planning sessions—she threw herself at Charles's feet and, hugging his legs in supplication, cried, "Noble Dauphin, hold not such, and such long, council but go to Rheims as soon as possible to receive a fitting crown." As before, her humbly dramatic appeal had a strong effect upon the king, who asked her to expand upon her thinking. "I remember that . . . the lords of the blood royal, and the captains, wanted the King to go into Normandy and not Rheims, but the Maid was still of the opinion that we should go to Rheims to consecrate the King, and she gave reason for her opinion saying that once the King should be crowned and anointed the strength of his adversaries would go on declining and that at last they would not be able to harm him or his kingdom," the Bastard remembered.

The source of Joan's fixation with a coronation at Reims—an objective that, until the crisis at Orléans, seems to have been her voices' primary concern—may very probably be traced to the enemy's humiliating reference to Charles as "the king of Bourges," and by the subsequent English promotion of Henry VI as the legitimate heir to Saint Louis. The duchy of Bar was very close to Reims, and every native of that area knew that the cathedral at Reims was where Saint Louis had been crowned; it stood to reason that Saint Louis's true heir would be crowned there as well. This was a piece of homespun philosophy that the English, unconcerned with the myriad ancient customs and ethos of the kingdom they happened to be occupying, had failed as yet to take into account.*

The problem with a coronation at Reims was that in order to achieve this goal, Charles was actually going to have to *go* to Reims, a coronation not being the sort of ceremony that could be handled by proxy or delegated to an inferior. This meant abandoning the royal court, which was located at a safe distance behind the enemy lines, and venturing out into far more risky territory. A great many English and Burgundian towns and soldiers stood between Orléans and Reims. To become king, Charles was going to need to act like one and follow the royal army as it fought its way to the cathedral. For a man who feared capture above all else, this must have been a truly frightening prospect. It is a measure of his faith in Joan, and the self-evident nature of her argument—"All rallied to her opinion," the Bastard reported—that Charles agreed to make the journey.

The duke of Alençon was placed in charge of the king's forces. His father had been killed at Agincourt and he himself captured by the English in 1424 at the battle of Verneuil, a predicament from which he had only recently extricated himself by raising the substantial sum of 80,000 gold saluts with which to pay his ransom. His wife, frantic for his safety, begged him not to accept the commission and appealed to Joan, an entreaty to which the Maid replied, "Lady, fear not, I will bring him back to you safe and sound and in such state or better than now he is." The army mustered at Selles-en-Berry, between Tours and Bourges, near Romorantin. "And arrived the Monday at Selles my lord the Duke of Alençon who had a very great company. . . . And it is said here that my lord the Constable is coming also with six hundred men-at-arms and four hundred men of draft [supply bearers] and that Jean de la Roche comes also, and that the King never had so great a company as are hoped for here," reported an eyewitness who participated in the campaign.

---

*Even when they were aware of a particular folkway, the English often discounted the significance of the habit. For example, it was a Parisian tradition that royalty feast the poor at Christmas. Under the English occupation, the duke of Bedford, wishing to save money, dispensed with this custom, an oversight that cost Henry VI the support of much of the Parisian populace.

This sudden influx of men and arms was directly attributable to the victory at Orléans. As news of the English defeat spread, many of Charles's former allies who had dismissed the king's campaign as moribund returned to his camp. Among these was the old duke of Brittany, who the year before, disgusted with Charles's lack of enterprise, had shifted his allegiance yet again to the English and Burgundian side. (This was the reason—exploited by Georges de la Trémoïlle—that the constable, Arthur of Richemont, had fallen from grace.) Now, just as Yolande and her faction had hoped, the duke of Brittany sent his confessor and a herald to congratulate Charles on his victory. The duke's confessor questioned Joan as to whether she had truly been sent by God to help the king. "If it be so," the confessor continued, "my lord the duke of Brittany is disposed to come to the King's aid with his service. . . . He cannot come in his proper person, for he is in a great state of infirmity, but he can send his eldest son with a great army."

On June 6, 1429, Joan, accompanied by the duke of Alençon and the king's soldiers, marched out of Selles to rendezvous with the Bastard and his men at Orléans. Again, the army was preceded by churchmen, in this case mendicant friars who were instructed by Joan to pray aloud as they walked, giving the company the air of a religious procession; she herself, arrayed in white armor and a hood, rode behind them on a spirited black stallion. This force met up with the Bastard just outside of Orléans on June 9. Also among those present were La Hire and Yolande's ally, the count of Vendôme, the lord who had escorted Joan into Charles's presence. Estimates of the size of the French army gathered at Orléans vary from five thousand to eight thousand men. The duke of Alençon reported the strength of the battalion at "about twelve hundred lances," to which must be added foot soldiers and archers, as well as a volunteer militia from within the city itself. On Saturday, June 11, these troops marched out of Orléans to meet the English.

The remains of the original enemy force, still under the command of the earl of Suffolk, had taken refuge in three of the neighboring towns—Jargeau, Meung, and Beaugency—that hugged the Loire. Upon being informed that a French army of significant size was on the move, the earl of Suffolk, with five hundred English knights and two hundred archers, barricaded himself in the town of Jargeau, just ten miles southeast of Orléans. Jargeau, much smaller than Orléans, was protected by a wall and towers; additionally the town boasted a bridge fortified by two tall stone strongholds.

No sooner had Joan and her troops arrived at the suburbs of Jargeau than word reached them that a large battalion of English reinforcements—the intelligence indicated a force of at least two thousand soldiers, under the direction of the feared English commander Sir John Fastolf—was approaching at a rapid pace. The duke of Alençon, who was young and inexperienced (he had fought in only two battles before being captured, which explains his wife's anxiety), lost his nerve and called for a war council. Some of the captains argued that they should break off the attack on Jargeau in order to intercept Fastolf; some advised abandoning the project altogether. Joan, however, insisted on maintaining their original target. "Be not afraid of any armed host whatsoever and make no difficulty of attacking the English, for Messire [God] leads you," she asserted. Separately, to the duke of Alençon, who worried it was too soon to begin the assault, she said, "Ah, gentle Duke, wast thou afeared? Knowest thou not that I promised thy wife to bring thee back safe and sound?"

The next morning, June 12, the people of Orléans having dragged some of their cannons to Jargeau, the French opened fire on the town and with three volleys destroyed the largest of the fortifications on the bridge. (For some reason Joan did not seem to object to beginning the attack on a Sunday as she had done previously; perhaps she had lost track of the date.) The English returned fire, and Joan, who had more battle experience than her commanding officer, advised the duke of Alençon, who had taken a position directly in the line of fire, to move. "That machine . . . will kill thee," she told him, pointing to one of the English guns. The duke of Alençon hastily changed locations, and another French knight who took up the duke's vacated position and was not lucky enough to have Joan looking out for him was killed instead.

With the English overwhelmingly outnumbered, the battle for Jargeau took only four hours. Again, Joan was a source of great inspiration to her troops. She climbed high atop a scaling ladder, banner in hand, and the French soldiers, following her lead, swarmed over the walls and overran the town. The earl of Suffolk tried to call for a negotiated surrender, but no one paid any attention to him and he was taken prisoner by a French squire. ("Are you a gentleman?" the earl asked his captor suspiciously after it was clear that he was cornered. The squire replied in the affirmative. "Are you a knight?" the earl pressed. Upon hearing the Frenchman was not, the earl promptly dubbed his antagonist. Honor and the social structure having been rescued, if not the town itself, only then did the earl surrender his glove and allow himself to be taken captive.) Those serving under Suffolk were not so fortunate. With the exception of the members of the garrison who were of sufficient rank to command a ransom, the entire English force at Jargeau was executed, and the town sacked.

That was Sunday; by Wednesday, the French had taken the bridge at Meung. By Friday, the entire English garrison at Beaugency had capitulated and as part of the terms of submission abandoned the city on Saturday morning, June 18, without a fight. However, as the French turned back toward Meung to finish retaking the town, new, disquieting information arrived. "And while the English [at Beaugency] were retreating came one from La Hire's company who said to me, as to the King's captains, that the English were coming, that we should soon be face to face with them, and that they were about one thousand men-at-arms in number," remembered the duke of Alençon.

It was Fastolf with the long-awaited reinforcements. La Hire's man must have underestimated this force, as the number of English men-at-arms bearing down on the French seems to have been double that of the original assessment. The English commander had been marching to the aid of Beaugency when, halting just outside of Meung, he met up with Captain John Talbot, who was leading what was left of the original army that had besieged Orléans—just forty lances, two hundred archers, and their foot soldiers, about three hundred men in all—in the hopes of intercepting Fastolf and making a united stand against the French. Hearing from Talbot that Beaugency had fallen, and having reports of the superior numbers of the French force, Fastolf counseled falling back on Patay, about fifteen miles north of Orléans. Talbot reluctantly agreed and the English soldiers were turned around and ordered to retreat northward.

News of the arrival of the English reinforcement army threw the French military leadership into its customary panic. The duke of Alençon abruptly reverted to his former, indecisive self—a less commanding commanding officer is difficult to imagine—and appealed to Joan for guidance. "Then the lord Duke of Alençon, in the presence of the lord constable, of myself and several others, asked Joan what he ought to do," recalled the Bastard. "She answered him in a loud voice, saying, 'Have all good spurs,' which hearing those present asked Joan: 'What say you? Are we going to turn our backs on them?' Then Joan answered: 'No. But it will be the English who will not defend themselves and will be vanquished and you will need good spurs to run after them.'"

By this time, the French were aware that the English were falling back in order to regroup to the north, and the decision was made to follow Joan's advice and pursue them. To prevent the enemy's getting away, the royal army was divided into three groups: in the first wave were approximately twelve hundred of the swiftest cavalry, under the direction of La Hire; then came the main body of troops, led by the Bastard and the duke of Alençon; and finally a rear guard headed by Joan and Arthur of Richemont. Joan was upset at being consigned to the back, but she was overruled; possibly she was not skilled enough to ride with the advance guard. In the end, it did not matter, for she had already given the French soldiery, and in particular La Hire, all they needed: the confidence that they could win. This would be his battle, not hers.

Riding at full speed, unburdened by heavy artillery, the French cavalry overtook Fastolf's men in the woods outside of Patay at about two o'clock in the afternoon. Some of the English bowmen, not realizing the enemy was so close, gave their position away by ballyhooing at a stag as it bounded through the forest. Seeing the French upon them, Captain Talbot hurriedly found what he believed to be an advantageous spot at which to arrange his troops. His strength was, as usual, heavily weighted to his archers, five hundred of whom, handpicked by their commander for their experience and ability, were instructed to dismount and dig their pikes into the ground in a long line, to make it more difficult for the French horsemen to pass. Fastolf and the rest of the English regiment ducked in behind the longbowmen and, searching for the high ground, scrambled to a ridge, ready to confront the main body of the French army when it arrived.

This battle plan was similar to that employed by the English at Agincourt to such devastating effect. But in the space of two short months, Joan had erased the stigma of defeat associated with that battle. Even though he had only a small force with him, La Hire did not have to wait for the rest of the army to catch up: he knew he could take Talbot's men on his own; he was not afraid to lead. Consequently, unlike at Agincourt, he did not stand by and allow the English longbowmen to set up so that they could then safely slaughter their French opponents at a distance. Instead, in a move decried by English historians as most unsportsmanlike, La Hire attacked at once.* The archers went down in a matter of minutes. The second wave of the French army arrived soon after and Fastolf, watching from the ridge, brought his men down to aid the fight. But no sooner did he get there than he saw that it was hopeless and, deserting his post, escaped with a handful of men. "And before he had gone, the French had thrown to the ground the lord de Talbot, had made him prisoner and all his men being dead, and were the French already so far advanced in battle that they could at will take or kill whomsoever they wanted to," testified an eyewitness. It took less than an hour for the main body of the French army to decimate their opponents; at the end of that time two thousand Englishmen lay dead.

Even more than the raising of the siege of Orléans, this encounter, called the battle of Patay, was decisive. Afterward, throughout the kingdom, the English occupiers were suddenly on the defensive; they were cognizant of being in danger of losing all of their gains; most important, the home country's attitude toward the war changed. "By the renown of Joan the Maid," wrote a Burgundian chronicler of the time, "the courage of the English was much impaired and fallen off. They saw, it seemed to them, their fortune turn its wheel sharply against them, for they had already lost several towns and fortresses which had returned their obedience to the King of France. . . . They saw their men stricken down and did not now find them of such or so firm and prudent words as they were wont to be." The erosion of the English commitment to the war may be dated from this moment. "Thus they were all . . . very desirous of withdrawing on to the Normandy marches, abandoning what they held in the country of France and thereabout," observed the chronicler.

The experienced military men among the duke of Alençon's command, understanding the significance of this victory and not wishing to give the English time to recover and regroup, pressed to continue the forward assault by marching on Paris and liberating the city, a strike that could have meant the end of the war. (The duke of Bedford was so sure that this would happen that upon hearing the news of the English defeat at Patay, he immediately went into hiding at the fort of Vincennes.) But it would have taken a bold leader to order such a move, exactly the sort of individual the duke of Alençon patently was not; moreover, Joan was against this and adamant

*"The French did not give the English archers time to drive their stakes into the ground (the normal order) but with their cavalry set themselves to overwhelm the little force," harrumphed the renowned English medievalist E. F. Jacob.

that Charles instead be crowned. "All that [pursuing the English to Paris] means nothing to me: now, we must go to Rheims," she said.

And so the royal army broke off the advance to the north in order to turn around and march south to Gien, where Charles (staying safely out of the fray) had moved his court. Even so, it took another two weeks for Joan to convince the king to make the journey, and this pattern continued even as they were en route. Despite being accompanied by a substantial army, Charles expressed fear every time they drew near a Burgundian city along the way— Auxerre, Troyes, Châlons—and sought to withdraw, but in each case was dissuaded from doing so by Joan, who "told the King to advance boldly and to fear nothing, for if he would advance courageously he would recover all his kingdom," remembered Simon Charles. She dictated letters to the various cities, informing them of the king's approach. "Loyal Frenchmen, come out to meet King Charles," she ordered written, "and if you do so . . . I promise you and certify on your lives that we shall enter with the help of God all the towns which should be of the holy kingdom, and there make good and lasting peace, let who will come against it." Most of the towns, although ostensibly loyal to the Burgundians, were quick to note the size of the king's army and opened their doors after a brief period of negotiation. (Auxerre, which came first, set precedent; there the inhabitants promised that "they would pay to the King the same obedience as should those of the towns of Troyes, Chalons and Rheims," a particularly adroit bit of diplomacy that neatly handed off the responsibility for choosing between the king and the duke of Burgundy to the next in line.) At Troyes alone was it necessary to engage in a brief show of force before the town capitulated.

As one by one the cities surrendered peacefully, it became clear that neither the English nor the duke of Burgundy would attempt to halt the king's progress. The realization settled in that the coronation would indeed take place, and excitement among Charles's supporters grew proportionately. People began pouring into Reims for the ceremony. "So many came that it would be an infinite task to describe, as would be the great joy that all felt," wrote an observer. Domrémy itself sent a small delegation, headed by Joan's parents, to witness the magnificent ceremony engineered by a daughter of the village, proving again that, despite its remote location, news of the king and his court did in fact penetrate to this outpost in a timely fashion. There is, however, no mention at all of Robert de Baudricourt's being in Reims on this occasion, which is surprising considering that he is credited with launching Joan's career. On the other hand, Yolande's son, René of Anjou, future duke of Bar and Lorraine, *was* reported as being in attendance.

Although initially Charles had wanted his wife to accompany him, neither Yolande of Aragon nor her daughter Marie was present at the ceremony, which took place on July 17 at the cathedral of Notre Dame in Reims. The journey was probably deemed too dangerous for Marie, who was pregnant again, although there is also the possibility that it would have been somewhat awkward to bring the queen as it might then be expected that she be crowned along with her husband, and it was important to maintain the focus on Charles as the heir to Saint Louis. Yolande stayed home to be with her daughter.

But just because she wasn't there didn't mean she didn't want to know all about it, so in her place Yolande sent three members of her household charged with the task of keeping her and her daughter informed of every particular. The report these agents sent back, addressed to both the queen of Sicily and her daughter, the queen of France, detailing the coronation ceremony and its aftermath, has survived. "Our Queens and most dread Ladies," their letter began. "May it please you to know that yesterday the King arrived in this town of Reims where he found complete and full obedience. Today he was anointed and crowned and the beautiful mystery was most striking to behold because it was as solemn and comprised of all the accoutrements that are essential to such a ceremony, as if it had been in preparation for a full year. . . . Our lords the duke of Alençon, the count of Clermont, the count of Vendôme, the lords of Laval and La Trémoïlle attended in their royal garments; his lordship d'Alençon conferred knighthood on the king . . . his lordship d'Albret held up the sword before the king . . . and our lord of Reims carried out the said mystery and hence the consecration." The holy oil used to anoint the king was carried in on horseback by four lords, magnificently attired and waving banners; the coronation lasted five hours, from nine in the morning until two in the afternoon. "And at the hour that the King was anointed and also when the crown was lowered onto his head, one and all cried out Noël! And the trumpets rang out in such a way that it seemed the church vaults might crack. And during said mystery [the mystical rite of coronation] the Maiden stood at all times by the King's side, holding her banner high in hand. And it was beautiful to behold the gracious manners of the King and the Maiden. God knows you were missed," the correspondents made haste to point out.

Having communicated the most important aspects of the coronation—
that it was splendid and solemn enough in all respects to convey legitimacy,
thereby wiping away the memory of the feeble ceremony at which Charles
had declared himself king immediately after his father's death; that the
abundance of participating lords meant that the old Armagnac alliance was
once again firmly in place; and that Joan's role in bringing about this
momentous event was publicly recognized by the king, as indicated by her
place at his side—the three operatives then reported on recent political
developments, an area of keen interest to both women. "Tomorrow the king
must leave in the direction of Paris," they wrote. "We hear in this town that
the duke of Burgundy went there and then on to Lyon where he is now. He
sent a messenger to the King as soon as he arrived. At this hour, we hope that
a solid treaty will be ready before they take their leave. The Maiden is confident that she will succeed at obtaining compliance from Paris."

This news was precisely what Yolande of Aragon had hoped for. Charles
had been persuaded to act and as a result his old allies had flocked to his side
and the diplomatic solution she had been advocating for so long—prying

The coronation of Charles VII at Reims.

the duke of Burgundy away from the English by arranging for a separate treaty—was in sight. More than this, her daughter's husband was now established as the true heir to the throne of Saint Louis and the legitimate king of France, which meant that Marie, coronation or no coronation, was the legitimate queen, and her offspring were the future heirs to the kingdom. From Reims, the army would go to Paris with every hope of victory. And all of this had happened as a result of the introduction of the Maid to the court at Chinon.

As for Joan herself, the hours spent at the coronation ceremony were a source of great pride. She had accomplished the impossible, the miraculous; she understood that her place nearest the king signified the tangible acknowledgment of her achievement. When asked later by her inquisitors, "Why was your standard more carried in the church at Rheims at the consecration of the King than those of other captains?" she answered simply that, as "it had borne the burden, it was quite right that it receive the honor."

CHAPTER 10

Capture
at
Compiègne

I shall last a year, hardly longer.

*—Joan of Arc to Charles VII at the
royal court at Chinon, 1429*

Y ALMOST ANY MEASURE, the coronation at Reims was a stunning political achievement. No longer was it possible for the English to sneer at Charles and dismiss his claims to the throne; afterward, as Joan had understood and predicted, the uncertainty regarding his legitimacy vanished and he was irrevocably Charles VII, king of France. Consequently, the war was no longer about whether he or Henry VI was rightfully heir to the kingdom but was instead recast as a struggle by a native population and ruler against an occupying force.* From seriously contemplating fleeing to Scotland, Charles now suddenly occupied a stronger position than he had in

---

*Too late the English recognized their error and the next year brought the young Henry VI to France to try to get him anointed at Reims as well—an enterprise at which they were unsuccessful, forcing him to be crowned instead in Paris at Notre Dame by the cardinal of Winchester on December 17, 1431. This ceremony did not fare well by comparison, being more English than French, and lacking the usual amenities expected by the general population. "The food was shocking, no one had a good word to say for it. Most of it, especially what was meant for the common people, had been cooked the previous Thursday, which seemed very odd to the French—the English were in charge of all this," sniffed a Parisian eyewitness.

a decade, when he had so rashly decided to assassinate John the Fearless on the bridge of Montereau.

But wars are not won solely by symbolic gestures, however brilliant, and whatever political gains were achieved at Reims were more than offset by the impairment of the king's military prospects caused by the interruption of hostilities. For no sooner had the duke of Bedford, hardly believing his luck, realized that the French army was not going to capitalize on its victory at Patay by immediately marching on Paris than he called urgently for reinforcements from England. A new army of some thirty-five hundred English knights and longbowmen, accompanied by their numerous attendant squires and foot soldiers, landed at Calais in early July, and by the day of Charles's coronation were within a week's march of Paris.

In this emergency, the attitude of Philip the Good, duke of Burgundy, toward the reinvigorated campaign by Charles was critical. If Philip could be induced to give up his English alliance, even if this meant his remaining neutral rather than openly embracing Charles's cause, the military odds might once again shift in the king's favor. The English could not expect to hold France without the support of the duke of Burgundy.

Philip knew this and exploited the opportunity to maximum advantage. Although a member of the French ruling dynasty by virtue of ancestry—his grandfather had, after all, been the brother of Charles's grandfather—when it came to his political standing, Philip did not consider himself French. Rather, he saw himself as an independent sovereign entity, much like the kings of Aragon or Scotland, whose participation in the war was elective. "Most redoubted lord, I recommend myself to you in all humility. I imagine that you and your councilors remember that it was at your urgent request that I took part in your French war," he would later write to Henry VI. Philip did, however, maintain strong feelings that he ought not to support the campaign of the man who had murdered his father—feelings he kept hidden in order to keep both sides bidding for his services.

Consequently, when, immediately following the ceremony in Reims, Charles made diplomatic overtures to him, Philip agreed to participate in talks. It is clear, however, that he had no intention of accepting the king's terms, no matter how generous. Unbeknownst to Charles and his counselors, during the week just prior to the coronation Philip had entered into a secret agreement with the regency government to help defend Paris against an attack by the royal army. The duke of Bedford, who had gone to the lengths of marrying Philip's sister in order to keep the alliance, was by this time familiar with his new brother-in-law's character and knew exactly which incentives to offer in order to secure his friendship. According to an eyewitness, he organized a solemn public ceremony at which he commemorated Philip's father, John the Fearless, and denounced his treacherous murder by Charles and the Armagnacs, calling for "a show of hands from all men who would be loyal and true to the Regent and to the Duke of Burgundy." At the same time, Philip the Good also received the munificent sum of 20,000 francs "by the command of my lord the regent of the kingdom of France [Bedford] . . . to spend and employ it in the payment of the men-at-arms and archers whom my said lord of Burgundy had the intention to bring into the parts of France from his country for the service of the king [Henry VI] against the enemies who at that time were advancing in force," according to the official register of English accounts. This two-pronged approach of appealing to both Philip's pride and his purse yielded the desired result. Together, the dukes of Burgundy and Bedford "promised . . . on their faith to defend the good town of Paris."

Under the circumstances, it was very much in the duke of Burgundy's interest to pretend to participate in diplomatic talks in order to ensure that Charles did nothing to further his offensive against Paris until such time as Philip and the duke of Bedford were prepared to move against him militarily. Here, he had a happy participant in the king. Charles positively excelled at doing nothing.

To encourage the promulgation of a peace treaty, Charles agreed immediately to a fifteen-day truce that specifically prevented him from marching on Paris. Georges de la Trémoïlle, whose brother, Jehan, was a high-ranking member of Philip the Good's entourage, was put in charge of the king's side in the negotiations, an appointment that more or less assured the complete subjugation of military considerations to the diplomatic process. In August, Charles's ambassadors offered Philip magnanimous terms in exchange for reconciliation: the king promised to make reparations and undertake acts of penance for the murder of John the Fearless; he would compensate the duke of Burgundy personally for his alliance with a substantial allocation of gold (which unfortunately at that moment he did not have) and territories; and Philip would be excused from having to do homage to Charles, which the king understood would be repugnant to him. Even after the fifteen days of the truce had passed, the king refrained from moving farther into the duke of

Burgundy's territory, "as much because some felt it strong in men-at-arms, as for the hope he had that a good treaty would be made between them," wrote the chronicler Monstrelet. Although his overtures to Philip were no doubt sincere, Charles's single-minded focus on these parleys also allowed him to mask his reluctance to pursue hostilities. In fact, the king had had enough of fighting. From Reims he simply wanted to retreat once again to the safety and comfort of Bourges and try to negotiate his way back to the throne.

This attitude put the king in opposition to Joan, who argued fervently in favor of marching on Paris at the earliest possible moment. Although Joan was aware that Charles's envoys were seeking a diplomatic settlement with Philip the Good, and approved this plan—she even wrote to him herself, requiring Philip to "make good firm peace which will last long"—she was deliberately not informed of the particulars, especially about the truce prohibiting an attack on Paris. To put her off and stall for time while he awaited the result of the negotiations, the king, accompanied by his entourage and the royal army, instead left Reims and began a very slow, roundabout tour of the neighboring area, stopping at all of the small cities along the route in order to parade through the streets to cries of "Noël!" Within a month, he had made it only as far as Crépy, about fifty miles to the west.

The duke of Bedford, of course, made optimum use of this respite. The English army arrived at Paris in late July and the city was fortified against assault. Cannons and ammunition were secured to the walls; trenches were dug outside the gates and the moats put into repair. The supplementary army promised by the duke of Burgundy arrived in due course. Suitably reinforced, the regent felt strong enough to challenge the king to battle in a letter that he took pains to make as humiliating as possible. "We, John of Lancaster, regent of France and Duke of Bedford, make known to you Charles of Valois who call yourself Dauphin of Viennois and now without cause call yourself King. . . . You who cause to be abused the ignorant people and take to yourself the aid of people superstitious and reproved, as that of a woman disordered and defamed, being in man's clothes and of dissolute conduct . . . choose in the country of Brie where you and we are, or in the Ile de France, some place in the fields . . . one day soon and fitting . . . at which day and place, if you would appear there in person with the aforesaid defamed and apostate woman, we, at Our Lord's pleasure, will appear in person," he wrote.

This letter, with its withering reference to Joan, would have stung Charles, but worse was the realization that the enemy had received substantial reinforcements, a state of affairs that became clear on August 15 when the king and the royal army, still on their goodwill tour, ran into the approximately eighty-five hundred English and Burgundian men-at-arms whom the duke of Bedford had brought up from Paris and who were camped just outside of Senlis, blocking the way south. Although neither side gave battle, just the threat was enough to cause Charles to turn around and retreat north, first back to Crépy and then farther to Compiègne.

It took Joan an additional two weeks to convince the king to finally make an attempt on Paris, and in the end she did it only by persuading the duke of Alençon to take the initiative and bring an advance party of soldiers within striking distance. "On the Friday following the 26th day of August, the Maid, the duke of Alençon, and their company were lodged in the city of Saint-Denis. And when the king knew that they were lodged [there] . . . with great regret he came as far as the city of Senlis. And it seemed that he was counseled against the will of the Maid, of the duke of Alençon, and of their company," observed a chronicler. Among this advance party of soldiers pressing Charles to listen to Joan and attack Paris was Yolande's son, René of Anjou, who after the coronation had thrown off his mantle of anonymity and openly joined the royal army "well accompanied by soldiers."

There followed a week or so of skirmishing, as the royal army looked for weaknesses in the Parisian defenses and tried to pinpoint the best location from which to launch an offensive. The duke of Bedford was so confident that he could hold Paris that he had left Philip the Good's forces alone to defend the capital and taken the English army to Le Mans, in Yolande's home county of Maine, to deflect an independent sortie led by Arthur of Richemont. (The constable was still in such disfavor with Charles that he had not been allowed to participate in the coronation, and so had struck off on his own to fight the enemy.) Finally, on Thursday, September 8, 1429, a little before noon, the royal army assembled in battle formation just outside the walls of Paris close to the Saint-Honoré gate. This time, no priests went praying and singing before the soldiers; no effort was made to evoke a crusade or holy war. The assault appeared to be just what it was: a full-scale attack by a secular, partisan military force.

Paris was the largest city in western Europe. A sprawling metropolis by medieval standards, home to some 200,000 people and heavily fortified, it represented a vastly more difficult target than anything Joan or the duke of Alençon had attempted before. Although the capital had in the past yielded to an invading army, this was generally achieved only with help from sup-porters within the city who could be counted on to unlock one or more of the heavy gates, saving the necessity of scaling the walls. While there were no doubt a substantial number of Parisians who favored Charles's cause over that of Henry VI, these people had been out of power for over a decade. Some effort seems to have been made to reach out to them, but they were not in a position to undertake so risky an enterprise as to steal the keys to the portals. Moreover, most of the citizens of Paris—or at least those in control of the city—were staunch Burgundians. To them, coronation or no coronation, Charles was just another incarnation of the old Armagnac party, which even after all this time they associated with government corruption, greed, and higher taxes. Further, taking history as a model, these people understood that if the royal army did succeed in entering the city they would all be hunted down and slaughtered. So, unlike at Orléans, where the citizens had rejoiced at the coming of the royal army and done everything they could to help, a majority of the Parisians scorned and loathed Joan and her forces. They had every incentive to fight against her, and they did.

The battle lasted all day and followed the by now familiar course. The king's forces arrived accompanied by heavy artillery and many wagons car-rying wood and branches that the soldiers hoped to use to dam the moats protecting the capital and thus provide a makeshift bridge to the walls. For hours, the royal army energetically assailed the city, firing its weapons while torrents of arrows and stone cannonballs rained down from the Burgundian men-at-arms and the citizen infantry stationed on high. "The assault, which was very cruel on both sides, lasted until four in the evening without it being known who would get the better," reported an eyewitness. As the afternoon wore on and night threatened without a definitive victory, the French soldiers began once again to tire and to think in terms of retreat, and Joan did what she always did when her troops' spirits flagged. With great courage, she moved to stand at the head of their ranks and held her standard high to signal a fresh assault, at the same time calling out in a loud voice to the Parisians on the wall, "Yield to us quickly, for Jesus' sake, for if you yield not before night, we shall enter by force whether you will or no, and you will all be put to death without mercy."

But this time the enemy forces did not fall back and tremble at her approach, thinking her a witch, as the outnumbered English men-at-arms had at Orléans. The citizens of Paris were not afraid of Joan; to them she was just a low, unpleasant, probably deranged Armagnac peasant woman from somewhere in the provinces. So when she planted her standard and called to them to surrender they simply answered her in kind. "Here's for you!" a Burgundian crossbowman shouted back. "Cackling bawd!" And he shot her in the leg. When Joan cried out and fell, her page grabbed her standard and bravely planted it again, at which point another crossbowman shot *him* in the leg. Then, as the page was lifting his visor so he could see to remove the arrow from his wound, a third archer shot him in the face and killed him, and in that instant Charles's chances of retaking the city of Paris died too.

Although Joan continued to try to rally her troops to press the attack, she was unable to rise because of pain, and seeing her down was a blow. The king's soldiers lost faith in themselves just as their enemies, noting her vulnerability, increased theirs. "A little after four o'clock the Parisians took heart and overwhelmed their adversaries with so many cannon balls and arrows that the latter were forced to retreat, to abandon the assault, and go away," wrote the same observer. Later, under cover of darkness, the injured Joan was retrieved from the moat into which she had fallen. Curiously, of all the knights who fought beside her that day, including those who had been with her from the beginning at Orléans, it was René who picked her up and carried her from the battlefield to the safety of his own quarters.

The next day, although both Joan and the duke of Alençon pressed to return to Paris to continue the onslaught, wiser heads prevailed and the army was ordered to fall back on Senlis, where Charles held court. A week later, with Paris still firmly in English and Burgundian hands, the king disbanded his army and retreated to the safety of his home base south of the Loire. "In September," wrote a Burgundian chronicler, "the Armagnacs came and assailed the walls of Paris which they hoped to take, but won there only grief, shame and misfortune. Many among them were wounded for the remainder of their lives who, before the assault, were in good health. But a fool fears nothing so long as he is successful. I say this for them who sweated ill-luck and bad faith . . . on the word of a creature in the form of a woman who accompanied them—who was it? God knows."

THE FIASCO AT PARIS—and it *was* a fiasco; only a disciplined, well-planned, sustained siege of the type Charles had no intention of engaging in could have taken the city—betrayed the precariousness of Joan's relationship to the king. Charles was not the sort of person to shrug off humiliation lightly. Insults rankled; he nursed grudges; worse, he was extremely sensitive and suspicious of possible slurs against his dignity. The chronicler Georges Chastellain summed up the king's principal character traits as "changeability, defiance, and above all, envy." Up until the coronation at Reims, Charles, surrounded by advisers who believed in Joan's godliness, had been protected by a cocoon of reassurance, but the scorn that had permeated the duke of Bedford's letter of challenge showed him only too clearly how his patronage of and reliance on the Maid were regarded by those outside his own circle. Charles had managed to shrug this off at first, but after the dismal sortie against Paris the English regent's barbs resonated with the king. Messengers from God were not supposed to lose.

To save himself further embarrassment, Charles separated Joan from the army. The duke of Alençon was sent home to his wife, while Joan was escorted to Bourges under the stewardship of Georges de la Trémoïlle's half brother, the duke of Albret. With the decline in Joan's fortunes came a corresponding reduction in the influence of Yolande's party as well. La Trémoïlle was once again firmly in control at court, and he made it his business to see that the Maid of Orléans did not have an opportunity to regain her former glory. When later that year the duke of Alençon put together another force with the intent of evicting the English from Maine and Normandy, he wrote specifically to the king asking Charles to please send him Joan as he would be able to recruit far more soldiers were she present to lead the troops. But "Messire Regnault de Chartres, [and] the lord de la Trémoïlle . . . who at that time governed the King's council and matters of war, would never consent, nor permit, nor suffer the Maid and the Duke of Alençon be together, and since then he has not been able to recover her," wrote Perceval de Cagny, the duke of Alençon's chronicler.

To distract Joan, in November 1429 La Trémoïlle sent her instead to besiege the town of La Charité-sur-Loire, about twenty miles east of Bourges, which had been captured by a local mercenary who had sided with the English (and who had, coincidentally, previously extorted a hefty ransom of 14,000 écus from La Trémoïlle). Joan was likely set up to fail; another chronicler reported that "the sire de la Trémoïlle sent Joan . . . in the depths of winter . . . with very few men, before the town of La Charité, and there they were for about a month and withdrew themselves shamefully without aid coming to them from inside and there lost bombards and artilleries."

Perceval de Cagny also commented on this aborted mission to La Charité. "When Joan had been there a space of time, because the King made no diligence to send her victuals nor money to maintain her company, she was obliged to raise her siege and depart from it in great displeasure," he wrote.

The failure to accomplish even this small objective destroyed whatever lingering credibility Joan might have retained at court as a true prophetess. To save face—both hers and his own—in December, Charles ennobled Joan and her family, and rewarded her for her contribution to the crown. She was given an additional five couriers and six horses for her stable along with a generous donation for the maintenance of a suitably aristocratic household. The wretched duke of Orléans, still a prisoner in London—he had spent nearly half his life, fifteen years, in captivity and the English still refused to ransom him—also displayed his gratitude for her efforts at this time by sending her a very expensive, exquisite ruby red gown adorned with the finest lace from Brussels. As a result, she was no longer the simple shepherdess Jeannette from Domrémy, nor the Maid of Orléans, but Joan of Arc, a lady of position and means. It was clearly hoped by both the king and those around him like La Trémoïlle that this bribe would be sufficient to induce Joan to hang up her armor once and for all, put on her pretty dress, and go away.

But Joan did not want to go away; Joan wanted to fight. Although her voices were no longer leading her—when asked later by her inquisitors if she had attacked Paris at the command of her angels, she replied, "It was at the request of the men of war that was made a valiance in arms against Paris and also against La Charité at the request of my King"—Joan was nonetheless determined to evict the English from France. Unaware that she had lost her influence, she chafed at the king's inaction, expressed her unhappiness openly, and continued to press Charles to send her with an army into those parts of the kingdom still occupied by England or allied to the duke of Burgundy. There is no question that despite her public popularity (which was considerable) she was during this period kept at arm's length and regarded as a nuisance and a potential liability by those in power at court. Later, Regnault de Chartres would write that Joan "did not wish to pay attention to any counsel and did everything at her own pleasure."

Matters came to a head in the spring of 1430. By March it was reasonably clear, even to Charles (although he would not admit it publicly for another two months), that Philip the Good was not really all that interested in making peace and had been prolonging negotiations only as a means of augmenting his power and territory. The duke of Burgundy had recently accepted the title of lieutenant general of France from the English, which put him second in command of the kingdom after his brother-in-law the duke of Bedford, and had also received the counties of Champagne and Brie from Henry VI's government. Yet another reinforcement English army, this one comprising two thousand men-at-arms, had landed at Calais, intending to retake Reims in preparation for the coronation of eight-year-old Henry VI, and a joint battle plan was drawn up between the dukes of Burgundy and Bedford. Intelligence reported that one of their first targets would be Compiègne, which, ironically, was one of the towns Charles himself had given Philip in order to entice him to sign a treaty, but whose citizens, inspired by Joan and the coronation at Reims, had refused to surrender to the Burgundians.

Joan met with the king at the beginning of March 1430, when he moved his court to Sully-sur-Loire, near Orléans, where she had been staying under the more or less watchful eye of La Trémoïlle at one of his family's castles. It seems to have been the first time in months that she had been allowed into Charles's presence, or participated in a meeting of the royal council. Predictably, she was unhappy with the endless discussions and lack of response to the military threat from the English. Finding herself unable to move the king as she had in the past, however, she instead determined to strike out on her own. "The King being in the town of Sully-sur-Loire, the Maid, who had seen and heard all the matter and manner which the King and his council held for the recovery of his kingdom, very ill content with that, found means to separate herself from them and, unknown to the King and without taking leave of him, she pretended to go about some business and, without returning, went away to the town of Lagny-sur-Marne because they of that place were making good war on the English of Paris and elsewhere," wrote Perceval de Cagny. Joan left with her remaining page, her brother, and a small band of some two hundred mercenaries led by an Italian bandit—a far cry from the previous year's royally sanctioned, well-manned Orléans expedition. Although Perceval de Cagny claimed that she slipped away by stratagem, it is likely that the court was aware of her movements but made no attempt to go after her, a sign that she had been officially cut loose. This way, if she succeeded in repelling the English, the king could take credit for her victory, but if she failed, as was more likely, she could be disavowed as having acted on her own initiative and against her sovereign's wishes.

Joan and her band of soldiers headed north to Compiègne, but it took them nearly two months to get there because they stopped to skirmish with whatever English and Burgundian resistance they met with along the way. At least two of these encounters were successful: in April, Joan managed to liberate the town of Melun from its small English garrison and soon afterward put to rout a platoon of Burgundians, capturing their captain outside of Senlis. However, by the time she arrived in Compiègne on May 14, 1430, the duke of Burgundy, bankrolled by his English brother-in-law, had managed to put together a substantial army and had already taken the small town of Choisy-au-Bac, just outside the city.

Joan was not alone in her desire to defend Compiègne from the machinations of Philip the Good. Charles had already dispatched Regnault de Chartres, archbishop of Reims, and the count of Vendôme to see what could be done to assist the city. The archbishop of Reims in particular cannot have been pleased to have Joan and her force turn up unannounced, but he had no choice but to accept her presence. To the citizens of Compiègne, who were on record as "resolute to undergo every risk for themselves, their children, and their infants, rather than be exposed to the mercy of the duke [of Burgundy]," Joan was still the Maid of Orléans, the holy woman who had delivered the king to his coronation at Reims, the Messenger who was celebrated throughout France for her famous deeds, and they welcomed her among them as a sign of divine favor.

For two days, Joan and her men assisted in maneuvers at Choisy-au-Bac intended to free the town from the Burgundians. These sorties were easily repelled by the enemy, who eclipsed the local forces in terms of both heavy artillery and numbers. To try to marshal more support, Regnault de Chartres and the count of Vendôme, accompanied by Joan and her mercenaries, left Compiègne for Soissons on May 18. However, when they did not receive the sort of welcome they were hoping for—the captain of Soissons refused to allow Joan's soldiers to come inside the gates, and later handed the town to the duke of Burgundy without a fight—the archbishop and the count understood that the cause was lost. The next day they fell back south of Reims, but were apparently unable to convince Joan to join them, and she and her men instead returned secretly to Compiègne in the early morning of May 23. It was to be a fateful decision on Joan's part. This could well have been what Regnault de Chartres meant when he complained later that she would not take counsel.

No sooner had Joan and her men arrived than they were enlisted by a local commander to help aid in an assault against Margny, which had recently been taken by the Burgundians. Margny was across the Oise River just to the north of Compiègne; it was reached by a drawbridge from the city. That very afternoon, Joan, dressed in her armor, "with a doublet of rich cloth-of-gold over her breastplate," as reported by a Burgundian chronicler, charged out of the city on a large gray steed and led a force of knights, the size of which is unknown (it was stated only that she was "well-accompanied by many noble men"), across the bridge to begin an attack on the outpost. Twice Joan and her men fell upon Margny and twice they were repulsed; she was regrouping for a third drive when the sounds of the battle reached John of Luxembourg, one of Philip the Good's leading generals, who sounded the alarm. Immediately, reinforcements arrived "and more assistance flowed towards the Burgundians than they needed"; the duke of Burgundy himself galloped toward Margny.

The knights accompanying Joan, fearing that they would soon be overwhelmed, fell back on Compiègne in a panic. Everyone rushed to the drawbridge at once; only Joan kept her head and worked to protect her men. Even the Burgundian chronicler was impressed: "The Maid, going beyond the nature of womankind, performed a great feat and took much pain to save her company from loss, staying behind like a chief and like the most valiant member of the flock," he reported. However, when the captain of the city saw that a large number of enemy soldiers were bearing down on Compiègne, he abruptly raised the drawbridge to prevent their penetrating the gate, leaving Joan and a small party of attendants alone and unguarded in the fields outside the city's walls. They were soon surrounded by Burgundian soldiers, at which point "an archer, a rough man and a sour [one], full of spite because a woman of whom so much had been heard should have overthrown so many valiant men, dragged her to one side by her cloth-of-gold cloak and pulled her from her horse, throwing her flat on the ground; never could she find recourse or succour in her men, try though they might to remount her," wrote the Burgundian chronicler, Georges Chastellain. At almost the same moment, a nobleman in service to Philip the Good rode up and demanded that Joan surrender to him.

Recognizing that she had no other choice, Joan reluctantly yielded.

• • •

The capture of Joan of Arc at Compiègne.

THE IMPORTANCE of Joan's capture was perceived instantly by all involved. Beyond the question of ransom, what did it mean that God had allowed her, his stated Messenger, to be taken? Just whose side was God on? The English "were very joyous at it, more than had they taken five hundred combatants," while the French at Compiègne were "doleful and wroth at their losses, and above all had great displeasure at the taking of the Maid," wrote Chastellain. The duke of Burgundy himself hurried to interview her and later sent a letter around to all of his territories, advising them that "by the pleasure of our blessed Creator, the woman called the Maid has been taken; and from her capture will be recognized the error and mad belief of all those who became sympathetic and favorable to the deeds of this woman. . . . Render homage to our Creator, who through His blessed pleasure has wished to conduct the rest of our enterprises on behalf of our lord the king of England and of France." The knight to whom she had surrendered could not believe his luck: "more joyful than if he had had a King in his hands," he made haste to whisk her off the battlefield and inside the stronghold of Margny for safekeeping.

To prevent a rescue attempt, she was quickly transferred to John of Luxembourg's castle of Beaulieu-les-Fontaines, north of Noyon. Charles's enemies need not have worried; to think that the king, who had been unwilling to take action on his own to relieve Orléans, or even to organize a decent army to defend Compiègne, would suddenly find the energy to raise a force strong enough to deliver a single prisoner was hardly creditable. Even a ransom agreement was unlikely. Charles, who had a war to prosecute and who had had to disband his army after Paris because he could not afford to pay his soldiers, was not going to throw away good money on Joan just so that she could come back to court and bother him again.* The king's distance from his former seer may be measured by the letter Regnault de Chartres wrote to the people of Reims in the immediate aftermath of Joan's capture. Joan, he wrote, "had become full of pride due to the rich garments she had begun to wear. She had not been doing what God had commanded her but her own will."

Neither would Yolande of Aragon have seriously entertained the thought of trying to deliver Joan from her captivity. By this time, the queen of Sicily had withdrawn from the royal court and was living at her castle in Saumur, where she could focus her energies in support of the duke of Alençon's campaign to free the important city of Le Mans in Maine, of which she was duchess. The previous year she had spent heavily on the expedition to resupply Orléans, and her finances had not yet recovered, for whatever income was derived from the county of Provence was reserved for the use of her eldest son, Louis III, in his campaign to win the kingdom of Naples. Nor would she have considered it her place to purchase Joan's freedom; ransom money was too precious to be wasted on anyone outside of the immediate family. This she had learned from Marie of Blois on her mother-in-law's deathbed. With one son at war in Italy and another fighting for the king of France, Yolande knew to preserve her assets.

But even if she had had the resources to free Joan it is unlikely that the queen of Sicily, or any member of her family, would have done so. Because Joan claimed to have appeared by the order of God, to interfere in her fate would have been akin to questioning a divine imperative. Familiar as she was with Jean of Arras's romance, Yolande would have remembered the passage

---

*Charles was notoriously stingy in these matters. Much later, when the English finally agreed to ransom the duke of Orléans, the king refused to contribute so much as a sovereign to free his cousin and the money had to be paid by others.

where Raymondin cried out over a sin committed by one of his sons and Melusine expressly reminded him that "God's will is inscrutable; the judgments of God are so secret that no human being can understand them." If God had decreed that Joan be captured, He must have done so for a reason; similarly, if she was to be freed, the angels, and not the queen of Sicily, would be responsible. And there was no telling that it might not be God's will that she remain a prisoner. Melusine had, after all, been betrayed by Raymondin in the end and fated to suffer.

And, in fairness to both Charles and Yolande, despite Joan's captivity, neither had reason to believe that the Maid was in any particular danger. Future generations have the advantage of hindsight, but what would befall Joan was unprecedented at the time. The medieval military code as regards capture, ransom, and imprisonment was dictated by the time-honored rules of chivalry. If during a battle a member of the nobility fighting for one side voluntarily surrendered to a member of the nobility on the other—and Joan, who understood the protocol, had made sure to do this—then that person was taken unharmed. A ransom would be set, and if that ransom was raised, the captive would go free; if not, he would remain unmolested in the castle of the lord who had claimed him until such time as it could be raised, or a prisoner swap arranged, or a peace treaty signed. Imprisonment was uncomfortable, certainly, but not life-threatening. Moreover, it happened all the time—both the duke of Alençon and the count of Vendôme, for example, had been captured in battle and spent some time in a cell, and they were none the worse for it. Of course, these rules did not apply to the foot soldiers or the members of the lower classes who risked their lives in battle, but Charles had taken care of that by ennobling Joan the previous December.

And for the first several months of Joan's captivity, this version of events played out exactly according to etiquette, and she was treated like an ordinary knight. Soon after being transferred to the castle at Beaulieu she tried to break out (and almost succeeded), but this was not due to maltreatment. "I have never been a prisoner in any place but I would try to escape from it. Being in that castle, I had shut up my keepers in the tower, excepting the porter who saw me and encountered me. It seems to me that it did not please God that I should escape that time," she later told her inquisitors, referring to this incident. Nor was she punished for the attempt, although as a further precaution she was moved even farther into Burgundian territory afterward, to another of John of Luxembourg's strongholds, the castle of

Beaurevoir. However, here too she was treated with respect, and even kindness. She was shut up in a tower room but was never shackled, and she was allowed the society of John of Luxembourg's wife and aunt for company. These two ladies tried gently to persuade her to put off her male attire and adopt women's clothing, and although Joan refused, she clearly held them in great esteem. "The demoiselle of Luxembourg and the lady of Beaurevoir offered me a woman's dress or the stuff to make one, asking me to wear that habit, and I answered that I had not permission from God and that it was not yet time. . . . Had it been that I was to wear women's clothes, I should have done so more willingly at the request of those women than of any other woman in all France excepting my queen," she later testified.

But this relatively benign state of affairs did not last. A conspiracy was afoot between two seemingly unrelated but nonetheless powerful entities— the University of Paris and the regency government—that would make a sham of all of the carefully constructed laws of chivalric behavior that governed prisoners of war. As a result, a nineteen-year-old girl would be subjected to treatment so barbaric, so inhumane, that its cruelty and horror still register today with an immediacy that belies the slow passage of many centuries.

CHAPTER 11

The Trial
of
Joan of Arc

❧

You say that you are my judge. Consider well what
you are about, for in truth I am sent from God,
and you are putting yourself in great danger.

—*Joan of Arc, in response to an inquisitor's question
at her Trial of Condemnation, 1431*

HE UNIVERSITY OF PARIS was without question
the most distinguished and influential school of theology in fifteenth-century Europe. Those of its stu-
dents who managed to survive the grueling course
of study—six years of preparatory work in the general arts followed by a further nine years under the
exacting tutelage of the faculty of theology—were
more or less assured a lucrative path to prominence among the priesthood.
An institution as vast and complex as the medieval Church had a never-
ending need for competent officials to tend to the administration of its many
benefices, and the best of these positions—canon, dean, bishop, archbishop,
cardinal—were disproportionately populated by masters of theology from
the University of Paris. As these ecclesiastic appointments all boasted an
income stream or "living" that was pocketed by their administrators, masters of theology could also hope to attain great wealth in addition to emi-
nence. Naturally, there was considerable competition for the better

assignments—the larger and more prestigious the diocese, the more profit-able the living. Moreover, those who succeeded in ascending to the upper regions of the Church hierarchy could expect to hold positions of authority in the courts of secular princes as well. High-ranking ecclesiastics and mas-ters of theology were in great demand as ambassadors and counselors, and were royally rewarded for their efforts with gifts of money or additional benefices. This symbiotic convergence of Church and state ensured that the University of Paris functioned as a political institution as much as an aca-demic one—perhaps more so.

Consequently, the school and its various officials did not stand coolly above the civil passions that gripped the rest of the kingdom. Rather, the masters of theology had played a prominent role in the war since its incep-tion. As in the general population, some of its members had favored the Armagnac position while others supported the Burgundians. The fortunes of each side had risen and fallen with the pace of the conflict, and with the triumph of Henry V, the Armagnac masters, even those who were revered for their erudition, had been forced to flee Paris and had taken refuge with Charles, who made use of their services. Similarly, the remaining masters, all Burgundian partisans, welcomed the English occupation and threw the full force of the university behind Henry V and his successors.

As might be expected, the influence of the Maid on the course of the war, her hold on the public consciousness, and in particular her assertion that she came as a messenger from God aroused the extreme umbrage of those Bur-gundian masters who now controlled the theological faculty. This ire had become further inflamed when some of their former colleagues, the exiled Armagnac masters acting for Charles, had examined Joan at Poitiers and approved her mission, in effect declaring her to be a prophetess. The crown-ing blow had fallen when, immediately following the raising of the siege of Orléans, the great Armagnac theologian Jean Gerson, a former chancellor of the university and the most esteemed academician of the period, published a prodigiously learned monograph on the subject of the Maid, in which, citing the relevant cases of Divine Law, he asserted that Joan was not forbidden from assuming male attire. His thesis was subsequently reinforced by the archbishop of Embrun, another Armagnac scholar, who justified Joan's ward-robe as not only necessary to her occupation but required as, in her case, being constantly in the presence of warriors, it was a matter of decency. It was at this point that the question of the divine nature of Joan's mission was raised to the level of a faculty disagreement, and the University of Paris was a place that took its faculty disagreements very seriously. In the previous century, a chancellor had been hauled up on charges before the pope and ultimately dismissed from his post over a dispute arising from the order of seating preference at the annual end-of-term banquet.

With the capture of Joan at Compiègne, the Burgundian masters saw their chance. They dispatched a letter to Philip the Good in the name of the Inquisitor of France entreating that the Maid be delivered to the university as soon as possible to stand trial for false doctrine. "Whereas all faithful Christian princes and all other true Catholics are required to extirpate all errors arising against the faith . . . and that it be now of common renown that by a certain woman named Joan whom the adversaries of this kingdom call the Maid, have been in several cities, good towns and other places of this kingdom, broadcast and published . . . diverse errors . . . we implore you of good affection, you, most puissant prince . . . that the soonest and most safely and conveniently it can be done, be sent and brought prisoner to us the said Joan, vehemently suspected of many crimes smacking of heresy, to appear before us and a procurator of the Holy Inquisitor, to answer and proceed as in reason bound," they wrote. The extent of the university's desire to repudiate their former colleagues' arguments may be measured by the speed with which they proceeded. Word of the Maid's apprehension reached Paris on May 25; the letter was dated May 26.

The duke of Burgundy, having received this communication, went to interview Joan on June 6 and there met with his vassal, John of Luxembourg. Although there is no record of their conversation, it is likely they discussed what should be done with her. Apparently this did not include simply handing her over to the university, as no move was made in that direction. The theological faculty, failing to obtain a satisfactory response to its first salvo, recognized that stronger measures were called for and handed the responsibility for securing Joan to a man uniquely qualified to accomplish the task: Pierre Cauchon, the bishop of Beauvais.

The career of Pierre Cauchon was a conspicuous example of the advantages to be drawn through the assiduous massaging of the shared ambitions of Church and state. A former rector—a position equivalent to head of school—and an impassioned mouthpiece for the Burgundian agenda, Cauchon had thrown the full weight of the university behind the duke of Burgundy and the English occupation. Under his supervision, the theological faculty had provided the intellectual and scholastic arguments, known as the "theory of the double monarchy," which had justified the crowning of Henry V, and he himself had helped to negotiate the Treaty of Troyes, by which agreement the dauphin had been disinherited. For these services, Cauchon had been rewarded with the bishopric of Beauvais by the duke of Burgundy. Since then, he had so ingratiated himself with the duke of Bedford that he succeeded in having himself appointed as a counselor to Henry VI, a position for which he was compensated by a stipend of 1,000 livres, paid by the English treasury.

Recently, however, Cauchon's career had stalled. Despite his best efforts to prove his worth to his English employers over the previous decade, he was still only a bishop. Still, Cauchon had hope, for just at the time of Joan's capture, the archbishopric of Rouen, a particularly valuable diocese, fell vacant. There would of course be strong competition for the posting, so the bishop of Beauvais knew that he would have to perform a meaningful service to the duke of Bedford to secure the appointment. The procurement of Joan for trial and punishment presented itself as a happy confluence of interests. It was no great secret that the English wanted the Maid delivered into their hands for execution.

And Cauchon had his own grudge against Joan. He had been in Reims just prior to Charles's coronation, and with the coming of Joan and her army had been forced to flee in a manner that he considered most unbecoming to his position. He had subsequently taken refuge in his home bishopric of Beauvais, only to be forced out a second time when, in the aftermath of the coronation, this city too had embraced Charles's side in the war. Even more ominously for Joan, the fall of Beauvais to the opposition did worse than ruffle Cauchon's vanity; it deprived him of the living associated with his bishopric, and Pierre Cauchon was not a man who took a loss of income lightly.

Thus inspired, the bishop of Beauvais fell to work, opening a channel of communication between the duke of Bedford and the University of Paris. Although there was some feeling within the English camp that the best strategy with regard to the Maid was simply to force the duke of Burgundy to hand her over, tie her into a sack, and drown her in the river, Cauchon was soon able to make his allies see the political advantages of the Inquisition's first publicly trying her and condemning her for heresy. By obtaining the imprimatur of the Holy Church—for Joan would certainly be found guilty—those among the opposition whom she had beguiled would be undeceived, and Charles and his Armagnac theological advisers discredited and humiliated. Moreover, as the punishment for heresy (which, as everyone knew, was to be burned at the stake) was always carried out by the secular authority within whose jurisdiction the trial was held, the English would ultimately have the satisfaction of executing Joan in the most painful way possible.

The merits of this plan to both sides were so obvious that it took very little time to work out the details. On July 14, 1430, at a private audience, Pierre Cauchon was able to personally hand John of Luxembourg an official summons. "It is by this that it is required by the Bishop of Beauvais of my lord the Duke of Burgundy and of my lord John of Luxembourg . . . in the name on behalf of the King our sire [Henry VI] and on his own behalf as Bishop of Beauvais: that the woman who is commonly called Joan the Maid, prisoner, be sent to the King to be delivered over to the Church to hold her trial because she is suspected and defamed to have committed many crimes, sortileges, idolatry, invocations of enemies and other several cases touching our faith and against that faith." The document was strongly worded, but it was not upon language that the bishop of Beauvais relied to ensure the success of his mission. With these papers came the offer of a ransom of 10,000 livres tournois drawn on the English treasury.

To have a ransom paid by the enemy was definitely not what the chivalric process had intended. As word of the offer leaked out, Charles was provoked to a semblance of action. He sent an embassy to the Burgundians in which he informed them sharply that "they should not for anything in the world lend themselves to such a transaction or, if they did, he would inflict similar treatment on those of their party whom he had in his hands." This was largely a hollow threat—it is unlikely that the king of Scotland, for example, would pay much for a Burgundian prisoner of war—but it demonstrates that this course of action was unusual enough that it had not been anticipated by the French side. The king also responded by sending military aid to Compiègne, which was being besieged by the Burgundians. It is true that Charles did not offer a competing ransom (not that he had the money), but to do so would have been pointless; the English would never have allowed the duke of Burgundy to return Joan to the French. They feared her effect on the civilian population and the war too much. The best result Charles could hope for was that she be allowed to remain where she was.

Ten thousand livres tournois was not a tremendous sum, but it was still a good deal of money, and gives a sense of just how badly the English wanted Joan delivered into their hands. And yet John of Luxembourg hesitated. He was surrounded by women who were sympathetic to Joan and who had no love of the English. He had married Joan of Béthune, whose first husband, Robert, duke of Bar, had been killed fighting against Henry V at Agincourt. Robert had been Yolande of Aragon's uncle, so Joan of Béthune was her aunt by marriage.* The Maid had an even stronger advocate in the person of John's elderly aunt, the lady of Luxembourg, who had stood as godmother to Charles VII at his christening, and appears to have promised her nephew that she would make him her heir if he would refuse the English offer. Joan herself reported, "The lady of Luxembourg asked my lord of Luxembourg that I not be delivered to the English."

Despite this promise of protection, Joan, who was under no illusions as to what Cauchon's offer meant, spent the summer and early fall in terror of being sold to her enemies and begged her voices to help her. "I would rather die than be put in the hands of the English," she told Saint Catherine, whom Joan claimed responded that "God would aid me and also the people of Compiègne." So overpowering was Joan's dread that despite her angel's reassurance and against her explicit instructions, the prisoner eventually despaired and threw herself from the window of the high tower in which she was being held. The injuries Joan sustained in this fall were so severe that at first her Burgundian jailers believed her to be dead, and it was several days before she recovered sufficiently to be able even to eat or drink. Asked later by her inquisitors, "What was the reason you jumped from the tower of Beaurevoir?" Joan replied, "I had heard that all the people of Compiègne beyond the age of seven would be subjected to fire and sword, and I preferred to die rather than to live after such a destruction of good people, and that was one of the reasons why I jumped; and the other was that I knew that I had been sold to the English, and I would have preferred to die rather than to be in the hands of the English, my enemies."

Her worst fears were realized when in autumn two events occurred that sealed her fate. On September 18, the aged lady of Luxembourg succumbed to overexertion and died while undertaking a fatiguing journey to Avignon, depriving Joan of her most formidable champion; and on October 24 the

---

*This was perhaps another reason why Yolande was not initially concerned for Joan of Arc's safety and was content to have her remain a prisoner of John of Luxembourg.

siege of Compiègne was lifted with the aid of an army sent by Charles under the leadership of the count of Vendôme and the lord of Boussac, who had fought beside Joan at Orléans. John of Luxembourg, who was in command of the siege for the duke of Burgundy, was obliged to retreat ignominiously from the field, leaving behind his heavy artillery. He returned to the castle of Beaurevoir in what might be expected to be none too fine a humor, and under pressure from Philip the Good and the regency government he at last accepted the English offer. The ransom payment was hurriedly forwarded on December 6 and Pierre Cauchon, gleeful at his success and anxious to claim his prize, arrived soon afterward to arrange for Joan's removal by an armed escort. "The Bishop of Beauvais whom I saw return after he had been to fetch her [Joan] . . . [gave] an account of his embassy . . . with joy and exultation," reported an eyewitness. By Christmas Joan had been transferred to Rouen, deep in the heart of English territory, there to await interrogation by the Inquisition on matters pertaining to the true faith in preparation for her trial on charges of heresy and witchcraft.

THE JUDICIAL ACTION against Joan of Arc began on January 9, 1431, and lasted nearly five months. During this period, both her jailers and the vindictive men who set themselves up as her examiners made every attempt to break her spirit by subjecting her to a continual stream of mental, verbal, and physical abuse. Although as a defendant in an Inquisition trial Joan had the right to be held in a Church prison and given access to the protection of nuns, she was instead consigned to the civil authorities, who placed her under a male guard in a tower cell of the castle of Rouen, owned by the English earl of Warwick. Under pretense of preventing her escape, she was kept shackled throughout the entire ordeal. "And I know for certain that at night she slept with two pairs of irons on her legs, attached by a chain very tightly to another chain that was connected to the foot of her bed, itself anchored by a large piece of wood five or six feet long. The contraption was fastened by a key," Jean Massieu, a member of the French escort responsible for conveying Joan back and forth from her cell to the courtroom, later testified. Joan was also kept fettered in irons during the day while at trial, and she was further threatened with imprisonment in an iron cage, specially built to hold her, in which she would be kept standing "fastened by the neck, the hands, and the feet," if she misbehaved or attempted flight. Of the five soldiers who guarded her, three were stationed inside her cell and two just outside the door; all were "Englishmen of the lowest rank, those who are called in French *houssepaillers* [abusers]," reported another eyewitness. When she first arrived, Joan had been required to expose herself to yet another intimate physical examination to confirm her virginity, this one conducted under the auspices of the duchess of Bedford (the duke of Bedford concealing himself "in a secret place" and peeping at her to satisfy his curiosity). The prisoner's maidenhood being established, the duchess "had the warders and others forbidden to offer her any violence." However, while this may have prevented Joan from actually being raped by her guard, it did not stop the soldiers from abusing her in other ways just short of that, or of attempting to humiliate her through lewdness, and they evidently were encouraged to give free vent to their contempt, as Joan was to complain of their behavior toward her throughout her captivity.

Again contrary to established procedure, she was given no counsel, and when both a leading Church lawyer and a local cleric objected to this irregularity, the one was ostracized and the other jailed. Pierre Cauchon dispatched a spy to Domrémy to obtain incriminating evidence about Joan's past that could be used against her in court; when the man reported back that he had found "nothing concerning Joan which he would not have liked to find about his own sister," the bishop flew into a rage and refused to pay him for his time and expenses, complaining that "he was a traitor and a bad man and that he had not done what he should have done and was ordered to do." Even more odiously, in a flagrant violation of canon law that stated clearly that only ecclesiastics from the diocese of Rouen had the authority to adjudicate the case, the bishop of Beauvais contrived to have himself named as the second of Joan's two judges. His appointment, condoned by the duke of Bedford, drew strong protest from the other principal magistrate in the case, the vice-inquisitor, that "as much for the serenity of his conscience as for a more certain conduct of the trial, he did not wish to be involved in this affair." Cauchon was forced to appeal to the chief inquisitor of France in order to compel his fellow judge to undertake his duty; the vice-inquisitor eventually appeared in court but continued to sulk throughout the trial, and his reluctance to officiate was obvious to all who participated in the inquest.

Although only Cauchon and the vice-inquisitor had the power to judge and pass sentence on Joan, dozens of other clerics, some sixty-three in all representing both England and France, including a prestigious contingent of masters from the University of Paris, took part in her examination and trial in an advisory capacity. Known as "assessors," many of these prelates were as anxious as Cauchon to play a visible role in Joan's conviction and so advance their careers. They made for such a noisy crowd on the first day of her interrogation that the notary responsible for recording the questions and answers couldn't hear to do his job properly. "The assessors with the judges put questions to her, and sometimes at the moment when one was questioning her and she was answering his question, another interrupted her answer so much so that she several times said to those who were interrogating her: 'Fine lords, ask one at a time,'" reported Jean Massieu.

Every deception and ruse that could be used to undermine her testimony was employed so shamelessly that even the administrative staff of the court protested. To ensure that the official record portrayed Joan's responses as being sufficiently heretical, two concealed priests, one of them a canon of Rouen, kept a separate, edited account of the proceedings. "At the beginning of the trial, during five or six days, while I set down in writing the Maid's answers and excuses, sometimes the judges tried to constrain me, by translating into Latin, to put into other terms, changing the meaning of the words or, in some other manner, my understanding," Guillaume Manchon, the official court notary, later complained. "And were placed two men, at the command of my lord of Beauvais, in a window near to the place where the judges were. And there was a serge curtain drawn in front of the window so that they should not be seen. These men wrote and reported what was charged against Joan, and suppressed her excuses. . . . And after the session, while collating what they had written, the two others reported in another manner and did not put down Joan's excuses." Manchon protested this surreptitious note-taking by insisting on highlighting the differences between the clandestine register and his own official record. "On this subject my lord of Beauvais was greatly enraged against me," he observed. This same canon of Rouen, a crony of Cauchon's, ingratiated himself with Joan, the better to betray her. "[He] pretended to be of the Maid's own country and, by that means, contrived to have dealings, interviews and familiar talk with her, by giving her news from home which were pleasing to her, and he asked to be her confessor," Manchon continued. "And what she told him in secret he found means to bring to the ears of the notaries." Again, the bishop of Beauvais made use of subterfuge and concealment in order to entrap Joan in the act of committing heresy. "In fact, at the beginning of the trial, myself and Boisguillaume, with witnesses, were put secretly into a room near to where there was a hole through which one could listen, so that we could report what she said or confessed to the said [canon]," complained the notary.

To these as well as all other attempts to confuse, deceive, intimidate, or degrade her, Joan responded with a degree of courage that surpassed any feat she had achieved on the battlefield. During the investigatory phase of the trial, which lasted from her first court appearance on February 21, 1431, until March 26, she would frequently spend up to seven hours a day—from eight o'clock in the morning until noon, with a second session following the midday meal—patiently answering the inquisitors' questions and often sparring with them verbally when the line of interrogation became too repetitive or inane. Fettered in irons throughout, she endured the assessors' unending, none-too-subtle probing into her early life and religious beliefs, after which she would be marched back to her cell in the evening, dragging her chains, to face the insults and depravity of her English guard. Still wearing the leg irons, she would then be clamped into a second set of iron restraints. In these she would snatch what sleep she could, conscious always of the presence of the soldiers by her bed and the need to fend them off if necessary, only to be dragged from her quarters early the next morning to face her accusers for another long day of interrogation.

Throughout, she never flagged. The inquiry emerged as a test of wills between Joan and her examiners as the assessors tried, often with a conspicuous lack of success, to break her down. The first session, for example, was almost entirely devoted to Cauchon's getting Joan to swear an oath "to speak the truth . . . in all matters on which you will be questioned," and to demonstrate her religious training by having her recite the Pater Noster. Joan countered that she could not take such an oath as "it may happen that you will ask me a thing which I shall not tell you," and declined to recite either the Pater Noster or Ave Maria unless Cauchon first agreed to hear her in confession and render absolution, an act that would have precluded the bishop of Beauvais from further participation in her prosecution. After persistent haranguing, the best Cauchon could do was to elicit a compromise from Joan: "About my father and mother, and everything that I have done since I took the road to come to France, I shall willingly swear; but never have I said or revealed anything about the revelations made to me by God except to Charles, my king. And even if you wish to cut my head off, I will not reveal them, because I know from my visions that I must keep them secret." Joan was equally unmovable when it came to Cauchon's second demand; as the bishop ultimately refused her request to hear her confession, she never declaimed the Lord's Prayer.

By the second day and for many of the sessions following, the inquiry shifted to Joan's childhood, the emergence of her voices, her journey to the royal court at Chinon, and her mission in France. This interrogation was handled by Master Jean Beaupère, another former rector of the University of Paris who, like Cauchon, was in the employ of the English king. It was Beaupère's job, as a man of superior theological learning, to trick Joan into a heretical statement. This he was unable to do despite repeated attempts. "This voice which you say appears to you, is it an angel or does it come immediately from God, or is it the voice of a saint?" he asked, and then, "Do you believe that it displeases God that the truth be told?" and, finally, "Do you know if you are in God's grace?" to which Joan famously replied, "If I am not, may God bring me to it; if I am, may God keep me in it," a statement of such obvious and forceful piety that Beaupère subsequently gave up on that line of questioning altogether.

Despite this setback, the following day Beaupère continued as Joan's principal interrogator. Under his direction, the inquiry now took an extremely curious turn. In a discussion of her childhood in Domrémy, the assessor suddenly asked Joan about the Fairy Tree and the spring.

"Asked about the tree: [Joan] replied, that quite near to Domrémy there was a tree that was called the Ladies' Tree, and which others called the Fairies' Tree, and nearby was a spring (*fontaine*) and that she had heard tell that people with fevers drank of it and that they visited this spring in this way seeking a cure. But she did not know whether or not they were cured. . . .

"That she had gone sometimes with other girls in summer time and made garlands for our Lady of Domrémy there . . . that she had heard from many old people, not of her own generation, that the fairies frequented the place; and that she had heard tell of one named Jhenne, wife of the mayor of the town of Domrémy, her godmother, that she had seen them there. Whether or not it was true she did not know . . . that she had never seen a fairy, as far as she knew, there or anywhere else."

By the fifteenth century, the language of witchcraft (for the English demanded that Joan be tried as a witch) was very specific. Evil sorcery was connoted by the Latin term *maleficium,* which referred in general to demons, necromancers, witches, and diabolism. From 1400 to 1430 there were at least seventy recorded cases of witchcraft that came to trial in Europe. The records of these proceedings invoked the devil, evil invocations, black magic, witches' sabbaths, sodomy, demon worship, attempted murder through sorcery, ritualized spells, bewitchment, incantations, conjuring, apostasy, cults, desecration, infanticide, phantasms, cannibalism, divinations, and secret compacts with Satan. However, the word "fairy" does not appear in any of them. "It has long been clear that most of the charges leveled against Joan were deliberate falsifications," wrote medieval witchcraft specialist Jeffrey Burton Russell. "But the irrelevance of witchcraft in her case is even more fundamental. . . . These charges . . . were quite removed from the usual witch tradition. Dancing with fairies or adoring them was an accusation drawn from old folklore, not from the thoroughly developed witch traditions from the mid-fifteenth century."

Yet the inquisitors hammered away on this point: the tree (standing in for the wood where Raymondin had wandered despondently after killing his uncle) and the spring (representing the fountain where he first met the fairy Melusine), and, later, whether Joan had interacted with anyone in addition to her godmother who had "erred with fairies." It is clear that the assessors, too, knew the story of Melusine, and were trying to taint Joan with it. Again and again she denied it. "She said that she had heard it said to her brother that they said in the countryside that she got her revelations from the tree and the fairies, but she did not and she had told him clearly to the contrary," the official record reported.

Beaupère's pointed probing of the Melusine mythology, so out of place in a late medieval witchcraft trial, remains one of the strongest pieces of evidence to date that the decision to introduce Joan to the royal court at Chinon had its genesis in this classic romance. Too many people, both on the king's side and within the French Inquisition, saw the parallels between the Maid's mission and Jean of Arras's well-known work for this to have been a coincidence. Only the Maid herself, illiterate and ignorant of the novel, did not make this connection. Joan's voices sprang from her deep spiritualism and unshakable belief in God; even if she had heard something of the tale of Melusine, she would not have associated the story with herself. Joan knew that she was not a fairy.

THE TRIAL DRAGGED ON. The assessors plumbed every incident of Joan's life in an attempt to elicit responses that could later be used against her in an indictment. She, in turn, demonstrated the quick tongue and passionate defiance that had so impressed Charles's religious advisers at Poitiers. Asked by her interrogators if Saint Michael appeared to her naked, she retorted, "Do you think that God cannot afford to clothe him?" When further probed as to whether or not the saint had hair, she asked, "Why should it have been cut off?" Time and again Pierre Cauchon tried to find out what sign she had given Charles to make the king believe her to be a messenger of God; time and again she refused to say until at last she snapped, "I have always told you that you will not drag that out of my mouth. Go and ask him!"

As might be expected given the Armagnac masters' defense of Joan's male attire, the Burgundian University of Paris assessors made sure to introduce this issue. Beaupère, the theorist, was again responsible for Joan's interrogation on this point. Responding to one of Joan's statements that she was forbidden by God from answering a certain question, he asked, "How do you know how to make the distinction when you answer on certain points and others not?"

"On certain points I asked permission [of her voices] and received it," she replied. "I would rather be torn apart by four horses than to have gone to France without God's permission."

"Did he command you to wear man's clothes?" Beaupère, seeing his chance, continued.

"The clothes are a trifle, the very least of things," Joan replied. "I did not put on man's clothes by the counsel of any man in the world and I did not put on the clothes and I did not do anything excepting by the commandment of God and the angels."

"Do you believe that you did right to put on man's clothes?" Beaupère pressed.

"All that I have done, I have done by God's commandment and I believe that I did right, and I expect from it good warrant and good succour."

"In the particular case of taking on man's clothes, do you think that you did right?" Beaupère insisted.

"Of what I have done in the world I have done nothing but by God's commandment," Joan replied, demonstrating her ability to answer honestly without straying into the heretical.

Much later, Beaupère would recall the Maid's dexterity in this regard. "She was right subtle, with a subtlety pertaining to woman," he observed with annoyance.

Sustained by her faith and her belief that her voices would save her, Joan maintained her self-possession and strength of character throughout the long weeks of relentless interrogation. The humble yet joyous piety that permeated many of her responses still resonates today. "Since your voices have told you that in the end you would go to Paradise, do you hold yourself assured of being saved and of not being damned in hell?" demanded one of her inquisitors. "After that revelation, do you believe that you cannot commit mortal sin?" "I know nothing about that, but in all things I trust in God," replied Joan. "That answer is of great weight," warned the inquisitor. "Wherefore I hold it to be a great treasure," Joan countered.

Of course, in the end, it didn't matter how well she answered or how pure her spirit or how innocent she was of the crimes for which she was being investigated. Joan was in the hands of the English, and the English wanted her condemned as a witch and burned at the stake. On March 26, the interrogatory phase of the proceedings ended and the next day a document officially charging Joan with heresy and witchcraft in seventy instances, of which three articles specifically referred to the defendant's interaction with fairies and six condemned her assumption of male attire "which the laws of God and man do forbid her to wear," was drawn up and read aloud by the clerk of the court.* The second phase of Joan's ordeal, in which the bishop of Beauvais and the vice-inquisitor would hand down their judgment on her, had begun.

THIS NEW STAGE in the legislative process focused not on the question of Joan's guilt or innocence but rather on trying to force Joan to recognize her errors and the authority of the Church to punish her. This Joan had so far steadfastly refused to do. "If the Church Militant [the Church of the living] tells you that your revelations are illusions or somehow diabolic, would you defer to the church?" she was asked. "In that case, I would defer as always to God, whose command I have always obeyed," she answered, "and should the Church Militant command me to do otherwise, I would not defer to any man of the world, other than our Lord, whose good command I have always done." "Have you received the command from your voices not to submit to

---

*The original seventy counts against her were later summarized and reduced to twelve for simplicity's sake.

the Church Militant, which is on earth, nor her judgment?" the inquisitors persisted. "They do not command me not to obey the church, God being first served," Joan replied.

This position—that through her voices Joan had received divine instruction that superseded the teachings of the established Church—infuriated her inquisitors, and they made the issue of bringing Joan to obedience the focal point of their efforts over the next months. Cauchon tried to force her into submission by forbidding her to attend mass or receive confession while she remained obdurate, and eventually threatened her with torture, to which Joan bravely replied, "Truly, if you pull my members apart and make the soul leave the body, I will not tell you anything else, and if I should tell you something, afterward I shall always say that you made me say it by force." The proceedings were delayed somewhat when Joan fell seriously ill in April from eating spoiled carp, but even in this extremity the bishop of Beauvais pursued his case. When Joan, apparently near death from food poisoning, begged to be allowed to receive the last rites, Cauchon saw his opening. "If you have the sacraments of the Church you must declare yourself a good Catholic and submit to the Church," he admonished sternly. "I am not able to say anything else to you at present," Joan replied. "The more you fear for your life because of the sickness which you have, the more should you amend your ways," Cauchon wheedled. "Since you ask that the Church give you the sacrament of the Eucharist, will you submit yourself to the Church Militant and a promise to give you that sacrament will be given you?" "I shall not do otherwise about that submission," she refused him again. Joan recovered soon afterward with the help of a number of prominent physicians who were hurriedly called in to attend her. "The earl of Warwick told us that Joan was sick, . . . and that he had summoned us to take care of her, because more than anything in the world the king [of England] did not wish her to die a natural death," one of these doctors later reported. "The king considered her very precious and had bought her dearly, and he did not wish her to die except at the hands of justice and he wished that she should be burned."

It was at this juncture, after almost losing her to illness, that the English government began to grow restive. The trial was costing the treasury a great deal of money and they had yet to see a conviction. The earl of Warwick invited Cauchon to a large banquet on Sunday, May 13, and told him to speed things up. On May 19, Cauchon, who had by this time also received the official sanction of the University of Paris to condemn Joan for heresy and witchcraft, brought all of the assessors together to conclude the proceedings.

But the Church had still failed in its primary objective, to break the heretic's spirit and bring her into obedience "for her own good," as one of the assessors observed, and this omission rankled. In a last effort to get her to admit her errors, on Thursday, May 24, Joan was subjected to what amounted to a dress rehearsal of her own execution. She was brought under guard to the cemetery of a nearby abbey where, against the backdrop of all the gravestones—a chilling reminder of the reality of these proceedings— her judges and assessors solemnly awaited her on a series of platforms specially erected for the occasion. In sight of the executioner, who was waiting to take her away in a cart, one of the masters from the University of Paris delivered a long, vengeful sermon against Joan and the Armagnacs. "O Royal House of France!" he thundered. "You have never known a monster until now! But now behold yourself dishonored in placing your trust in this woman, this magician, heretical and superstitious," impelling Joan to cry out, "Do not speak of my king, he is a good Christian."

At the end of his harangue, the master turned to Joan and demanded that she publicly repent. Joan pleaded that her case be submitted to the pope. This was denied. The master ordered her again to admit her errors. "I appeal to God and to our holy father the pope," Joan reiterated.

A piece of parchment was suddenly thrust into her hand. On it were written some eight lines in Latin. As the master exhorted her to abjure a third time, Joan was instructed to sign the document. "Do it now, otherwise you will end your days by fire," the master threatened. Not knowing what the writing said, she at first drew a circle on the paper. As this was deemed insufficient, her hand was guided by one of the clerics to form a cross. As she made the mark "a great murmur arose among those who were present." She had signed a letter of retraction.

> *I, Joan, called the Maid, a miserable sinner, having now realized the sink of error into which I had come and having by the grace of God returned to the holy church our mother, in order that it may be seen I have returned to her not half-heartedly but with a good heart and will, do confess that I have grievously sinned, by claiming lyingly that I had revelations from God and his angels St. Catherine and St. Margaret, and all those my words and acts*

which are against the church I do repudiate, wishing to remain in union with the church, never leaving it.

By the testimony of my sign: X

The document was subsequently read to her, and the person who did so remembered much later that it said also that "in future she would neither carry arms, nor wear men's clothes, nor cut her hair short." Although Joan was reported to have laughed when the letter was first read to her, she did not repudiate it and that day let her hair down and exchanged her male attire for women's clothing.

The English were furious. Having recanted, Joan could not now be condemned and burned at the stake. In their view, the entire trial had been a waste of time, money, and prestige. Cauchon lost his archbishopric in that moment. "The king has spent his money very badly on you," a member of the earl of Warwick's entourage was said to have hissed at him afterward.

But the bishop of Beauvais recovered quickly. He had spent months interrogating Joan; he knew her character. She may have broken down in the pressure of the moment, but he knew her admission would gnaw at her. The Church's purpose had been served by publicly forcing Joan to recant; Charles's "prophetess" had admitted that she had basely lied and deceived her supporters, and had violated the laws of the true religion by assuming male attire; the Armagnac masters who had condoned such behavior were refuted and humiliated. Now the bishop could satisfy the English appetite for vengeance. To the earl of Warwick, who complained bitterly that "it would go badly for the king because Joan would escape them," Cauchon and the other masters had a ready answer. "My Lord, do not worry; we will catch her again."

THE PROBLEM was how to do it quickly, for the English were in no humor to wait. Again, Cauchon was forced to circumvent established procedure. Once Joan had renounced her former errors and returned in full obedience to the Church, canon law required that she now be delivered from the civil authority. She seems to have understood this as, after the ceremony, she asked that "some of you men of the church take me into your prison so that I be no longer in the hands of these Englishmen." But Cauchon made a point of restoring her to her English jailers. "Take her back to where you found her," he ordered.

And so Joan, still chained but now wearing a woman's gown supplied by a seamstress who worked for the duchess of Bedford, was returned to her cell at the castle of Rouen. There she remained under the same male guard, the only difference being that she had lost whatever spiritual comfort or symbolic protection she had formerly acquired from her male garb.

The English waited two days for her to relapse into heresy on her own. When she did not, they forced the issue. The knight's clothing that Joan had worn had not been removed from her cell but instead had been stuffed into a sack and kept at hand. On Sunday morning, May 27, Joan awoke and as usual asked for her clothes so that she could rise to go to the bathroom. The guard, who had hidden her gown the night before, instead shook the male attire out of the bag and threw it at her. Joan resisted at first—"Gentlemen, you know that it is forbidden me, without fail I will not wear it"—but they continued to withhold her approved apparel, and it became a question of rising naked to urinate or accepting men's garb. Modesty won the struggle, and the second she put on the proscribed clothing, Cauchon was informed that she had relapsed into heresy.

The next day, her two judges, the bishop of Beauvais and the vice-inquisitor, along with a group of assessors visited her in her cell and sealed her fate by forcing her to confront the significance of having publicly recanted. "You said, upon the scaffold and the tribune, before us, judges, and before others and before the people, when you made abjuration, that it was falsely that you had boasted that those voices were the voices of Saints Catherine and Margaret," Cauchon reminded her. "I did not mean to do and say so," Joan fatally replied. "I did not say or mean to revoke my apparitions. . . . I would rather make my penitence once and for all, that is to say die, than to suffer any longer the pain of being in prison. I have never done anything against God and against the faith, whatever I may have been made to revoke; and for what was contained in the *cédule* of abjuration [the parchment she signed], I did not understand it. I did not mean to revoke anything unless provided it pleased God. If the judges wish it I will resume woman's clothes; for the rest, I will do nothing about it."

This was the admission Cauchon had been waiting for. Her reply was duly noted and recorded. As he and the others left the cell, the bishop of Beauvais turned to the English officials who were waiting in the hallway. "Farewell, it is done," he said.

And so came the morning of Wednesday, May 30, 1431, the day established by her judges for her public condemnation and execution. To accommodate the earl of Warwick, the bishop of Beauvais had wasted no time and called an immediate meeting of the assessors, at which Joan's relapse was confirmed by majority vote. The English used the intervening hours to erect raised platforms for the officers who would attend the burning and to construct a low circular stone barricade in the middle of the public square of the Old Market of Rouen, the venue deemed most suited to accommodate the expected crowd. Into this a stake was driven.

Joan was informed of her impending death when she awoke that Wednesday by Brother Martin Ladvenu, who had been sent by Cauchon to hear her confession, another irregularity, as the prisoner's heresy should have prohibited her from receiving this solace. This time there would be no reprieve, and Joan knew it. "'Alas! Do they treat me thus horribly and cruelly, so that my body, clean and whole, which was never corrupted, must be this day consumed and reduced to ashes! . . . Alas! Had I been in the ecclesiastical prison to which I submitted myself, and been guarded by men of the Church and not by my enemies and adversaries, it had not so wretchedly happened to me as now it has! Ah! I appeal before God, the Great Judge, from the great wrongs and grievances being done to me.' And she complained marvelously in that place of the oppressions and violences which had been done to her in the prison by the gaolers and by others who had been let in against her," remembered an eyewitness. Nor did Joan fail in her despair to identify her true adversary. After her confession, Cauchon himself visited Joan for one last interview. "Bishop, I die by you," she cried out passionately as he entered her cell.

She was made to put on the long robe and hood of the condemned and in this costume was paraded down to the Old Market. The English, taking no chances, surrounded her with some eight hundred soldiers equipped with blades and axes; more were waiting at the square. By nine o'clock when she arrived, the platforms were already filled by her judges and assessors, as well as numerous English officials, and a great crowd had gathered, some in the marketplace, others hanging out of windows or perched on roofs.

Again, she was first made to endure a protracted sermon on the evils of heresy and the need for all true Christians to snuff it out without mercy, lest the one infect the whole; but this time she was not offered the chance to recant. Instead, as soon as the pastor had finished, Cauchon stepped forward and delivered the judges' verdict:

"We declare that thou, Joan, commonly called the Maid, art fallen into diverse errors and diverse crimes of schism, idolatry, invocation of devils

The execution of Joan of Arc.

and numerous others. . . . And thereafter, after abjuration of thine errors, it is evident that thou hast returned to those same errors and to those crimes, your heart having been beguiled by the author of schism and heresy. . . . Wherefore we declare thee relapsed and heretic." Then the bishop uttered the words that the English had been waiting for since they had first laid down their 10,000 livres tournois the previous December. "By this sentence . . . we rule that like a rotten limb you be cut off and rejected from the unity of the church and we remit you to secular justice."

Again by precedent, Joan ought to have at this point been handed over to the sheriff and taken to a civil court, there to go through the official process of sentencing and punishment, but the English were in no mood for formalities. No sooner were the words out of Cauchon's mouth than she was seized by the executioner and dragged to the stake.

And it was at this point that Joan broke: Joan who in an effort to exhort her men to victory had so often in the past defiantly planted her standard in the name of God and king, enduring with steadfast purpose a rain of arrows and cannonballs by the enemy; Joan who had met without fear or doubt those who were her superiors in age, learning, and lineage, expertly trading barb for barb, subtlety for subtlety, for months on end without losing her composure; Joan who by nineteen had suffered deprivation, humiliation, and oppression such as the most hardened soldier of fortune had not experienced and who yet never lost the clear song nor sweet joy of her faith, finally succumbed to the terror and anguish that lay before her. Piteously shrieking and crying, "imploring and invoking without cease the aid of the saints of paradise," so that she moved the hearts of even those who supported the English cause, she was bound to the stake and the fire lit. Because of her youth and vitality, and the low stone parapet encircling the stake, which prevented the fire from over-taking her at once, the duration of Joan's agony was prolonged even beyond that which was common for the ordeal. In the over half an hour that it took for her to die in the smoke and flames she continued to beg her angels for mercy and to proclaim her faith in God: "Once in the fire, she cried out more than six times, 'Jesus!' and especially in her last breath, she cried with a strong voice, 'Jesus!' so that everyone present could hear it; almost all wept with pity," recounted an onlooker. After this, her head fell forward, the flames finally overcame the stone parapet that surrounded her, and she perished.

The English remained cautious of Joan even in death, so much so that after the fire died down, the executioner was ordered to throw her heart, which had remained intact, along with the rest of her ashes, into the Seine. This prevented their being used as relics but also, according to witnesses, "because they feared lest she escape or lest some say she had escaped."

Still, the English had gotten what they had paid for: the Maid who had so humbled their army had been made to suffer torments and was now gone. But at least one of those present had an inkling of what the victory over this single, transcendent French soul had cost them. Master Jean Tressard, secretary to Henry VI, witnessed the execution and returned afterward to the castle much troubled.

"We are all lost," he said.

PART III
After Joan

The French battle the English in the final stages of the Hundred Years War.

CHAPTER 12

Of Politics
and
Prisoners

T WOULD BE GRATIFYING to be able to confirm the
widespread belief that this one act, the terrible
martyrdom of Joan of Arc—so unjust, so cruel, so
iniquitous—resulted, as Master Jean Tressard predicted, in the immediate vanquishing of the English
and the triumphal return of Charles VII to his
hereditary throne. Or even that, if not quite the
catalyst for a precipitous surrender, Joan's execution at least marked the
moral turning point in the conflict, the moment at which the native French
population, repulsed by the deed, turned against the occupation and began
the slow process of throwing off the yoke of the invaders. And yet the sad
truth is that Joan's death *had absolutely no effect* upon the war, or the politics
of the period, or the eventual outcome of the struggle about which she had
cared so deeply and in which, for a very brief period, she had played so
critical a role. To her contemporaries, Joan's condemnation and slaying,
while deplored by those whose political leanings coincided with her own,
represented little more than a sideshow, a momentary diversion—fleetingly
noted and just as quickly forgotten.

In part, this uninterest was due to a lack of information regarding the
more troubling aspects of her trial. The official record of the proceedings
was kept secret at Rouen. This did not stop both the English and the University of Paris from disseminating as much incriminating evidence and
hearsay as was necessary to gain support for their actions. Within a month

of Joan's execution, Henry VI sent a letter around addressed to "the prelates, dukes, counts, and other nobles and to the cities of his kingdom of France," commanding them "through preaching and public sermons and otherwise" to trumpet the story of her many impieties, emphasizing that before she had burned, the Maid had acknowledged her voices to be shams; the University of Paris masters penned a similar letter to Rome. These measures of course influenced popular opinion. To the outside world, Joan's words and actions had been impartially reviewed by high-ranking and learned members of the clergy and had been found (as many who adhered to the Burgundian side in the war had already suspected) to be heretical. An anonymous Burgundian chronicler, known simply as "un Bourgeois de Paris," devoted a lengthy passage in his journal to Joan's philosophy and execution that is instructive as to the manner in which she was viewed by ordinary people of the opposing camp. "She rode with the King every day, amongst very many men-at-arms, no woman with her, wearing men's clothing, points, and armor, and carrying a great stick in her hand," he wrote. "If any of her men did anything wrong, she would wallop them hard with this stick, like a very brutal woman. . . . In several places she had men and women killed, both in battle and in deliberate revenge, for she had anyone who did not obey her letters killed immediately without pity whenever she could. She said and affirmed that she never did anything except at God's command, as given to her frequently by the archangel St. Michael, by St. Catherine, and by St. Margaret, who made her do these things—not as Our Lord did to Moses on Mount Sinai, but themselves, personally, told her secret things that were to come; that they had ordered and did order everything that she did, her clothes and everything else.

"Such and worse were my lady Joan's false errors. They were all declared to her in front of the people, who were horrified when they heard these great errors against our faith which she held and still did hold. For, however clearly her great crimes and errors were shown her, she never faltered or was ashamed, but replied boldly to all the articles enumerated before her like one wholly given over to Satan," the chronicler concluded.

As difficult as it is to believe today, this unsympathetic view of Joan as a hardened, rather distasteful, unrepentant sinner was the one that in the aftermath of her execution was seemingly destined to prevail. To understand the heroism of the Maid it was necessary to hear her voice, to feel the force of her piety, to reflect on the magnitude of her courage and achievements, and all of this stood in great peril of being lost or deliberately destroyed by her enemies. To rescue Joan from this fate, three exceedingly unlikely events had to occur: Charles VII had either to win a major battle decisively (a dubious prospect at best) or somehow find a way to get himself recognized as the legitimate king of France by those municipalities, most especially Paris, currently occupied by his enemies; the English had subsequently to be expelled from all of their strongholds on the continent; and, finally, a conscious effort had to be made to discredit and overturn the heretical conviction of the Church, not an institution particularly known for changing positions or admitting errors. This was a daunting agenda for any sovereign, let alone one whose abilities were as limited as Charles's.

For all Joan's courage, then, and despite the undeniable political legitimacy conferred upon Charles by the coronation at Reims, there was no indication at all at the time of her martyrdom that her king would ultimately prevail in his struggle against the English. The proof of this was that the war would drag on for a further *twenty years*. In the end, it would fall to another woman entirely, one unacknowledged by history, to take on the task left unfinished by the Maid.

IRONICALLY, in terms of the war effort, the period of Joan's captivity— from May 1430 to her death in May of the following year—marked the most productive and active interval of Charles's reign. The council meetings convened at Sully-sur-Loire in March 1430 (from which a frustrated Joan had slipped away, choosing instead to act independently rather than endure what she considered to be endless talk) had for once actually produced something approaching a coordinated plan of attack. The king had finally been made to realize that Philip the Good had not really been negotiating for peace but rather had only been using Charles's offers to improve the terms of his alliance with the English. Above all, Charles did not like to be taken for a fool, and his anger was palpable in a letter issued on May 6, 1430, to his supporters, in which the king disdainfully referred to Philip the Good as "our adversary of Burgundy." The duke, the king fumed, "has, for some time, amused and deceived us by truces and otherwise, under the shadow of good faith, because he said and affirmed that he wished to arrive at the well-being of peace, the which, for the relief of our poor people who, to the displeasure of our heart, has suffered and every day suffer so much for the matter of the war, we greatly desired and do desire, he has set himself with certain forces to make war upon us and upon our countries and loyal subjects." Charles's bitterness over this duplicity had prompted him to approve an aggressive military campaign, much of it aimed directly at those areas held or desired by the duke of Burgundy. La Hire was sent into Normandy, the lord of Barbazan to aid the duke of Bar in Champagne, and the marshal Boussac and the count of Vendôme to Compiègne. Many of their efforts met with success. René besieged and won the Burgundian town of Chappes, which was heavily defended by an army sent by the marshal of Burgundy; the Bastard of Orléans joined La Hire in Normandy, worrying the English in Louviers, close to the Burgundian border to the north; and the lord of Boussac and the count of Vendôme not only raised the siege of Compiègne but won a further victory at Peronne.* Philip the Good suddenly found his participation in the war to be a good deal more onerous than had previously been his experience.

But the energy displayed by the French military belied the poisonous nature of the royal court, which was rent by rivalry, intrigue, and corruption. Two principal political parties had formed, one under the leadership of Georges de la Trémoïlle, who, having vanquished Joan, once again occupied his former position as Charles's closest and most influential adviser, and was very busy exploiting this advantage to maximum profit. The other, composed of the Angevins and their allies, focused on reconciling the king to Arthur of Richemont, Charles's formerly rejected constable, as a means of obtaining a meaningful coalition with his brother, the ever-vacillating duke of Brittany. Bringing Arthur of Richemont back into Charles's good graces meant restoring the constable to a dominant role at court and within the royal council, an appointment that La Trémoïlle, jealous of his authority (and riches), was desperate to prevent.

Although Yolande of Aragon was still Arthur's primary supporter and the ostensible leader of the Angevin party, by the spring of 1430 the queen of Sicily seems to have been in the process of retiring from the day-to-day

---

*This is perhaps why Regnauld de Chartres expressed such frustration with Joan when she acted independently at Compiègne: she had been told that a French army was being assembled and yet she refused to wait for it. At Orléans, when she had wanted to attack before the relieving troops had had a chance to return with the second cargo of supplies, the Bastard had been able to talk her out of it; not so here. This was particularly unfortunate, as had she been induced to wait and join the main body of troops, she would have had much more protection and might have eluded capture.

workings of the court. She was, after all, nearly fifty years old and had been a dominant force in French politics since 1415, when the battle of Agincourt had thrust first her husband, and then herself, into a position of power within the old Armagnac coalition. Her great coup, the introduction of Joan to Charles at Chinon, had succeeded beyond all expectations. Orléans had been delivered from the enemy and by the coronation at Reims her daughter Marie's position as the legitimate queen of France was established. More-over, as a result of Joan's intervention, Charles was no longer in doubt as to his parentage, and seemed well on his way to recovering his kingdom. Yolande's third son and chosen political successor, Charles of Anjou, was nearing adulthood. She had never sent him away as she had Louis III to Naples or René to Bar and consequently he had had the benefit of her polit-ical experience and advice since childhood. He was familiar with the work-ings of the royal court and was a trusted confidant of both his sister, Marie, the queen, and her husband. The political situation had stabilized to the point where the aging queen of Sicily could begin the process of edging toward a quieter, more peaceful existence. On March 30, 1430, by letters patent, sixteen-year-old Charles of Anjou took his place as an official mem-ber of the royal council and his mother retreated to her castle in Saumur.

With this transition, Georges de la Trémoïlle saw his chance. In April, ambassadors from the duke of Brittany arrived to discuss the possibility, yet again, of the duke's coming to a formal alliance with Charles VII. Charles of Anjou, not yet his mother's equal at intrigue, was easily outmaneuvered by La Trémoïlle and seems to have been left out of these talks. He was there-fore not in a position to protest when the ambassadors decided to cement the affiliation between the French king and the duke of Brittany by marrying the duke of Brittany's daughter, Isabelle, to the count of Laval, a close friend of the constable's, as a means of further protecting Breton interests at the royal court.

Ordinarily, Yolande would have been very happy with these negotia-tions. After all, she had been trying to separate the duke of Brittany from his English and Burgundian allies and bring him into an alliance with Charles VII for years. There was, however, a slight problem with this new arrangement: Isabelle of Brittany had been very publicly affianced for years to Yolande's eldest son, Louis III, currently away in Italy and so conve-niently unavailable to defend his marital rights. To sever the relationship was an act of treachery (not to mention highly reminiscent of what Yolande herself had done when she had so abruptly and dismissively returned Louis III's first fiancée, the duke of Burgundy's daughter, those many years ago). Georges de la Trémoïlle was well aware of the offending nature of this arrangement and suggested that the king send Arthur of Richemont himself to Saumur to break the news to the queen of Sicily, hoping to cause a rupture between the constable and his most powerful supporter.

He very nearly succeeded. Yolande was above all committed to the welfare and advancement of her children, and, as the lord of Trémoïlle had expected, she reacted to the breaking of the marriage alliance between her eldest son and the daughter of the duke of Brittany as a profound insult. The woman who had taken with equanimity the murder of John the Fearless, the disinheritance of her son-in-law the dauphin, and the trials of a decades-long war with England, who had counseled forbearance and diplomacy in the face of nearly every emergency, lost all of her sangfroid and self-discipline when this news was delivered to her by her hapless protégé. "When the constable came, in the name of his brother, to see Yolande, accompanied by the count of Etampes and the Breton ambassadors, to obtain her agreement [to the marriage of Isabelle to the count of Laval] she became violently angry and it almost came to an open declaration of war," reported G. du Fresne de Beaucourt, Charles VII's definitive biographer. Although the constable managed to salvage his relationship with his patron, the queen of Sicily was reconciled to this betrayal only when Charles VII later appeased her by agreeing to a face-saving replacement marriage between her second daughter, Yolande of Anjou, and the duke of Brittany's eldest son. She must have directed some choice words, too, at her youngest son for allowing himself to be outwitted, because Charles of Anjou later took his revenge in a way that implied he had strong feelings about the matter. But the principal outcome of this episode was that Yolande of Aragon was jolted out of retirement, and in this La Trémoïlle seriously miscalculated, for, once roused, the queen of Sicily made for a dangerous enemy.

She did not recover her former influence at once; La Trémoïlle's power over Charles VII was still too strong. Through a combination of excessive solicitude for his well-being and an adroit manipulation of his many weaknesses, the councillor had made himself seemingly indispensable to the king. (One of the many services the lord of Trémoïlle provided to his sovereign was to openly encourage and enable Charles's frequent infidelities. As might be expected, this did not endear him to the queen.) The planned marriage

René at home in his castle at work on a book of chivalry.

between Isabelle of Brittany and the count of Laval went through despite Yolande's vociferous objections. Although the expense of underwriting the elaborate coronation at Reims had severely depleted the royal treasury's resources, Georges de la Trémoïlle continued to reap substantial rewards, both in terms of tax revenues and outright gifts of gold and property, from the king in exchange for "the great, notable, profitable and agreeable" tasks that he performed for Charles's benefit.*

---

*For example, by letters of May 1431, Charles granted La Trémoïlle a duty of fifteen deniers on every cask of wine and every hogshead (barrel) of salt that passed, either by land or by water, in front of a specific castle near a well-traveled commercial route near the Loire. This at a time when the crown could not afford to pay its soldiers for their service in the war.

How long it might have taken to dislodge this favorite using the custom-ary methods of politics is anyone's guess. But in the summer of 1431 another Angevin family crisis arose, this one involving René, that, even more than the severed marriage contract, forced Yolande of Aragon to intervene once again in the management of her son-in-law's kingdom, and by so doing win the war.

THAT RENÉ, who had been Joan's earliest (if clandestine) supporter, should be the means, however backhanded, of the accomplishment of her goals is somehow fitting. After the disaster at Paris, René had remained loyal to his brother-in-law the king and had pursued the struggle against Charles VII's enemies from his home duchy of Bar and Lorraine, an enterprise that coin-cided nicely with self-interest, as he got to keep everything he conquered. As a further encouragement to this helpful relative, Charles sent him troops and an experienced captain, the lord of Barbazan, so that René might launch an offensive into the neighboring county of Champagne. In 1430 this strat-egy resulted in a major victory against the Burgundians, when René seized the town of Chappes, a feat for which he was approvingly described by a chronicler as "a brave knight of great heart who showed himself to be proud and courageous."

Then, at the beginning of the succeeding year, on January 15, 1431, just as Joan's trial for heresy was beginning in Rouen, René's father-in-law, the old, gouty, philandering duke of Lorraine, finally succumbed to his various illnesses and René at last came into his inheritance. He was now officially titled duke of Bar and Lorraine (his uncle, the cardinal, had died the previ-ous June), with all of the advantages that the distinction implied: overlord-ship of a large swath of land supplemented by the wealth of its rents and a highly prestigious position in the world.

Unfortunately, the dispensation of lucrative legacies such as the old duke had agreed to bestow on his son-in-law were frequently challenged by other family members who considered themselves cheated by these arrangements, and the duke of Lorraine's estate was no exception to this rule. René's father-in-law had had a younger brother, and this younger brother had had a son, Antoine, and Antoine thought that no matter what had been agreed to in the past, he was far more entitled to his uncle's estates than was René. To buttress his position, Antoine appealed to Philip the Good, who was already none too pleased that René had brazenly invaded Champagne and taken the town of Chappes away from him. Consequently, the duke of Burgundy was only too happy to provide Antoine with an army of approximately four thousand warriors. On July 2, 1431, Antoine's forces met René's near Bulgnéville, about ten miles southeast of Neufchâteau.

Although René, still accompanied by the lord of Barbazan, commanded the larger force—some seventy-five hundred men in all—Antoine had the benefit of position. The Burgundians were entrenched behind a stream and had taken the precaution of digging trenches and erecting the customary line of stakes behind which stood a crack troop of four hundred archers lent by Philip. Antoine had also thought to bring along some heavy artillery. René had no bowmen to speak of and was without guns altogether, serious drawbacks that the more experienced Barbazan took pains to point out. But René, with one victory under his belt, was overeager for a second and was the superior in rank. He overruled Barbazan and ordered his men to cross the stream and attack. René would later defend this decision by observing that he felt that "he had so many men that it seemed that he could fight all the world for a day."

This sentiment proved optimistic. René's forces charged directly into a thumping bombardment of cannonballs and a storm of lethal arrows. It was one of the shortest battles in French history. The poor lord of Barbazan died alongside his men in the first wave of the assault. René himself was struck in the face and went down soon thereafter. Seeing their commander incapacitated, the remainder of René's forces deserted, allowing Antoine to claim victory in a record fifteen minutes (although it took a further two hours for the Burgundians to chase down and slay the fleeing opposition). In the resulting chaos, the wounded duke of Bar and Lorraine was initially claimed by an ignominious squire intent on making a profit from his noble captive, but Antoine soon discovered the identity of the prisoner and took possession of René himself. But even Antoine was to be denied so great a prize, and René was almost immediately consigned to the duke of Burgundy, who had him carted off to Dijon and sequestered in a high tower cell at one of his castles, there to await his fate.

The defeat and capture of René of Anjou had infinitely more impact upon the court of Charles VII than had the burning of Joan of Arc six weeks earlier. "Intelligence of this defeat was spread throughout the countries of Bar and Lorraine, and that their lord had been made prisoner, which caused the severest grief to all attached to him," wrote the chronicler Enguerrand de Monstrelet. Not that anyone close to him feared for his life. The difference in René's experience of captivity and Joan's is striking. The duke of Bar and Lorraine was a man of high birth and position. The laws of chivalry had been expressly developed to safeguard such a lord as he, and he received the full benefit of their protection, even though he had somewhat broken the rules and surrendered to a mere squire and not a member of the nobility as was the proper etiquette. René was never shackled in irons nor threatened by his jailers. Nor was it conceivable that he would ever be sold to the English no matter what the sum offered; the very idea was ridiculous; the duke of Burgundy would never have lived down the dishonor. And although René was of course made melancholy by his confinement, he was certainly never reduced by terror to such despair that he felt the need to throw himself out the window. On the contrary, he was allowed visitors and furloughs. He seems to have whiled away most of his time in prison painting pictures on the walls of his room and preparing sketches of stained glass windows.

But to have the queen's younger brother a prisoner of "our adversary of Burgundy" was a bitter pill to Charles VII. Philip the Good was fully cognizant of the boost that had been given to his bargaining position and would not in the beginning even consider setting a ransom for his hostage. To convince him otherwise, Charles was moved to real action. The military offensive against Burgundian territory, in both the north and east, was stepped up significantly in the wake of René's capture. By a letter of July 22, the lord of Albret was named to replace the deceased Barbazan and sent to Champagne to continue to try to reclaim the area for Charles. On July 20, the duke of Austria was finally induced to declare war on Philip and began a series of border strikes that, while not seriously endangering his duchy, nonetheless forced the duke of Burgundy to divert resources to this area. Charles even sent ambassadors to the Holy Roman Emperor, who had his own territorial disputes with Philip, to arrange an alliance against Burgundy.

But above all else, René's capture served to convince his mother that the time had finally come to separate Philip the Good from his English allegiance. She had always believed in and worked toward this goal, but now it acquired a new urgency. A truce alone was no longer acceptable; there had been truces in the past and these had been implemented merely as a means of stalling for advantage; they were easily made and just as easily broken. What was required now was a firm peace treaty between the king of France and the duke of Burgundy, for only in this way could her son be assured of his freedom. Keeping military pressure on Philip might encourage the duke to come to terms, but it could be only one component of the overall strategy. Of equal importance would be the opening of a confidential diplomatic channel between the two courts, aimed at assessing the duke of Burgundy's state of mind and exploiting any potential friction between Philip and the regency government in France. The question was only how best to do this, and the prisoner himself soon provided the answer.

As it happened, by the summer of 1431, just at that critical juncture in the war when he had so fortuitously captured René, Philip the Good was in fact experiencing some deep reservations about his dealings with England. This was entirely based on the sudden realization by the English exchequer that the war in France was costing a great deal of money. In the Middle Ages, foreign conquests were undertaken as much for the expectation of profit as for glory; the whole point was to ravage the enemy and bring home whatever spoils could be conveniently appropriated. But in France, the English baronage was beginning to suspect, the reverse was true. It was the French who were making all the money! French priests and officials were on the English payroll; there was a seemingly endless demand for more soldiers, more supplies, more arms; after Charles's coronation at Reims, the English treasury had been required to pay for a competing enthronement ceremony for ten-year-old Henry VI in Paris. The French, it seemed, could do nothing for themselves: the government had even to foot the bill for the purchase and prosecution of that Armagnac witch who had caused so much trouble in Orléans. For most of the 1420s, while the English were winning and Charles's resistance was feeble, the war had more or less paid for itself. But in 1429, with the arrival of Joan of Arc, English outlays suddenly exceeded receipts by a distressing 10,000 pounds. And since that time, the trend had continued, and for precious little return, at least as perceived by the native English baronage. Henry VI's forces held less territory in France in 1431 than they had in 1428 and there was apparently need of significant funds just to ensure against further losses. Although she never realized it, Joan's most meaningful blow against her enemies was in *making the war expensive.*

And when it came to allies who expected to be paid for their assistance, no one's hand reached deeper into the pocket of the English treasury, the regency government noted, than Philip the Good's. The duke of Burgundy had already been much enriched—outlandishly so, it was believed by some in England—in terms of both authority and territory as well as by currency. And yet in November 1430, he had had the temerity to write a letter to Henry VI complaining that Compiègne had been lost because he hadn't received his money quickly enough and that if his expenses weren't met soon Burgundy would refuse to participate in the war altogether! "It is . . . true, most redoubted lord," the duke of Burgundy had written disagreeably to the boy king, "that, according to the agreement drawn up on your part with my people, you ought to have paid me the sum of 19,500 francs of royal money each month for the expenses of my troops before Compiègne, as well as the cost of the artillery. . . . It was under the impression that this would be done on your part, and especially that the said payment would be made without fail, as agreed, that I had my men stationed before Compiègne all the time. But, most redoubted lord, these payments have not been kept up by you, for they are in arrears to the tune of two months. . . . My most redoubted lord, I cannot continue without adequate provision in future from you . . . and without payment of what is due me."

The English response to this irksome dunning came addressed to Philip in a long letter issued by the regency council from Rouen on May 28, 1431, just two days before Joan's execution. It was a masterpiece of evasion. "And firstly, with regard to . . . the great damages, outlays, and expenses which my said lord of Burgundy and his lands . . . have sustained by occasion of the wars; the king [Henry VI] is as much annoyed therewith as if they had been in his own country," the letter began diplomatically, before going on to address, at some length, "the great diligence" with which the English king was prosecuting the war, and how much he was doing and had already done on Philip's behalf. The issue of the outstanding debt owed to the duke was referred to only at the end of this extensive missive. "To the tenth article, which makes mention of what is demanded by my said lord of Burgundy in consequence of his troops who have been before Compiègne, and the artillery which has been there employed, the king will cause to be inspected the indentures and arrangements which have been made and taken in these matters . . . and if it shall be agreeable to my said lord of Burgundy to send him some of his people, he will cause such an arrangement to be made as ought reasonably to be satisfactory," the English council concluded. Apparently what was satisfactory to the king of England did not involve actually paying Philip his money, because the duke had to remind Henry VI quite forcefully again six months later by a letter of December 12, 1431, that he still was not in receipt of his funds. "Notwithstanding all letters, statements, requests, and supplications, I have been unable to obtain from you, not even the payment of what you clearly owe me by the account made with your people, which amounts to a large sum. . . . In consequence of which I have been compelled to disband the said armies . . . and have been constrained to consent that certain truces and abstinences of war should be made in my said countries, and especially in my countries of Burgundy, with your said enemies and mine," Philip finished ominously. To further communicate his displeasure at this unwarranted disruption to his cash flow, the duke of Burgundy pointedly did not attend the coronation of Henry VI that was held in Paris later that month, but instead made good on his threat to collaborate with the enemy by signing a truce (which he had no intention of keeping, of course) with Charles's representatives at Lille in order to prevent further incursions into his territory while he regrouped and waited for reinforcements.

In the past, this behavior had always resulted in England's capitulating to his demands, with perhaps some additional monies, territories, or honors thrown in as an extra incentive to remain true to the alliance. The duke of Burgundy no doubt waited confidently for this to happen; it must have come as quite a shock when it didn't. And just as Philip came to the recognition that, inexplicably, a bribe would not be forthcoming, his chancellor, a man named Nicolas Rolin, who was the duke of Burgundy's most trusted adviser ("it is he who does and decides everything, and through whose hands everything passes," an eyewitness reported), found a convenient loophole in the treaty between Burgundy and England. According to Nicolas's understanding of international law, Philip wasn't obligated to maintain his allegiance to the English king, on the grounds that Henry V had died prior to the demise of the mad king Charles VI. Nicolas (who had tallied the devastation to the duke's property caused by the war and had decided that peace would be far more profitable for all concerned, including himself) argued that although Henry V had been *named* Charles VI's chosen successor, he had never actually *assumed* the French crown, being already dead when the reigning French monarch had died and passed it on. Therefore, as Henry V had never worn the crown of France, his son could not have inherited it from him, a legal nicety that had somehow been overlooked for the past decade while the English were winning and still paying.

While all of this was going on, in February 1432, Philip finally met face-to-face with his captive in order to hammer out the conditions of René's release. The negotiations lasted off and on until April. No ransom figure was agreed on at this time, but René was required to marry his eldest daughter (four years old at the time) to the son of his rival, Antoine. The duke of Bar and Lorraine was allowed temporary freedom from his cell, but only on the condition that he pay an upfront installment of 20,000 gold pieces and substitute his two young sons (the eldest was six) as hostages in his place. This René did, and he was released on April 30. René was then required to travel to Brussels to continue discussions with Antoine under the mediating influence of Philip the Good as to who would inherit Lorraine after his death. Nicolas Rolin, Philip's chancellor, also attended these meetings and was responsible for drawing up the documentation.

As a result of all of these negotiations, René got to know Philip the Good and Nicolas Rolin quite well. It didn't take him long to figure out that the duke of Burgundy was not all that happy with his English allies, and that the duke of Burgundy's chancellor had found a way out of their treaty arrangements. (Actually, it seems likely from later events that Nicolas deliberately leaked this information to René as a means of opening a backdoor diplomatic channel to Charles's court.) Whichever way René came to this information, however, the message was the same: the glimmer of an opportunity to dislodge Philip from his heretofore unshakable adherence to England had suddenly appeared.

The exploitation of so rare an opening was too important and sensitive to leave to routine officials. Upon completion of the talks in Brussels in February 1433, René did not go directly home to his wife in Nancy. Rather, he went to see his mother.

CHAPTER 13

The Queen
Takes
Control

 OLANDE OF ARAGON was a sufficiently astute politician—after nearly two decades, perhaps the most experienced diplomat on Charles's side in the war—to grasp instantly the implications of René's intelligence. If what her son told her was true, the Burgundian chancellor was signaling that the duke might be receptive, or at least that the timing was propitious, and that Philip the Good might be coaxed into considering a separate peace agreement with Charles VII. And she also understood why this communication had come to her through René, and had not gone directly to the royal ambassadors. It was because Nicolas Rolin did not trust Georges de la Trémoïlle, and everybody on both sides of the French and Burgundian courts knew that the queen of Sicily opposed the lord of Trémoïlle as well, and openly advocated that he be replaced by her candidate, the constable Arthur of Richemont.

Nicolas Rolin's misgivings about Charles's favorite councillor were well founded. La Trémoïlle had completely misread the situation; instead of trying to work with Rolin, he was trying to get rid of him. La Trémoïlle's idea of a diplomatic initiative was to have Nicolas kidnapped or killed, and he had already botched one attempt to ambush the Burgundian chancellor. Nicolas had been forced to surround himself with an escort of twenty-four bowmen whenever he appeared in public. He did not appreciate having to exercise this level of caution, and thought that perhaps the queen of Sicily might be able to do something about it.

Yolande was well aware of La Trémoïlle's unsavory tactics. Arthur of Richemont had been targeted for political assassination by the lord of Trémoïlle as well, and only escaped death during a hunting party in the fall of 1430 when the three agents assigned to perpetrate the crime were betrayed and arrested before they had a chance to execute the plot. More than this, La Trémoïlle was deliberately impeding Yolande's efforts to recover her properties in Anjou and Maine by sending in mercenaries, not to combat the English, but to battle the constable's troops, who were fighting on her behalf. "La Trémoïlle's . . . one thought was to overthrow Richemont and get rid of the Queen of Sicily, Queen Marie of Anjou, and her brother Charles of Maine," the great French medievalist and specialist in the Hundred Years War, Edouard Perroy, stated flatly.

As tempting as René's intelligence was, Yolande moved cautiously. She looked first for proof of the estrangement between Philip the Good and his English allies. It was not long in coming. On November 14, 1432, Anne of Burgundy, the duke of Bedford's wife and Philip the Good's sister, died in Paris, severing the important familial link between the regent and the duke of Burgundy. The duke of Bedford remarried in April of the following year. He did not bother to consult Philip, as was customary, before entering into this contract. This insult did not recommend the regent to his ally. By the next month, May 1433, the coolness between Bedford and his former brother-in-law was publicly observed when the two arranged to meet for talks in the Burgundian town of Saint-Omer. Both men arrived at the appointed time and place, but they never met or spoke as neither would stoop to call upon the other. "The duke of Bedford expected that the duke of Burgundy should come to him at his lodgings, which he would not do," the chronicler Enguerrand de Monstrelet reported. "Many of their lords went from the one to the other to endeavor to settle this matter of ceremony, but in vain. . . . Within a short time, the two dukes departed from Saint-Omer without anything further being done, but more discontented with each other than before," the chronicler noted.

This was all the proof Yolande needed. In June 1433, soon after the episode at Saint-Omer, Georges de la Trémoïlle was given a taste of his own methods. The king was back in Chinon and La Trémoïlle was with him, housed as was customary in the castle of Coudray. Late one night, four men, all of them in service to Yolande of Aragon, having previously subverted the guard, quietly entered the castle through an ulterior doorway and made their way to La Trémoïlle's chamber. They surprised the councillor in his bed, and when he made a move to resist, they made use of their swords, but only to injure, as the councillor survived and quickly surrendered. (The chroniclers claim that La Trémoïlle was protected from their knife thrusts by his considerable fat, which prevented his enemies' blades from penetrating too deeply into his organs.) Bleeding from his wounds, the king's favorite adviser was hustled out of the castle and out into the grounds where a larger group, numbering some dozen men-at-arms in all, were waiting. "They made him prisoner, and carried him away, taking him from the government of the king," Enguerrand de Monstrelet reported. "He afterward, by treaty . . . promised never to return to the king, yielding up many forts that he held as security for keeping the said treaty. Shortly after, the constable [Arthur of Richemont] was restored to the good graces of his monarch, who was well satisfied to receive him, although he was much vexed at the conduct that had been held to the lord de La Trémoïlle."

Although another chronicler, Jean Chartier, assigned the responsibility for this successful maneuver to Yolande's nineteen-year-old son, Charles of Anjou, the organization of so efficient an operation bore all the trademarks of his far more capable and sensible mother. Overweight or no, it was four against one and the councillor could easily have been killed; the fact that he was not indicated that the conspirators had been told to exercise restraint. It was not Yolande's way to murder her opponents. Assassinating people was what had gotten the French into this mess in the first place.

To ensure a smooth political transition, Yolande also enlisted the aid of her daughter Queen Marie, who was only too thrilled to see the last of this particular adviser. Charles VII was angry at first, thinking that Arthur of Richemont had planned and executed the coup for his own purposes, but Yolande had been clever enough to keep the constable out of it. Marie made her husband realize that Arthur was not among those who had spirited his favorite away, and calmed him down so that he could hear the charges against La Trémoïlle. It turned out that the chamberlain had been engaged in some rather unorthodox financial transactions that were much to the detriment of the king and the royal treasury. The disclosure of these indiscretions was exactly calculated to turn the king's anger away from the perpetrators of the coup and toward its victim. Charles VII was quickly resigned to his loss and "Yolande [of Aragon] resumed all her lost ascendancy over her son-in-law, and the Constable . . . returned to favor," Edouard Perroy reported.

Two months later, at a council in Basel that had been convened earlier in the year by the Church to discuss the conflict between France and England, the duke of Burgundy suddenly and without warning ordered his representatives, who had been sitting for the past months on the same bench with the delegation representing England, to change their seats and remove themselves from their English counterparts. The process of reconciliation with France had begun.

WITH YOLANDE OF ARAGON and her protégé Arthur of Richemont once more in control of the court, Charles VII's diplomatic policy focused on an all-out effort to isolate England by coming to a separate peace arrangement with Philip the Good. But this time, the king did not, as he had after his coronation at Reims, make the mistake of suspending French combat efforts during the negotiations in order to induce the duke of Burgundy to come to terms; rather, he increased the pressure, both diplomatically and militarily, on his adversary. After so many years spent in conflict, even Charles had learned how to prosecute a war.

And so raids continued to be conducted into English and Burgundian territory, penetrating as far as the capital. "The war got worse and worse," the anonymous chronicler known as the Bourgeois of Paris complained in 1434. "Those who called themselves Frenchmen [Charles VII's supporters]—at Lagny and the other fortresses around Paris—came every day right up to the gates of Paris. They stole, they killed. . . . There was no news at this time of the Regent or of the Duke of Burgundy; they might have been dead. Every day the people were told that they were coming very soon, now this one, now that; meanwhile the enemy came every day and plundered right outside Paris because no one . . . did anything to stop them." As a result of the perpetual conflict prices rose and food became scarce; an epidemic of plague struck the city, and the death rate increased alarmingly. In the face of such horrendous conditions, even those Parisians who had supported the regency government began to turn against the English.

The French royal court also secured a major diplomatic coup by coaxing the Holy Roman Empire into the conflict. In April 1434 the emperor, who claimed suzerainty over Lorraine, declared René to be its legitimate duke, dashing Antoine's hope of assuming power. Philip the Good was so incensed by this decision that he demanded that his hostage, who had been granted a temporary leave of absence from captivity in order to negotiate the terms of his ransom and permanent release, return at once to his prison cell in Dijon, an order that the hapless René, bound by the code of chivalry and honor, was reluctantly compelled to obey. This act of pique on Philip's part, while no doubt emotionally satisfying, turned out to be somewhat less effective diplomatically. The following month the emperor retaliated by signing a treaty with Charles VII in which Philip was labeled as a "dis-obedient rebel, self-styled duke of Burgundy," an unpropitious turn of phrase that was followed six months later by a formal declaration of impe-rial war.

THE PROSPECT of having to fight the French and the empire simultaneously was sufficiently unpleasant that in January 1435, strongly encouraged by his chancellor, Philip the Good agreed to participate in a series of secret meetings with key ambassadors from Charles VII's court, including the constable, Regnault of Chartres, and the duke of Bourbon (formerly the count of Clermont). The talks were held in the Burgundian town of Nevers. The duke of Bourbon, who was specifically chosen for this assignment because he had the good fortune to be married to another of Philip's sisters, sent his wife and children to Nevers in advance of the negotiations to soften the duke of Burgundy. The stratagem worked: "At length the duchess came, accompanied by her two sons and a brilliant attendance of knights, esquires, ladies, and damsels," reported Enguerrand de Monstrelet. "The duke of Burgundy went out of the place to meet her, and received her with much affection and joy, for he had not seen his sister for a long time, and showed the same love to his nephews, although they were very young. . . . On the next day a council was held, when it was determined that Arthur of Brittany, constable of France, and the archbishop of Reims, should be sent for." In due course these gentlemen arrived and the parley began in earnest. To everyone's great relief, the pros-pect of peace, so long elusive, began to take shape. In fact, Philip experi-enced such a change of heart at these meetings, and demonstrated such goodwill and hospitality toward his former enemies, that a Burgundian knight, observing his master's behavior, complained aloud that "we are very foolish to risk our bodies and souls at the will of princes and great lords who, when they please, make up their quarrels, while we oftentimes remain poor and in distress."

In this congenial atmosphere, which could easily have been mistaken for a joyous family reunion rather than a serious political conference, the duke of Burgundy at last overcame his aversion to treating with his father's killer,

Portrait of Philip the Good.

and allowed himself to be munificently bribed. In exchange for formally abandoning England and allying with Charles, Philip got 50,000 gold crowns, payable on signing of the peace treaty. He was allowed to keep all the territory he had already been given by the English, and the French ambassadors even threw in some new property, including the lucrative Somme towns and the county of Ponthieu (although these could be redeemed in the future by Charles for 400,000 gold crowns). Charles would issue a formal apology acknowledging any emotional hardship the duke of Burgundy might have suffered as a result of the murder of his father, and although Philip would officially recognize Charles as the legitimate sovereign of France and become his vassal once again, in deference to any lingering sensitivity he was absolved during his lifetime from having to do personal obeisance to the king.* (The duke of Burgundy's heirs would, however, have to pay homage to future kings of France.)

Nor was the Burgundian architect of this peace forgotten. On July 6, 1435, Charles VII wrote from his castle in Amboise to Nicolas Rolin and others on Philip the Good's council: "Charles, by the grace of God, king of France, greetings to all those who see these letters. Be it known that we, having heard on good authority . . . of the good will and affection which Nicolas Rolin, knight . . . and chancellor [of Burgundy] and the lords of Croÿ, Charny and Baucignies, councilors and chamberlains of our cousin of Burgundy, and other servants of his, cherish for the reconciliation and reunion of us and our cousin . . . bearing in mind that this peace and reconciliation is more likely to be brought about by our cousin's leading confidential advisers, in whom he places his trust, than by others of his entourage . . . we grant and have granted by these present letters the sum of 60,000 gold saluts . . . to divide between them as follows: To the said Nicolas Rolin, 10,000 saluts, to the said lord of Croy, likewise . . . to the said lord of Charny, 8,000 [saluts] . . . to the lord of Baucignies, 8,000."

After the agreement of Nevers, there remained only the uncomfortable task of Philip's informing the unsuspecting English that, alas, he was no

---

*The apology was eventually ingeniously worded as follows: "The king [Charles] will declare . . . that the death of the late lord John, duke of Burgundy . . . was iniquitously and treacherously caused by those who perpetrated the deed, and through wicked counsel, which was always displeasing to him, and continues to be so in the sincerity of his heart. That if he had been aware of the consequences, and of an age to have judged of them, he would have prevented it; but at the time he was very young, having little knowledge, and inconsiderately did not prevent it."

longer their ally. Sensitive to the charge that his behavior might be construed as falling somewhat short of the cherished chivalric ideal of honor—Philip was, after all, secretly conspiring with Charles VII while still pretending to remain faithful to his sworn oath to support Henry VI—to save face the duke of Burgundy insisted that Charles at least try to make peace with England by calling for a general conference, at which all sides would be present, to be mediated by representatives of the Church. He even offered to host the event, and it was decided, before everyone left Nevers, to issue an invitation to the English to meet later in the year in Arras. "Within a few days many councils were held respecting a peace between the king of France and the duke of Burgundy; and various proposals were made to the duke concerning the murder of the late duke John that were agreeable to him, insomuch that preliminaries were agreed on, and a day appointed for a convention at Arras to put a final conclusion on it," reported Enguerrand de Monstrelet. "When this was done, they separated most amicably; and news of this event was published throughout the realm, and other countries: notice of it was sent to the pope and the council at Basel, that all persons who chose might order ambassadors to attend the convention at Arras."

THE CONGRESS OF ARRAS, universally recognized as the turning point of the Hundred Years War, began in August 1435. It was a grand affair, as opulent and illustrious as the great wealth of its sponsor, the duke of Burgundy (whose estate had recently been given a significant boost by his secret deal with the French), could provide. The three participating nations—France, England, and Burgundy—all sent multiple ambassadors accompanied by impressively large, resplendent entourages, so that the total number of emissaries, including bureaucrats, secretaries, servants, and other minions associated with each embassy, reached nearly a thousand people apiece. The French delegation, headed by Philip's brother-in-law the duke of Bourbon, was composed of the leading members of the royal council: Regnault of Chartres, Arthur of Richemont, and the count of Vendôme, among others. Although she did not herself attend, Yolande maintained her influence over these proceedings through her servant, the treasurer of Anjou, who was one of the principal negotiators for the French. The queen of Sicily also sent separate representatives charged with protecting her specific interests and those of her family.

The English, who had been kept deliberately uninformed of the earlier conference at Nevers, and who were consequently surprised by the invitation to attend a general peace summit, had to scramble to come up with a sufficiently prestigious deputation. They at first asked Philip the Good to lead their embassy, but the duke of Burgundy, for reasons that would become obvious to his former allies only later, delicately declined to undertake this responsibility. The duke of Bedford, seriously ill in Rouen, was unable to attend, so the English ended up with Cardinal Henry Beaufort (Henry VI's great-uncle and one of the most influential men in the government) and the archbishop of York as its lead negotiators instead. However, as it was important to demonstrate that Henry VI was the legitimate king of both England *and* France, a number of Frenchmen were included as principal envoys as well. These were more difficult to find, as many of the regency's formerly loyal subjects, sensing the change in mood, had already defected to Charles VII. But there were still a number who, as a result of the salaries paid them, could be relied upon, and of these the most prominent was none other than Pierre Cauchon. Subsequent to his successful prosecution of Joan of Arc, Cauchon had received the consolation prize of the bishopric of Lisieux—not quite so prestigious a posting as archbishop of Rouen, for which he had initially hoped, but a profitable benefice nonetheless. So enthusiastic a collaborator was he that when the archbishop of York fell ill early in the proceedings it would be Pierre Cauchon who would speak for the English in their negotiations with the French.

The duke of Burgundy of course brought his own entourage, which included some 115 noblemen and their respective households from throughout his domains. He was not a mediator in this instance—two cardinals and bishops assumed that role—but rather the hospitable provider of lodgings and the master of entertainment, an avocation into which he zealously threw himself. There were succulent feasts and late-night suppers accompanied by music, wine, and dancing, and parties at which were played amusing games of chance; the crowning event was an elaborate tournament, where a pair of knights in magnificent armor jousted for the benefit of spectators. The entire affair was staged exactly as though a brilliant medieval wedding was taking place—which in a sense it was, except that, unbeknownst to the English, one of the suitors was about to get jilted at the altar.

Care was taken by the duke of Burgundy to obscure the true state of his relationship with France. Under the guise of providing due protection—after

all, the French and the English were enemy combatants, and since each delegation had arrived with an armed guard, the possibility that violence might
erupt was not inconsequential—the envoys from England and France, and all
of their retinues, were housed at a substantial distance from each other. The
English were given their lodgings in the center of the city proper, while the
French stayed alongside their host in the comfortable village adjacent to Philip
the Good's castle. During the entire length of the congress, the ambassadors
from England and France, along with their numerous respective counselors,
never met face-to-face but communicated only by presenting their cases and
proposals to the mediators, who passed them along to the opposite side and
vice versa. The only member of the English delegation ever to venture into
the French or Burgundian living space was the duke of Suffolk, who made a
ceremonial appearance on the day of the jousting.

While this separation prevented the English from observing the secret
meetings between Philip the Good and Arthur of Richemont (which took
place nightly), it did not entirely disguise the growing cordiality that existed
between the delegations of Burgundy and France. By the end of the second
week of August, the English began to notice that their French counterparts
heard mass daily with their Burgundian hosts and later made merry, drinking and carousing until the early hours of the morning, and generally behaving like the best of friends, and that Philip the Good showered many marks
of affection and courtesy on those who were, at least in theory, his sworn
enemies. "The English ambassadors were not well pleased at these entertainments; and from the frequent intercourse that took place between the French
and the duke, they suspected some treaties were in agitation that would not
be for the advantage of their country," Enguerrand de Monstrelet reported.

The format for the talks had been established in advance and the conference proceeded according to the agreed-upon routine. On August 12, 1435,
Pierre Cauchon presented the first peace proposal on behalf of the English
to the mediators in a large room in the abbey of Saint-Vaast that had been
assigned for this purpose. The arbitrators took notes, after which the English
delegation, having finished its presentation, filed out, the signal for the
French embassy, which had been waiting in another room, to file in. The
French envoys were then informed of the details of the opposition's offer by
the cardinals and the two bishops. The English overtures were derisively
rebuffed; and so it became the turn of the French to put forth a counterpro-
posal, which proposition was duly and laboriously recorded by the

mediators. Then the French filed out, and the English, who had been waiting in another room, filed in, and the whole process began over again.

As the English were unaware that their military and diplomatic position
had been seriously undermined at Nevers, and the French were only too
cognizant that the balance of power had shifted seriously in their favor and
that consequently there was no need for them to concede to any of the enemy's terms, there was not much overlap between the various proposals. The
issue of sovereignty, as might be expected, was particularly divisive. The
English held fast to the theory of the double monarchy and insisted that
Henry VI be recognized as king of both England and France. They were
willing to allow Charles VII to keep his lands south of the Loire, but only
if he did homage to Henry VI for them, which meant that Charles would
become Henry's vassal. They absolutely refused to consider surrendering
any of the territory currently under occupation, including Normandy,
Maine, and Paris, although as a concession they threw out the idea of a marriage between Henry VI and one of Charles's daughters, the implication
being that by joining the two bloodlines the conflict would be resolved
when the crown passed to Henry's progeny.

The French proposals were naturally in diametric opposition to those
proffered by the English. The French considered Henry VI to be a mere
interloper and demanded that he immediately renounce any pretension to
the throne of France, reminding the mediators that this honor had already
been conferred upon Charles VII, the legitimate sovereign, by the coronation at Reims. Further, they were adamant that England, which kept a garrison in Paris, must vacate the capital at once. They were reluctantly willing
to allow Henry VI to keep his possessions in Normandy, provided he did
homage to Charles VII for them, but they preferred to simply pay him to
get out, and offered the English 150,000 saluts of gold to leave the kingdom
altogether.

As the French conditions were deemed as unsatisfactory to the English as
the English propositions had been to the French, the prospects for the signing of a general peace, which had not been particularly promising to begin
with, faded altogether in the waning days of August. Despite the best efforts
of the mediators, the two sides failed to come to any agreement whatever,
and eventually the English lost patience with the enterprise and withdrew
from negotiations. According to Enguerrand de Monstrelet, the delegation
representing Henry VI left the conference on September 6, 1435, and

returned to England in a bitter mood, "for they had perceived, while at Arras, that great cordiality existed between the duke and the French, which was far from pleasing to them." The following week, on September 14, in a further harbinger of looming collapse, the indomitable duke of Bedford, who in the thirteen years since the sudden demise of his brother Henry V had held the English occupation of France together, often by sheer force of will as regent, died of his illness in Rouen.

A week after that, on September 21, 1435, timed to fall on Saint Matthew's Day, at a very grand and solemn ceremony at the abbey of Saint-Vaast attended by the Church mediators and all of the most important officials of both the French and Burgundian delegations, Philip the Good signed a separate peace agreement, known as the Treaty of Arras, with the ambassadors from France and publicly swore to "acknowledge our aforesaid lord king Charles of France as our sovereign lord, in as much as regards the land and lordships we hold in that kingdom, promising for ourself and our heirs on our faith and bodily oath, on the word of a prince, on our honor, and on the loss of our expectations in this world and in that to come, to hold inviolate this treaty of peace." And just like that every city, town, village, castle, fortress, military unit, vassal, and government official in those territories loyal to the duke of Burgundy, whether high or low, rich or poor, rural or urban, peasant or aristocrat, instantly abandoned his or her allegiance to Henry VI and instead embraced Charles VII as the rightful sovereign.

Three days later in Paris, the once notorious queen of France, Isabeau of Bavaria, who for her own comfort had engineered the disinheritance of her last surviving son so that the English might advance into the capital and thereby take possession of the kingdom, died alone and penniless, of an illness brought on by sharp poverty and distress, in the Hôtel Saint-Pol, at the age of sixty-five. She lived just long enough to see her life's work undone by the Treaty of Arras.

THE NEWS that the duke of Burgundy had signed a separate peace agreement with Charles VII fell like a stone cannonball on the court of Henry VI. Philip the Good himself sent messengers and high-level ambassadors to England, armed with letters explaining this action, which were read aloud at a council meeting. "All persons were very much surprised," wrote Enguerrand de Monstrelet, "and the young king Henry was so much hurt at their contents, that his eyes were filled with tears, which ran down his cheeks. He said to some of the privy counselors nearest to him, that he plainly perceived since the duke of Burgundy had acted thus disloyally toward him, and was reconciled to his enemy king Charles, that his dominions in France would fare the worse for it." Astonishment turned to vexation, and vexation to anger. Violence broke out in London against people whose only crime was that they were identified with Flanders, Brabant, or Hainaut, and several were murdered before the king put a stop to it. The royal council determined to fight for its possessions in France, and preparations were made not only to retake territory lost to Charles VII but to declare war on Philip the Good as well.

But it would take time to raise the necessary reinforcements, and in the interim Charles's forces struck. "When the French or Armagnacs realized that they could not reach an agreement [with England at Arras], they began to make war again more strongly than ever," wrote the anonymous Bourgeois of Paris. "They entered Normandy in force and soon captured some of its best seaports, Montivilliers, Dieppe, Harfleur, and a number of other good towns and castelries. Then they came nearer Paris and took Corbeil, Bois de Vincennes, Beauté, Pontoise . . . and other towns and castles near Paris. Thus nothing could come into Paris from Normandy or anywhere else, so that in Lent all goods were very dear, especially pickled herring." By April, five thousand troops led by Arthur of Richemont and the Bastard of Orléans had surrounded the capital. To forestall a prolonged siege, the constable approached the gate at Saint-Jacques at the head of his force and advised those who guarded the city to open the doors and "let us into Paris peacefully, or you will all die of famine." Joan had issued much the same appeal when she had assaulted these very same walls at the head of an army seven years before, but that was when the duke of Burgundy still stood with England. This time, those addressed "looked over the walls and saw so many armed men that they would not have thought all King Charles' resources could have paid for even half the troops they could see; frightened at this and fearing an outbreak of violence, they agreed to let them into the town," the Parisian chronicler reported. Some of the inhabitants loyal to Charles supplied ladders suitable for scaling, and the Bastard of Orléans, with a few of his men, climbed over the walls and opened the gate, allowing the French army to pour into the city. The English garrison, whose numbers had already been severely weakened by desertions, was so obviously outnumbered that its soldiers were allowed to leave the capital unharmed, provided they did so peacefully. The men formed into three companies and marched out of the city to the hoots and taunts of the Parisians, never to return.

And then something unprecedented happened. The constable, acting on behalf of Charles, *issued immunity to all Parisians, even those who had supported the regency government, and forbade all acts of retribution.* "My good friends," he was reported to have said, "the good King Charles gives you a hundred thousand thanks, and so do I on his behalf, for having so peaceably returned the chief city of the kingdom to him. If anyone of any rank, present or absent, had done any wrong to our lord the King, it is entirely forgiven him." For the first time in three decades, the government of Paris changed hands without the massacre of a single citizen, Burgundian or Armagnac; and in that one act of enlightened statesmanship, the civil war was at long last resolved and Charles truly became king of France. "The Parisians loved them for this and before the day was out every man in Paris would have risked his life and goods to destroy the English," the anonymous Bourgeois of Paris, a confirmed Burgundian who had reviled the Armagnacs for decades, wrote happily, obviously including himself in the general euphoria.

It took several more months to thoroughly secure the surrounding area, but on November 12 of the following year, after being so long denied the city, Charles VII was finally able to enter Paris safely. To mark the solemnity of the occasion, he arrived in great state at the head of a long procession, and was met outside the walls by a large delegation of townspeople, who presented him with the keys to the city. Following this ceremony, a canopy of azure silk, embroidered all over with fleurs-de-lis in gold thread, which had been specially made for the occasion, was raised over his head and the king was formally escorted into the city proper. Present with Charles for this important occasion were his eldest son, Louis, now dauphin of Vienne, and all the most eminent noblemen of the kingdom, the men who had fought for this moment, their names now familiar to all—Arthur of Richemont, the count of Vendôme, the Bastard of Orléans. Even La Hire "in very grand state" rode with Charles at the head of the procession. In one of those pinpoint turnabouts of fealty at which medieval societies were so practiced, the king was celebrated with a degree of warmth that utterly belied the events of the recent past; no one viewing the scene who did not know the circumstances would ever have guessed that this reception was the result of the most savage conflict of the age. "Thus nobly accompanied, did the king make his entry into the city of Paris by the gate of St. Denis," Enguerrand de Monstrelet recorded. "Three angels supported a shield bearing the arms of France over the gate . . . and underneath was written in large characters,

"Most excellent and noble king,
The burghers of this loyal town
To you their grateful offering bring,
And bow before your royal crown."

The procession proceeded into the city to noisy acclaim; prayers were said, and then Charles and all his company paraded through the capital to his father's palace, the Hôtel Saint-Pol. "The crowd of common people was so great that it was difficult to walk the streets; and they sang carols in all the squares, and other places, as loud as they could, for the welcome return of their natural lord and king, with his son, the dauphin. Many even wept for joy at this happy event," the chronicler enthused.

Charles VII parades triumphantly into Paris.

The entrance of Charles VII into Paris, while an important milestone, was largely ceremonial. The military conflict was far from over—the English were still firmly entrenched in Maine and Normandy, where they remained a significant threat to the rest of the kingdom—but to have retaken Paris was an undeniable accomplishment that cemented Charles's rule and added greatly to his luster. The king himself recognized the moment as such, and that was why he had taken such pains, prior to his entrance, to surround himself in procession with those of the nobility to whom he felt an obligation, as a reward for services rendered. And so on that historic day in November 1437, every person of consequence in Charles's regime was present to savor the king's triumph at Paris—except, of course, the two women who had put him there: Joan of Arc and Yolande of Aragon.

CHAPTER 14

The Road
to
Rouen

⚜

ITH THE TREATY OF ARRAS and the surrender of Paris, the first of the three conditions necessary to establish Joan of Arc's place in history was achieved. In a stunning reversal of English interests, Charles was now not only the acknowledged sovereign of France, but for the first time during his reign actually in possession of three-quarters of his kingdom. Henry VI might still call himself king of France, but barring a string of further military successes, this was an empty title. For this reason, England clung to its holdings on the continent, and particularly Normandy, with a ferocity that made clear its government's intentions to stay and fight for the legacy left by Henry V. And in the heart of Normandy lay the capital city of Rouen, in which the damning evidence of Joan's trial was locked away. Without those records nothing could be done to rehabilitate her image.

Not that Charles at this point demonstrated any particular interest in reviving Joan's memory. The king's overriding aspiration was to put the war behind him, either by defeating the English in battle or by bribing them to leave, two alternatives at which, in the years following his dramatic entrance into Paris, and despite Charles's having finally matured into a much more effective ruler, he was remarkably unsuccessful. It would fall once again to Yolande of Aragon and her family, and in particular the hapless René, to help him to finish the war and, in so doing, reclaim the Maid for posterity.

• • •

THE QUEEN OF SICILY'S second son certainly made for an unlikely hero. In the years following his defeat at Bulgnéville and subsequent imprisonment by the duke of Burgundy, René's career bore an unfortunate resemblance to the sort of fairy tale generally associated with the Brothers Grimm. The most deplorable luck dogged his heels even as the greatest of honors were showered on his head; he, who would help usher the Renaissance into France, was the recipient, often simultaneously, of the best and the worst the medieval world had to offer. Here was a man who by nature and inclination reveled in music, painting, and literature, but whose advancement lay in the mastering of the martial and political arts, a personal combination that resulted in disaster with an almost staggering consistency.

It was therefore entirely symptomatic of René's lot in life that, having done so much to advance his own cause by furthering the peace negotiations between Charles and Philip the Good, he would see his bargaining position with the duke of Burgundy suddenly deteriorate in an alarming fashion by virtue of an unlooked-for promotion. On November 12, 1434, just before the reconciliation talks at Nevers, while René still languished in his prison cell in Dijon, his older brother Louis III died unexpectedly of fever in Calabria, at the southern tip of the kingdom of Naples. Poor Louis had lived in Italy for over a decade, with only brief excursions home to France to see family and friends, while he waited impatiently for the reigning queen of Naples, Joanna II, to die and pass along his inheritance. Unfortunately for Yolande's eldest son, his benefactor outlived him by three months, and as Louis died childless, Joanna II instead named René as her successor. So when she too passed away on February 2, 1435, all of Louis III's many titles and appendages fell to his younger brother, and Philip the Good suddenly found himself in possession not simply of René, duke of Bar and Lorraine, but of René, king of Sicily, duke of Anjou and Maine, and count of Provence—a transformation that represented, in the rank-sensitive hierarchy of medieval prisoners, a stunning upgrade to a *much* more valuable hostage. Moreover, the duke of Burgundy knew, as everyone did, that Joanna II's will would be contested by the king of Aragon, and that René could be assured of this fabulous inheritance only by raising an army and going to Naples as soon as possible in order to claim his kingdom and defend his rights. That meant that every day René spent in Philip's prison cell would make him that much more desperate to get out, and the more desperate René became, the duke of Burgundy reasoned with undeniable logic, the more his captive would be willing to pay for his freedom.

Consequently, despite a concerted effort on the part of Yolande, Charles VII, the duke of Bourbon, Arthur of Richemont, and Regnault of Chartres to have René freed as a condition of the peace treaty of Arras, Philip the Good absolutely refused to consider this option. He had, by the purest stroke of good fortune, got a king rather than a mere duke in hand, and he wasn't about to give up what was likely to be the most lucrative acquisition of his career just to make peace with his father's killer. In the end it came down to reconciliation or René, and reconciliation won. The Treaty of Arras was signed without mention of the duke of Burgundy's illustrious hostage, and the new king of Sicily remained miserably in prison.

In this emergency, friends and family alike rallied to René's cause. He was extremely fortunate in the determined character of his wife, Isabelle of Lorraine, who upon being informed of the situation in Naples volunteered to go to Italy to hold and administer the kingdom while René negotiated for his release. This seemed like a good plan, and so by letters of June 4, 1435, issued from Dijon, René appointed his wife lieutenant general of his southern Italian kingdom. Isabelle immediately picked up her two youngest children, Louis and Margaret, aged eight and five respectively (her eldest son, John, was a hostage along with his father, and her older daughter, Yolande, had already been promised to Antoine's son and was living with the family of her betrothed), and sped down to Provence to assemble a fleet. She set sail from Marseille in a small convoy of five galleys, her children apparently still with her, at the beginning of October 1435, and by the eighteenth of the month had arrived at the capital city of Naples. A woman who clearly understood the importance of first impressions, no sooner had she disembarked than Isabelle made a point of parading all over town in great state under a velvet-and-gold canopy before appropriating a prominent royal castle as her living quarters, a bravado performance that, together with her five warships, won over the local population and allowed her time to establish her claim as ruler of the kingdom in her husband's place.

While René's wife secured his holdings in Italy, his mother guarded his property in France. Isabelle had left the bishops of Metz and Verdun in charge of administering Bar and Lorraine, but in the absence of their legitimate overlord the civilian populations were plagued by incursions from roving mercenaries. The bishops appealed by a letter of March 10, 1436, to

Yolande of Aragon for military aid—"expressing a confidence in her abilities second only to God," René's authoritative biographer, A. Lecoy de la Marche, observed drily—and the queen quickly convinced Charles VII to send both troops and artillery to protect her son's territory. Yolande, of course, also acted as regent for René's lands in Anjou and Provence, keeping the peace and defending against further inroads by the English, as she had for his older brother Louis while he was alive. Most important, she kept pressure on Philip the Good to release her son, enlisting the aid of not only the king of France and all of the extended royal family but also the pope and the most senior members of the Church in this effort.

Philip, however, intent upon wringing the most from his prize, responded to these various entreaties with a series of startling exorbitant demands. First, he wanted three million gold ducats, then two million, then the duchy of Bar, all of which were completely unreasonable, and so poor René sat in his prison cell, literally growing a long gray beard and feeling very sorry for himself, throughout the long months of 1436. Finally, casting about for a new enticement, his supporters floated the rumor that Joanna II had left a great treasure at her castle in Naples that could be claimed only by her heir, and the duke of Burgundy began to think that letting his hostage go and collect this sum might be a better strategy after all than having him simply pine away, and perhaps even die of unhappiness, in his tower in Dijon.

And so at the beginning of the following year, these two great lords met in Lille one last time to hammer out acceptable terms for René's release. On February 11, 1437, a treaty highly favorable to the duke of Burgundy was finally signed. By this document, in exchange for his permanent release from captivity, René agreed to pay Philip the Good the whopping sum of 400,000 écus in four yearly installments of 100,000 apiece, and he and his mother had to cede all of their rights to their territories in Flanders. (Yolande was made to sign the treaty as well.) René was allowed to keep the duchies of Bar and Lorraine but had to put up several towns, including Neufchâteau, as surety against the payment of the ransom money. Many of his most important vassals, including Robert de Baudricourt, had also to indemnify payment and go to prison in René's place in the event of default, and the marriage between his eldest daughter and Antoine's son was again confirmed. As René was already substantially in debt and did not have 10,000 écus to his name, let alone 400,000, he had to engage his eldest son, John, to the duke of Bourbon's daughter, who fortunately came with a dowry of 150,000 écus, to make the first payment.

The agreement represented a staggering financial blow, but at least the new king of Sicily had his liberty. He had to spend the rest of the year fundraising, scrounging off friends, begging for funds from Anjou and Provence, and appealing to Charles VII for help from the royal treasury, but eventually he scraped together enough money to assemble a small army. Isabelle sent back her five galleys to Marseille for her husband's use, and René, in the company of his eleven-year-old eldest son, who had been released with him, finally embarked for Italy and by May 1438 was in Naples. In a chivalric gesture that he no doubt came quickly to regret, knowing that he would soon have to fight the king of Aragon for his title, he gallantly sent his wife and children home to Provence, even though Isabelle was by this time far more familiar than he with the local baronage and serpentine ways of Neapolitan politics. Soon after his family sailed, the new king of Sicily, alone in a city of which he understood precious little, whose previous experience of warfare was limited to three battles, the last of which had ended in debacle, nervously barricaded himself in a castle while he waited for the enemy forces to mount an attack.

YOLANDE OF ARAGON was in her late fifties, a venerable age for the period, by the time her son René was at last released from his prison cell and free to pursue his all-important Angevin Italian inheritance. Although the queen of Sicily was nearing the end of her life, there is no indication of her slowing down in any way, or retiring from public affairs, or losing her influence at court. On the contrary: at the important representative meeting of the États généraux held in October 1439 in Orléans, convened to discuss military reforms and the implementation of a permanent tax to help finance the war effort, *two* thrones were set up for the opening convocation—one for the king of France, and the other for his mother-in-law.

Although certainly subject to personal tragedy—the death of her eldest son, Louis III, in 1434 was followed by the untimely loss of her youngest daughter in 1440—Yolande of Aragon could look back over her career with satisfaction. Despite the continued presence of the English in Maine and Normandy, the great work of her life, the reclamation of the throne of France for her daughter and son-in-law, had been accomplished. Charles VII's legitimacy was unquestioned; his eldest boy, Louis, Yolande's grandson, would inherit the kingdom at his death; the line of succession was firmly established. As Raymondin, with Melusine's aid, had taken over his cousin Aimery's lands and risen to become a richer and more powerful lord than he whom he had murdered, so had Charles VII, by the Treaty of Arras, taken over his assassinated cousin's lands and been acknowledged to be a greater lord than Philip the Good. And just as Melusine had provided her husband with sons who would go on to perform great feats that brought honor to the family's name, so too would Charles's descendants rule gloriously after the king's demise.

Nor in achieving this remarkable turnaround had the queen of Sicily neglected her other children, or her husband's legacy. After René's release from prison, she had not only given him as much of her own money as was available but used her influence in Anjou and at court and within the Church to help him secure the funds necessary to raise his army. Similarly, by her efficient elimination of Georges de la Trémoïlle, Yolande had placed her third son, Charles of Anjou, count of Maine, in a position of great power at court. No sooner had the previous favorite left than the count of Maine took his place in Charles VII's affections. The king could not do without him, and kept the younger Charles beside him always as his closest adviser, calling him "a brave prince, a true man of war endowed with a remarkable beauty." So influential was the count of Maine that he provoked the jealousy of the other barons, and the duke of Bourbon tried more than once to unseat him at court. But between them, Charles of Anjou and his mother had managed to defeat these conspiracies, and by 1439 very little could be accomplished in France without the support of the count of Maine.

There was, in fact, only one circumstance for which Yolande of Aragon could reproach herself: the loss of the duchy of Maine, which included the capital city of Le Mans. The English occupation of this important Angevin holding had occurred during her regency, and she could not reconcile herself to its forfeiture. She had tried to retrieve it militarily, by working with Arthur of Richemont and the duke of Alençon, both of whom had sporadically sent in commando units to try to force the English out, but these had been unsuccessful. At the time of the Treaty of Arras, when hopes of peace ran high throughout the occupied territories, artisans at the cathedral of Le Mans were at work on a stunning stained glass window depicting the figures of Louis I and his wife, Marie of Blois, and Louis II and Yolande of Aragon alongside the duke of Bourbon, a touching symbol of the faith the community still had in its lineage and in particular its surviving duchess. To have this cathedral (which she still supported financially) in the hands of the enemy was a provoking reminder of her impotence, and the queen of Sicily was not a woman who liked to lose.

Coincidently, toward the end of the decade—the exact date is not known, but certainly by 1439—she had one of her granddaughters, René's younger girl, nine-year-old Margaret, sent back from Italy to live with her. Margaret, who was dowered with the duchy of Bar, had been promised to the son of the count of Saint-Pol on March 25, 1437, as part of René's ongoing effort to keep his property out of the hands of the duke of Burgundy. The usual procedure was of course for the girl to go to live with her intended's family, as her older sister had done. But this did not happen in Margaret's case; instead, she was given over to the care of her indomitable grandmother. It might have been that René felt the need to have his mother safeguard the fate of the duchy of Bar, or it might have been that Yolande herself was not entirely happy with this alliance and, observing that strong-willed, intelligent Margaret was developing into something of a beauty, wished to try for a more prestigious match. Certainly, the queen of Sicily took pains to train her granddaughter, of whom she would become very fond, to be a great lady, and did not neglect to instruct her in all the skills necessary to the administration of a noble appendage. At the age of eleven, Margaret was already checking payments and learning to balance the accounts of her grandmother's treasury.

Margaret's arrival at her grandmother's chateau in Saumur seems also to have coincided with a new round of diplomatic talks between England and France that occurred in July 1439 at the port of Gravelines, northeast of Calais. "In this year, many noble ambassadors were assembled. . . . They held several meetings to consider if they could not bring about a general peace between the two kings and their allies, and also respecting the deliverance of the duke of Orléans, who had remained a prisoner in England since the battle of Agincourt," reported Enguerrand de Monstrelet. The English again floated the idea of a long-term truce supported by a royal marriage between the two kingdoms, but as they still insisted that Henry VI be recognized as king of both England and France, "they could not agree on any conclusion worth speaking of; for the English refused to treat with the king of France unless the duchy of Normandy, together with all their other conquests, remained to them independent of the crown of France," the chronicler observed. However, this was the second time that marriage had been mentioned as a means to peace, and with good reason. The conflict had by this time lasted so long that Henry VI, who had been an infant when the crown passed to him through his father, was now eighteen. It began to occur to those on the French side that the king of England would be married, and married soon, and that whom he married—what allies might yet be brought into the fray on the side of their enemies through matrimony—could very likely determine the direction of the war.

ALTHOUGH ENGLAND's public position as regards Henry VI's sovereignty over France did not waver at the conference at Gravelines, there was strong and growing disillusionment among the English baronage with the war effort, which cost so much and returned so little. A movement toward surrendering the dream of the double monarchy and protecting what was left of England's holdings on the continent by bringing the conflict to an honorable end was taking hold among a number of Henry VI's counselors. That by the beginning of the next year their influence began to dominate the government is evidenced by the decision in 1440 finally to ransom the duke of Orléans, in the hope of using this gentleman to promote peace.

The wisdom of selecting as a goodwill ambassador an individual who had just spent the past twenty-five years in an English prison cell might ordinarily be questioned, but in fact the duke of Orléans was at this point so wretched, and had been disappointed so many times in the past, and had so lost all hope of rescue, that he was willing to agree to almost anything his captors suggested. The ransom figure was set at 200,000 écus and, in another implausible twist of history, was actually paid by Philip the Good, whose father had started the whole mess by murdering the duke of Orléans's father three decades earlier. Philip had no problem meeting the English demands because he happened to have a sizable cash outlay on hand owing to René's having paid the first two installments on *his* ransom. "While these negotiations were pending, and afterward, the duke of Burgundy had a great desire to aid the duke of Orléans in his deliverance, as well from their near connection by blood, as that, on his return to France, they might remain good friends, forgetting all former feuds that had existed between their houses," Enguerrand de Monstrelet observed. "He caused him to be sounded, whether he would be willing to marry his niece . . . and also, in case of his deliverance, if he would agree to ally himself with the duke of Burgundy, without taking any measures in times to come against him or his family, in consequence of the former quarrels between their fathers. . . . The duke of Orléans, considering the long imprisonment he had suffered and might still undergo, readily assented to these propositions."

And so the duke of Orléans, at the age of forty-five, was finally liberated and immediately married Philip's niece at a lavish wedding paid for by the duke of Burgundy, well attended by both great nobles from France and ambassadors from England. But instead of being a force for unity, the reintroduction of the duke of Orléans into the fragile balance of power surrounding France became a source of division. "For . . . the king [Charles VII] had been informed of the whole conduct the duke had held since his return from England—of his oaths and alliance with the duke of Burgundy—of having received his order—how grandly he was accompanied—of his having admitted into his household numbers of Burgundians, who had formerly waged war against him and his crown," explained Enguerrand de Monstrelet. "The king was also told that these connections had been formed in opposition to him and his ministers—and that many great lords, such as the dukes of Brittany and Alençon, had joined the two dukes, with the view of forming a new administration. . . . The king, who was ever inclined to suspicion, and to listen to such information, from the many plots that had been formed against him during his reign, readily believed what was now told him."

Nor were these idle rumors. The duke of Burgundy had indeed joined in a new triple alliance with the dukes of Orléans and Brittany, which left open the possibility of a rebellion against Charles that could potentially be exploited by England. Also at this time the count of Armagnac, old ally of the duke of Orléans, offered one of his daughters to Henry VI in marriage without bothering to consult the king of France. Such an alliance could strengthen England's position on the continent and put the southern portion of the kingdom at risk.

It had been more than ten years since Charles VII had vacillated, irresolute and conflicted in the face of the English threat, unable to act until Joan had appeared. He was now a different man, a man inured to threats to his rule, a king convinced of the legitimacy of his cause, and with the experience to lead. Consequently, he did not wait for the conspirators to make a move but at the first hint of collusion acted with energy to protect his government. "King Charles of France now assembled a very large body of men from different provinces of his realm, and ordered those captains . . . to join him instantly with their troops," reported Enguerrand de Monstrelet. "When all were collected on the banks of the Loire, the king departed from Bourges in Berry, attended by the dauphin, the constable of France, the lord Charles of Anjou, and lords without number." In 1441, the king himself took command of this army and invaded Champagne, reaching to the out-skirts of Burgundy, and achieved the submission of the major forts and the town of Troyes, an act that reestablished and confirmed the population's obedience to the crown. From Champagne, Charles continued to accom-pany the royal militia north of Paris, where he attacked and won the city of Pontoise, despite its being defended by an English garrison under the highly experienced command of Captain Talbot, one of the original members of the besieging force at Orléans and the commander who later fought against Joan and La Hire at the battle of Patay. Encouraged by these successes, the king continued his offensive the next year, moving against the English occu-pation in Guyenne, in the heart of the Aquitaine.

In England, the political faction committed to the war roused itself and succeeded in convincing Henry VI to raise a new army to repel the French attack and take back the kingdom. During the winter of 1442, an imposing force of some seven thousand men-at-arms was recruited for a spring offen-sive. And this was where matters stood in France when René lost Naples.

RENÉ'S SOJOURN in his southern Italian kingdom had been plagued by his customary perverse luck. Although initially the forces he commanded were of equal strength to those of his opponent, the king of Aragon, and he had some early successes, his fortunes fell when he lost one of his best command-ers, a man named Jacopo Caldora, who was killed leading an assault in 1439. Jacopo was succeeded by his son, Antonio, who had neither his father's stra-tegic skills nor his sense of loyalty. Antonio was more of an entrepreneur—he regarded war as a moneymaking activity and was happy to switch sides at a moment's notice depending upon whose offer was the most lucrative. This did not make him the most reliable soldier, particularly as René's funds were already running low. The king of Sicily had to write home to his mother for more silver.

Matters came to a head in 1440 when René's troops encountered the king of Aragon's at the interior city of Benevento and lost due in large part to the nonparticipation of Antonio, who was too busy being bought off by the enemy to bother to fight. The fickle commander and his men eventually defected to the Aragonese side altogether. It was at this point that René sent Isabelle and his two sons back to Provence, an act that did not exactly instill confidence in his abilities among his Neapolitan subjects.

By the spring of 1442, the king of Aragon's forces had surrounded the capital, and his fleet had cut off food supplies to the city. The population began to suffer from hunger, and what support René and Isabelle had managed to garner in the past eroded. On June 1, a company of Aragonese soldiers quietly infiltrated Naples through an underground well by bribing the local guard; a second squadron followed the first; and by the next morning enough enemy soldiers were inside the city to open two of the gates. The king of Aragon's army poured into the streets of the capital. There was very little resistance from the starving population; on the contrary, most people welcomed the intruders, and a group of nuns even went so far as to toss ropes to the enemy soldiers in order to help them scale the high walls of the city.

René rushed out of his castle with a small band of loyalists. Fighting in the streets, he made an attempt to repel the invaders, but soon saw that it was hopeless and escaped to a waiting galley. "Were I certain of death I should not care, but I fear being taken prisoner," he gasped as his final poignant farewell to his men. In the confusion of the assault his ship managed to elude the enemy fleet, enabling the last in the long line of Angevin pretenders to the throne of Naples to watch from beyond the shore as the army of the king of Aragon took control of the capital—and with it, the kingdom.

By the end of the year, René was back in Provence and reunited with Isabelle and his sons. He arrived in Marseille depressed, defeated, and insolvent, just in time to hear that his mother had passed away.

YOLANDE OF ARAGON was sixty-one years old in 1442, the year she died. She was such an extraordinary presence that it must have seemed to her vassals that she was indestructible. The year before her death, the bishopric of Angers fell vacant, and she nominated her secretary to the position as a reward for his long years of loyal service. Charles VII made the mistake of trying to overrule her, and put his own candidate into the office. The queen of Sicily, in a fury, let it be known that if the king's appointee made an appearance in Angers she would have his head cut off. The king backed down. Yolande's candidate got the position. Clever little Margaret, still living with her grandmother, took it all in.

Yolande must have been very close to her granddaughter by this time, because her last public act was an attempt to elevate Margaret's nuptial prospects. It happened that the Holy Roman Emperor himself was looking for a wife, and had heard of the exceptional beauty of King René's younger daughter. Ambassadors were sent to Saumur to inspect the girl and make an offer. They arrived in September 1442. The queen of Sicily was noticeably failing in health, but she roused herself to one last great effort. Yolande's own dressmakers were called in, and Margaret was outfitted in a sumptuous robe made of cloth of gold and trimmed in white fur. In the account book of the period it was specifically noted that the queen of Sicily had ordered that no expense be spared as she wanted her granddaughter to look "dazzling." The imperial representatives were presented, Margaret was observed in all of her finery, and afterward everyone was treated to a series of extravagant feasts and entertainments. Although nothing definite could be concluded in her father's absence, the ambassadors were clearly impressed and no doubt made an extremely positive report of the young lady's charms upon their return to Germany.

By the time the envoys left Saumur at the beginning of October, the energy it had taken to entertain on such a lavish scale had begun to take its toll. Aware that she was terminally ill, Yolande sought refuge in religion and affiliated herself with a monastic house as a layperson or oblate. Practical to the end, on November 12, 1442, while staying at the chateau of the lord of Tucé, the queen of Sicily signed her last will and testament. In it, she divided the rights to her lands between her two surviving sons, René and Charles of Anjou. As remembrances, she gave René some important tapestries, and to her daughter Marie, some jewelry. Again, there is evidence of her deep affection for Margaret, as she alone among Yolande's grandchildren was also willed a special ornament. But there was no great pile of coins or saved hidden fortune with which to surprise her heirs, as had been the case with her own mother-in-law, Marie of Blois. In fact, there was no money at all—the queen of Sicily had held nothing back but had unstintingly, over the course of twenty-five years, given her entire fortune to the prosecution of two wars. Conscious of the meagerness of her legacy, she made a point of explicitly explaining the lack of gold and the absence of silver plate and precious stones in her will. "The most beautiful and the best of these were used for

Stained glass window of Yolande of Aragon at the cathedral in Le Mans.

the purposes of the kingdom of Italy and given to King Louis," Yolande of Aragon wrote simply.

Two days later, the queen of Sicily died. She was buried in the cathedral Saint-Maurice of Angers, next to her husband, and with her death the last and the greatest of the Armagnac leaders of her generation passed away.

THE LOSS OF HIS MOTHER, who had ever been a source of strength and aid, deprived René of his most powerful supporter. Impoverished by his abortive campaign in Italy, already in arrears on the final two payments of his ransom due to the duke of Burgundy, and desperate to stay free of that prison cell in Dijon, René turned to his brother-in-law, Charles VII. In March 1443, he reunited with the king when the royal court convened at Toulouse. Charles had already raised a large body of soldiers and was intending to march them into Normandy in anticipation of the enemy counterattack. But when the formidable new English army, numbering some seven thousand men, landed at Cherbourg in April, its commander, the earl of Somerset, a man of excellent political connections but very little military experience, inexplicably shunned a decisive battle with his French counterpart. Instead, he stayed timorously within the occupied lands of the duchy of Maine, wreaking havoc and marching his men haphazardly through its own territory before ending up for no apparent purpose in Brittany, which was not in contention. (The earl of Somerset, challenged by his own staff on this questionable course of action, refused to explain his strategy, declaring somewhat enigmatically, "I will reveal my secret to no one. If my shirt knew my secret I would burn it.") Whatever his secret was, it clearly did not involve an offensive strike against the French, as the earl of Somerset stayed in Brittany for only a few weeks, just long enough to extort some money from the duchy, before turning tail and sailing back to England.

This was the end of the war party's influence in London. A substantial English army, once so feared by the French that the threat of fighting alone had brought the kingdom to submission, had retreated without even giving battle! At the beginning of 1444, the English sent a new embassy to Charles VII, this one led by the earl of Suffolk, the leader of the faction that argued in favor of a general peace in combination with a royal marriage. Henry VI was by this time referring to Charles VII as "our dear uncle of France."

In April, Suffolk and his emissaries met with their counterparts in the

French court at Tours and an agreement was hammered out. The issue of sovereignty was left unresolved but a two-year moratorium on all hostilities was successfully negotiated. "The meetings for peace were, during this time, continued with much activity at Tours, whither came many of the high nobility of France and England," Enguerrand de Monstrelet wrote. "A general truce on the part of the king, our sovereign lord, and his kingdom, as well by sea as by land, his vassals and subjects, including those most powerful princes the kings of Castille and Leon, of the Romans, of Sicily, of Scotland; the dukedoms of Anjou, Bar, and Lorraine; the dauphin of Vienne; the dukes of Orléans, Burgundy, Brittany, Bourbon, Alençon; the count of Maine; and generally the whole of the princes of the blood-royal of France . . . including, likewise, all their vassals, subjects, and adherents . . . promising, on oath, to preserve the truce inviolate." The agreement was signed on May 20, 1444, and was known as the Truce of Tours.

That left only the issue of the royal marriage, a far thornier solution, at least on the French side, than would first appear. To give one of Charles VII's daughters to Henry VI was out of the question; it would only prejudice the dauphin's chances of inheriting the throne peacefully after his father's death, since any male offspring of such a marriage would inevitably claim rights to the kingdom through his mother. Charles wasn't about to conclude a marriage that might start the whole Hundred Years War over again in the next generation. In fact, for this very reason, no daughter of a king of France was wed to an English sovereign for the next two centuries, an astute policy that had the added undeniable benefit of saving the head of at least one French princess during the reign of Henry VIII.

But neither could the king of France simply walk away from the possibility of a marriage alliance and allow Henry VI to choose his own bride— there was too much risk that one of Charles VII's many enemies might use this device to try to amass power in order to challenge his rule. What was needed was the daughter of a nobleman upon whose loyalty the king of France could unquestionably rely; someone of very high rank who was nonetheless not a threat; someone who could perhaps be bullied into taking this on, as nobody really wanted to marry his child to Henry VI and send the girl over to live with the hated English. There was only one candidate who fit all of these requirements: René of Anjou's daughter Margaret. "The marriage of Margaret was concluded . . . in the interest of Charles VII and at his demand," René's biographer stated flatly. Without his mother to support him, René was in no position to deny the king this or, for that matter, any request. A short time after the signing of the Truce of Tours, Margaret's engagement to the son of the count of Saint-Pol was officially broken, the Holy Roman Emperor's advances were courteously but firmly denied, and Yolande of Aragon's favorite granddaughter was affianced to the king of England.

And so fifteen-year-old Margaret of Anjou, descended from the line of remarkable Frenchwomen that included Marie of Blois and Isabelle of Lorraine, and a girl who had just spent three years in the home and under the watchful tutelage of perhaps the most astute and powerful politician in the kingdom, was launched at the unsuspecting English aristocracy and married to Henry VI, a monarch so unsuited to his position that he made Charles VII look like a tower of energy and strength by comparison. The lessons acquired at her grandmother's side bore fruit almost immediately. Margaret was crowned queen on May 30, 1445, at Westminster, promised in a letter of December 17 of the same year to do all she could to retrieve Maine for France, and by December 22 Henry VI had officially renounced his rights to the entire duchy, including the capital city of Le Mans, in favor of his father-in-law, René.* Even more provocatively, Margaret would later be credited by many with starting the infamous Wars of the Roses, a bitter civil conflict that would consume England for thirty years. Not quite retribution for Agincourt, of course—but close.

By the summer of 1444, when he was forced to accede to his daughter's marriage, René's position was especially vulnerable. The citizens of Metz, just north of Nancy in Lorraine, encouraged by the duke of Burgundy, had revolted against René's authority, and some of its inhabitants had even had the temerity to steal his wife's luggage when she had visited as part of a pilgrimage. Impecunious René had not the resources to strike back on his own, and needed to convince the king of France to lend him his army to help him subdue the town quickly lest the duke of Burgundy gain a foothold in the duchy. Also, he was hoping to induce the king to intervene on his behalf with Philip the Good to settle the outstanding debt associated with the payment of his ransom. Accordingly, René invited Charles VII and all

---

*There was such an outcry in England over this decision that the government tried to appease public opinion by delaying the actual transfer of Maine to René for several years. In the end, Charles VII sent troops into the duchy in June 1448 to besiege Le Mans, and the English soldiers stationed there surrendered their positions and fell back on Normandy.

of his court to Nancy, where he feasted the king and introduced him to one of his wife Isabelle's ladies-in-waiting, a notorious beauty by the name of Agnes Sorel, who would very quickly become the king's mistress.

It was customary to present the visiting monarch with a memento on these occasions out of gratitude for the distinction conferred by the royal presence. René must have known that it would be helpful if he could give Charles something that would discreetly remind the king of everything that René and his family had done for him and the kingdom over the long course of the war. Being of an artistic nature, the duke of Lorraine ceremonially bestowed upon Charles VII a beautifully bound volume specially produced to commemorate the event. It cannot be by mere chance that, out of all the works of literature, history, and theology that were available, René elected to present Charles VII with a copy of *The Romance of Melusine*.

The following year, Charles took his army to Metz and helped René bring the city back to obedience. Afterward, the king hosted a conference attended by the duchess of Burgundy, who was empowered to act for her husband, at which the payments owed on the final installments of René's ransom were forgiven.

FINALLY, IN 1449, citing infringements of the truce, Charles VII, encouraged by the reacquisition of the duchy of Maine, sent three separate armies into Normandy in one last great push to rid the kingdom of the invader. Although the English still maintained an overall advantage in terms of superior numbers of soldiers and garrisons, their commanders were caught by surprise. The native French population was jubilant. The regency government had never been popular, and the local people welcomed Charles's advancement, joined his units, and in many cases did not even wait for the king's soldiers to arrive but rose up against the occupiers independently. From Beauvais in the north came forces commanded by the counts of Eu and Saint-Pol, which compelled the surrender of Lisieux on August 16; from Verneuil in the south swept the Bastard and the duke of Alençon and their soldiers, who, joining troops commanded by Charles himself at Louviers, fought their way east into the heart of Normandy, securing Argentan in October; and from the west out of Brittany came the constable, Arthur of Richemont, with enough men-at-arms to conquer every fortress between Coutances and Fougères, the last of which fell on November 5.

At length, on October 9, French forces fought their way to within a few miles of the English capital of Rouen, which was defended by a garrison of twelve hundred men under the command of the duke of Somerset and Captain Talbot. A week later, on October 16, the Bastard led a frontal assault but was pushed back by the English soldiers, and after that the population took matters into its own hands. There was rioting in the streets, the garrison was forced to take cover in the royal castle, and the gates were thrown open to the Bastard and his army. The French immediately surrounded the castle and prepared for a siege, but the duke of Somerset preferred to cut a deal: promising to pay a substantial fine and leaving poor Talbot behind as a hostage to his good intentions, he and the rest of the English garrison slunk out of the fortress and retreated to Caen, leaving the former capital of the regency government in the possession of the French.

A month later, on November 20, 1449, Charles VII ceremoniously entered the city of Rouen. And a mere three months after that, on February 15, 1450, one of his principal theological advisers, a man named Guillaume Bouillé, who was the dean of Noyon, received an assignment that came directly from the king:

"As heretofore Joan the Maid was taken and seized by our ancient enemies and adversaries the English . . . against whom they caused to take place a certain trial by certain persons . . . in the process of which they made and committed many falsifications and abuses, so much so that, by means of this trial and the great hatred that our enemies have against her, they caused her death iniquitously and against reason, very cruelly indeed," Charles VII wrote. "For this reason we wish to know the truth of the aforesaid trial, and the manner according to which it was conducted and carried out. We command you, instruct you, and expressly enjoin you to inquire and inform yourself well and diligently on what was said; and that you bring before us and the men of our council the information that you have gathered on this event under a closed seal . . . for we give you power, commission and special instruction by these presents to carry this out."

CHAPTER 15

The Rehabilitation
of
Joan of Arc

❧

I know well that my King will win the kingdom of
France and I know it as well as I know that you
are before me as my judge.

—*Joan of Arc, in response to her inquisitors, 1431*

HE SPEED WITH WHICH the royal decree of Rouen
was issued, and the vehemence of its language,
would naturally seem to imply that the impetus for
the inquiry had originated with the king himself;
that Charles VII, overcome by emotion upon entering the city, or perhaps responding to eyewitness
reports of the cruelty of Joan's death, had at last
remembered all the Maid had done for him, and had impulsively called for
the seizure and subsequent reexamination of the records of her trial. But this
explanation gives Charles far too much credit for self-reflection and gratitude. The driving force behind this investigation was not the king but the
man charged with its prosecution: Guillaume Bouillé, Charles's theological
adviser. It was Bouillé who, over an unspecified period of time but certainly
longer than three months, had finally convinced Charles to undertake this
task, and his motive for doing so is not difficult to penetrate. So much of life

is fleeting, ephemeral: seasons change; civilizations rise and fall; people are born, they live a little, they die.

But faculty disagreements endure.

The renewal of the theological argument surrounding Joan had its genesis a full fourteen years earlier when Charles's forces, under the leadership of Arthur of Richemont, the constable, had retaken Paris in 1436. Not simply the ordinary citizenry but all of the capital's governmental and quasi-governmental institutions had abruptly transferred their allegiance from Henry VI to Charles, and this included the faculty of the University of Paris. Suddenly, the theory of the double monarchy and all of its proponents were out, and a new generation of doctors of theology who supported the rule of the French king and adhered to the old Armagnac views were in. The year after Charles made his grand entrance into Paris, the university had obligingly appointed a new rector to reflect the altered political climate, and this new rector was none other than Guillaume Bouillé.

Almost immediately, the scholastic discussion over the propriety of Joan's assuming male dress had resumed with all its former intensity as if the long years of war, and even the victim's own martyrdom, had not intervened. Bouillé, as rector, was in the thick of it. He could not let Pierre Cauchon's logic stand; it was as important to him to clear Joan's name so that his English and Burgundian colleagues' theories would be refuted as it had once been for Cauchon to convict Joan in order to demonstrate the superiority of his own thinking versus that of the old Armagnac scholars. Bouillé would eventually pen a treatise in which he returned to the arguments first promulgated by the revered Armagnac theologian Jean Gerson, justifying a woman's use of male dress if it was undertaken from the perspective of modesty when forced to live among soldiers. Bouillé's defense of Joan went even further, however. Highlighting the reality of Charles VII's now assured sovereignty, Bouillé contended that Joan had license to don male apparel if instructed to do so by divine revelation, and compared her to a number of similarly garbed female saints.

And therein lay Bouillé's dilemma. So long as the Inquisition's condemnation of Joan stood—so long as her voices were officially deemed heretical rather than divine by the Church, and she herself had acknowledged them to be so, as had been proclaimed by Cauchon and the English after her death—he could not win his argument. The only way to eclipse the old theologians was to have the decision against Joan reversed, and for this he needed first the king, and then the pope.

And so Bouillé went to work on Charles VII just as Cauchon had once wheedled the duke of Bedford. Their arguments were mirror images of each other. Where Cauchon had pointed out how much more effective politically it would be for the English to demonstrate that Charles VII and the French populace had been taken in by a heretic before killing her, Bouillé stressed how important it was to reverse what was obviously a tainted decision—"an iniquitous, scandalous sentence which threatens his [the king's] crown," he called it—as a means of undermining the enemy's position. Everything Joan had predicted had come true, Bouillé asserted: the English had been forced out of the kingdom, and by the grace of God, Charles VII was king. Hindsight demonstrated that the Maid had been telling the truth about her voices. How then could the sentence of heresy be allowed to stand? That would imply that Charles was king (heaven forbid!) by the work of Satan. No, no, it had been *the English* who had been deceived into doing the devil's work, and their errors must now be acknowledged and corrected.

By the time Rouen fell to the French, Charles had enough distance from the events of his early reign to no longer worry about his dignity or feel embarrassment over his relationship with the Maid, and Bouillé's arguments held a definite appeal. Despite the French king's recent military successes, the war was not yet over completely. The English still occupied some (albeit much-reduced) territory on the continent, and anything that could be done to further decrease their influence or demoralize their troops should be attempted. That it would also be personally satisfying to turn the tables on his enemies by pointing out that they had behaved atrociously and against the word of God was just an added incentive.

And who better to conduct the royal inquiry than the man who had urged it in the first place? By putting Bouillé himself in charge, Charles was as assured that the commission would find in favor of Joan as the duke of Bedford had once been certain, by appointing Pierre Cauchon to a position of authority, that the Inquisition would find against her.

Bouillé threw himself into his work and within three weeks of receiving the king's decree had already begun to query Joan's former assessors as to her treatment during captivity and the protocol associated with her condemnation. Since it had been almost twenty years since her trial, many of these people were no longer living. Cauchon, her chief tormentor, had died eight years before, from being bled by an overly enthusiastic physician. Her other judge, the vice-inquisitor, was nowhere to be found and presumed dead. A number of their collaborators had also succumbed in the intervening years, including the priest who had delivered the haranguing sermon just prior to Joan's execution, and who had subsequently expired, fittingly, from leprosy.

Bouillé's investigation was therefore limited to interviews with just seven people over a period of two days. Of these seven, all but one distanced themselves from the proceedings, laying the blame for Joan's execution squarely on her judges, who, as one of the witnesses testified, "[acted] more through love of the English and the favor they had from them . . . than through zeal for justice of the Faith." The only holdout was the elderly theologian Jean Beaupère, whose question "Do you know if you are in God's grace?" had elicited perhaps the most eloquent of Joan's responses during her trial: "If I am not, may God bring me to it; if I am, may God keep me in it." In his seventies, Beaupère was apparently too old and crotchety to change his opinion for the sake of political expediency and insisted that Joan had gotten what she deserved.

On the basis of these seven interviews, Bouillé found enough improprieties as regards Joan's treatment and sentencing to strongly recommend to Charles that a more thorough inquiry be conducted with the goal of having her condemnation revoked. The secular authority had now done all it could to redeem Joan. Because the verdict had been delivered by the Inquisition, the question of Joan's heresy was, as it had always been, in the hands of the Church. Somebody was going to have to approach the pope.

THE POPE IN 1450 was an Italian scholar who took the name Nicholas V. Nicholas, who loved books and art and whose principal achievement would be the establishment of the Vatican Library, had inherited a host of world problems from his predecessors. As a result of decades of internal conflict, the papacy's reputation had been seriously weakened. A council in Basel had elected an antipope; the emperor was trying to assume powers regarding the dispensing of benefices and other Church offices that had traditionally resided solely with the pontiff; the Turks were threatening to overrun the ancient city of Constantinople. On a more mundane level, 1450 was a Jubilee year, which meant that thousands of pilgrims and other tourists would be descending on Rome in anticipation of spending their hard-earned savings and visiting the more important religious sites, and it was the pope's responsibility to see to it that the city and its monuments were spruced up and sufficient accommodations made available to capitalize fully on the money-making potential of this event. Obviously, with so much to do, the question of whether some obscure French peasant woman had been unfairly accused of heresy two decades earlier did not occupy a position of prominence on Nicholas's agenda.

However, the pope did need the English and French to stop fighting each other so that the attention of Christendom could be turned toward addressing what Nicholas considered to be the real threat: the aggressive military posturing of the Turks and the vulnerability of Constantinople. So he sent a legate, Cardinal Guillaume d'Estouteville, to France to negotiate a peace treaty. Cardinal Estouteville did not exactly qualify as an impartial arbiter. He was a native Frenchman, originally from Normandy. A number of the members of his family had fought against the occupation and lost their property to England, and the whole clan was consequently staunchly loyal to Charles VII. Moreover, Estouteville was an old University of Paris man himself (during his visit from Rome he took time off from his official duties to reform the teaching schedule there) and understood Bouillé's point perfectly. Before any peace could be concluded, the king must be absolved of the charge of having gained his throne through the interference of a condemned heretic, and the only way to do this was to have the sentence against Joan officially overturned. "I know that the matter greatly concerns your honor and estate [and] I am working on it with all my power . . . just as a good and loyal servant should do for his lord," the cardinal hastened to assure Charles in a letter of 1452.

On his own initiative, Estouteville secured the services of the then Inquisitor of France, a man named Jean Bréhal, who was also by coincidence originally from Normandy, and who similarly loathed the English and was a loyal partisan of the king. The two churchmen established themselves in Rouen at the end of April 1452, where they studied the transcript of Joan's trial and listened to the testimony of witnesses. This pair was even more efficient than Bouillé. By May 4 they had produced an official document noting the existence of some twenty-seven instances of irregularities associated with Joan's trial. As a result, they concluded that "the preceding and other points being weighed, the case and the sentence are both null and most unjust," and recommended that the question of Joan's heresy be reexamined in the light of these errors.

By the next year, Estouteville had given up all pretense of negotiating a peace between England and France (there never was an official treaty marking the end of the Hundred Years War) and had returned to Rome. But neither he nor the inquisitor, Bréhal, ceased in his efforts to have Joan's sentence reversed. Seeking to authenticate his findings, Bréhal spent the next two years soliciting opinions from theologians from as far away as the University of Vienna, while Estouteville tried to get Nicholas to authorize a retrial. But by this time Constantinople had fallen to the Turks and the pope had far more serious matters to attend to; also, it was likely he did not wish to offend the English, whose help he still hoped to gain against the Eastern threat.

It wasn't until after Nicholas's death in 1455, and the election of a new pope, Calixtus III, that Estouteville was able to make progress. By this time, he and Bréhal had revised their approach. In the process of seeking opinions from other theologians, Bréhal had received this piece of valuable advice from a sympathetic faculty member at the University of Paris: "Although many persons could be plaintiffs, as all those whom the thing concerns could be so considered . . . and the thing concerns many persons in general and in particular . . . it seems to us that the near relatives of the deceased Maid must have an advantage over the others and ought to be . . . prosecuting [bringing suit] for the injury done to one of their family." Joan's mother and two of her brothers were still alive, so Bréhal approached them to inquire whether they would be willing to petition the pope for a retrial. The result was a new application to Rome in the name of Joan's family, seeking redress for the injuries done to the Maid and her lineage and demanding that her case be retried before "a tribunal of rehabilitation."

Calixtus was already seventy-seven years old when he was elected pope in 1455. He would live only another three years, and during that time he would devote himself almost single-mindedly to organizing a crusade against the Turks for the purpose of recovering Constantinople. For this, he knew he would need the support of the French king and was probably persuaded by Estouteville (erroneously, as it turned out) that reopening the case against Joan would please Charles VII sufficiently so as to cause that monarch to consider aiding the new pope in his military venture. Also, Calixtus "loved to converse upon legal matters, and was as familiar with laws and canons as if he had but just left the University," observed distinguished papal scholar Dr. Ludwig Pastor. The lawful petition from Joan's family and the massive supporting scholarship from Bréhal impressed him. On June 11, 1455, Calixtus replied favorably to Joan's family's request and called upon three prominent members of the Church in France to work with the inquisitor to reopen proceedings in order to determine the validity of the Maid's former sentence of condemnation.

By 1455, Joan's mother, Isabelle, was in her sixties and widowed. She had been left in poverty by the death of her husband and was subsequently invited by the citizens of Orléans, who to their great credit never forgot what Joan had done for them, to take up residence in their town. The municipal government even provided Isabelle with a monthly stipend to help her meet her expenses and paid for a doctor to visit her when she became ill. Her son Pierre, who had fought with Joan, lived with her. Upon his return to France, the duke of Orléans, in recognition of the role Joan and her family had played in saving his birthright from the English, had awarded Pierre a small island in the Loire near Rouen.

In the fall of 1455, aware that a new tribunal had been commissioned to take up the question of her daughter's trial and execution, the aging Isabelle, in the company of Pierre and a group of supporters from Orléans, made her way to Paris in order to plead personally for justice on her daughter's behalf. On November 7, she and her entourage appeared at the cathedral of Notre Dame. They were ushered into the presence of Inquisitor Bréhal and the three ecclesiastics appointed to aid him in his inquiry, and Isabelle was allowed to present her case for rehabilitation. Because hers was the name on the papal petition, and it was she who was bringing suit against the former findings, the old woman's passionate appeal for redemption for her child was recorded as part of the official proceedings. It remains today as perhaps the most searing and poignant expression of the indefensible atrocity of the case. Joan is in every word.

"I had a daughter, born in legitimate marriage, whom I fortified worthily with the sacraments of baptism and confirmation and raised in the fear of God and respect for the tradition of the church, as much as her age and the simplicity of her condition permitted," Isabelle testified. "So well that, having grown up in the middle of the fields and of the pastures, she went frequently to church and every month, after confession, received the sacrament of the Eucharist despite her young age and gave herself to fasting and to prayer with great devotion and fervor, on account of the necessities then so grave in which the people found themselves and with which she sympathized with all her heart.

"Nevertheless," the mother continued, "certain enemies . . . betrayed her in a trial concerning the Faith, and . . . without any aid given to her innocence in a perfidious, violent, and iniquitous trial, without shadow of right . . . they condemned her in a damnable and criminal fashion and made her die most cruelly by fire." With that, Isabelle threw herself at the feet of the commissioners and burst into tears, waving the document she had brought to validate her suit; her grief was so profound that those who had accompanied her also cried out, and it was reported that the tribunal, visibly moved, accepted her petition.

So began the Church proceedings that would result in the rehabilitation of Joan of Arc.

IN CONTRAST to the earlier inquests by Bouillé and Cardinal Estouteville, which were rushed and superficial affairs designed only to prompt further action, this official retrial of the Maid of Orléans by the Inquisitor Bréhal and his three eminent colleagues was a painstakingly comprehensive examination carried out over a period of eight months. Determined that the judgment rendered by his tribunal be considered authoritative, and so permanently discredit and erase the previous ruling, Bréhal brought the same careful, thorough scholarship to the process that he had used when first researching the question of Joan's alleged heresy. A diligent effort was made to solicit statements from all those who were still living who had ever known or come into contact with the Maid, or who could shed light upon the events in question, and the result was that scores of people testified on her behalf—some 115 in all. Moreover, as it was recognized that many of these witnesses were now older and might find it difficult or inconvenient to travel, the inquisitor made the innovative decision to physically move the court from place to place, and in particular to those towns where Joan herself had appeared, on the grounds that it was at these venues that the judges would be most likely to find informants. Additionally, in order that no evidence be overlooked or neglected, the proceedings were made public and the sessions opened to spectators, of which there were many, for persons of both the very highest and lowest birth were heard with equal attention. In a further effort to reach the largest audience possible, proclamations were read out in all the public squares by the local town criers well in advance of the tribunal's visit, summoning anyone who could give testimony to appear before the court on a specific date.

The result was a collective catharsis staged at the national level, in which not only Joan but the entire French populace achieved redemption. The inquisitor remained in Paris throughout November 1455, and it was here that spectators were treated to the stirring eyewitness reports of great men like the Bastard (now raised to the count of Dunois) and the duke of Alençon, who relived in vivid detail the mesmerizing, miraculous events leading up to the lifting of the siege of Orléans and beyond to the coronation at Reims, in what each now recognized to be among the most glorious adventures of the kingdom's long history. From Paris, the tribunal moved to Rouen, where it sat in session from the twelfth of December through the twentieth and where the audience was electrified by the evidence of Guillaume Manchon, the notary from Joan's Trial of Condemnation, who testified that Pierre Cauchon and others had deliberately conspired to falsify the official records, offering as proof a number of original documents that he had retained for over two decades, and which he now placed into the hands of the inquisitor. In January, Bréhal sent a representative to Joan's home village of Domrémy to take depositions from her neighbors and childhood friends, as well as acquaintances and supporters from around the region, including two of the men who had made up the Maid's original escort from Vaucouleurs to the royal court at Chinon in 1429. The final location was Orléans, where so many witnesses came forward that the tribunal was forced to stay in session for a full three weeks, from February 22 to March 16, in order to hear all the evidence.

Out of these numerous and passionate attestations, the portrait of Joan as she is known today was recorded for history and seared into the consciousness of the kingdom like an engraving etched into a metal plate. There was brave Joan again on the banks of the Loire as the Bastard first remembered her: "Bearing in her hand her standard which was white and upon which was the image of Our Lord holding a fleur-de-lys in his hand, and she crossed with me and La Hire the river of the Loire, and we entered together the town of Orléans." And again with the duke of Alençon just before the decisive battle of Patay: "Many of the King's men were afraid [and] Joan said: 'In

God's name, we must fight them, were they hung from the clouds, we should beat them. . . . The gentle king will have this day greater victory than he ever had and my counsel has told me that they are all ours." And later at Troyes, with the Bastard again an eyewitness: "Then the Maid came and entered the council and spoke these words or nearly: 'Noble Dauphin, order that your people go and besiege the town of Troyes and stay no longer in council, for, in God's name, within three days I will take you into the city of Troyes by love or by force or by courage, and false Burgundy will stand amazed."

And just as powerfully, from the humble people there arose the image of Joan as one of their own, unpretentious and generous: "Willingly did she give alms and gathered in the poor and she would sleep beneath the hood of the hearth that the poor might sleep in her bed." "I often heard it said by Messire Guillaume Front, parish priest during his lifetime at the town of Domrémy, that Joan, called the Maid, was a good and simple girl, pious, well brought up, fearing God, so much so that she had not her equal in the town." "I was, in those days, churchwarden at the church of Domrémy and often did I see Joan come to church, to Mass and to Compline. And when I did not ring the bells for Compline, Joan would catch me and scold me, saying I had not done well; and she even promised to give me some wool if I would be punctual in ringing." Over and over they testified. And, finally, from the transcripts of her Trial of Condemnation, came Joan in her own words: "I call upon God and Our Lady that they send me counsel and comfort and thereafter they send it to me"; "It pleased God thus to do, by a simple Maid to drive out the King's enemies"; "As for the Church, I love her and would wish to sustain her with all my power for our Christian faith. . . . I abide by God who sent me, by the Holy Virgin and all the saints in paradise. And I am of opinion that it is all one and the same thing, God and the Church, and of that one should make no difficulty. Why do you make difficulty over that?" And at the last, her enduring defiance in the face of her tormentor, Pierre Cauchon: "And me, I tell you, consider well ere you call yourself my judge, for you are assuming a great charge."

The tribunal returned to Rouen in May; on the last day of the month provision was made for those who wished to speak in defense of the original condemnation. No witnesses came forward.

On June 10, the investigatory portion of the trial ended, and Jean Bréhal and his fellow judges retired to review the evidence in preparation for delivering a verdict. Ever the scrupulous academic, the inquisitor spent the next

Joan of Arc in her time.

month composing a highly detailed summary of all the material collected, in which the testimony from the retrial was compared point by point with the evidence and arguments obtained from the transcripts of the Trial of Condemnation and the heretical charges were refuted in every case.

At last the judges reached their decision. On July 7, 1456, at nine o'clock in the morning, they convened in the great hall of the palace of the archbishop of Rouen. To emphasize the import of their findings to the kingdom at large, they were attended by the archbishop of Reims and the bishop of Paris among other dignitaries. The archbishop of Reims, as the most senior Church member present, read the verdict aloud to the expectant crowd that had assembled to witness the ceremony:

"In consideration of the request of the d'Arc family against the Bishop of Beauvais, the promoter of criminal proceedings, and the inquisitor of Rouen . . . in consideration of the information . . . and juridical consultations . . . we, in session of our court and having God only before our eyes, say, pronounce, decree and declare that the said trial and sentence [of condemnation] being tainted with fraud, calumny, iniquity, contradiction and manifest errors of fact and of law, including the abjuration, execution and all their consequences, to have been and to be null, invalid, worthless, without effect and annihilated. . . . We break and annul them and declare that they must be destroyed. . . .

"In consideration of Joan's appeal to the Holy See . . . we proclaim that Joan did not contract any taint of infamy and that she shall be and is washed clean of such and, if need be, we wash her clean of such absolutely."

As these words were delivered, a copy of the original transcript of the Trial of Condemnation was dramatically held aloft and torn to pieces as a literal expression of the act of nullification.

The next day, in front of an even larger crowd, and to loud prayers and general rejoicing, the verdict of absolution was repeated at the Old Market, site of the Maid's terrible execution, and a cross erected in her memory.

"And thereafter my voices say to me: 'Take it all in good part, do not whine over thy martyrdom; by it thou shalt come at last to the kingdom of Paradise,'" Joan had once passionately declared to her inquisitors in response to their skepticism and attempts to undermine her commitment to her voices and state of grace. "[And] I firmly believe what my voices have told me, to wit that I shall be saved, as firmly as if I was there already."

Epilogue

✤

IN THE ABSENCE of a formal peace treaty, the verdict delivered in Rouen in 1456 exonerating Joan marked the symbolic end of the Hundred Years War. The last battle against the English had been fought three years earlier at Castillon, in Gascony, near Bayonne. An English force of between seven thousand and ten thousand soldiers, led by the redoubtable Captain Talbot, who had been freed from his Rouen prison in exchange for the peaceful surrender of the town of Falaise in 1450, attacked an entrenched French army, heavily fortified with artillery "both small and great," on July 17, 1453. "The attack commenced with great valor, and each party fought manfully, so the business lasted a full hour; at the end of which, the men-at-arms of the duke of Brittany . . . were sent to relieve the French who had been thus long engaged at the barriers," the successor to Enguerrand de Monstrelet's chronicle reported. "On their arrival, by the aid of God and their own prowess, the English were forced to turn their backs and were beaten down, with all their banners, by these Bretons." The majority of the English army was on foot; only the seventy-five-year-old Talbot remained mounted, and as such made an easy target. The old man's horse was soon struck by a cannonball and fell atop his rider; as Talbot struggled to free himself from the animal's weight, "he was put to death by the French, as he lay under him." With the demise of that extraordinarily valiant commander died the last of England's hopes for the reconquest of France. Bordeaux surrendered on October 19, and in the end only Calais remained to the English, as a sad souvenir of the once glorious legacy of Henry V.

Joan's prophecies were thus fulfilled, and Charles VII recovered his kingdom and remained sovereign of France until his death on July 22, 1461, at the
age of fifty-eight. From a *very* unpromising beginning, Charles matured in
his later years into a competent ruler. He is even credited with implementing
various exemplary reforms, the most significant of which was the maintenance of a standing royal army, an innovation that protected the civilian
population from being preyed on by the many soldiers and mercenaries left
unemployed by the cessation of formal hostilities. It is not difficult to see
where Charles came up with this idea. In January 1457, several years after the
decisive battle at Castillon, he was still haunted by fears of a surprise attack,
for he wrote to the king of Scotland that he was forced "to watch all the
coastline daily . . . from Spain to Picardy, which amounts to more than 450
leagues of land; in which he has continually to keep men-at-arms in great
numbers and in great strength, pay their wages, who do not move from the
said places, and in such a way that all the revenue of Normandy (which is one
of the finest parts and greatest revenues of this kingdom) could not suffice by
100,000 francs to pay the men-at-arms detailed to guard the same." Although
the king died estranged from the dauphin, Queen Marie, who survived her
husband by two years, helped her eldest son arrange for a peaceful succession,
and Yolande of Aragon's grandson ascended to the throne as Louis XI. This
time around, the royal family wasn't taking any chances: the coronation ceremony was held with much pomp and solemnity at Reims within the month.
In a suitably droll twist of historical irony, Philip the Good himself placed
the crown on Louis's head and proclaimed him king.

Despite overwhelming evidence, the role Yolande of Aragon played in
the defeat of the English and the preservation of the French monarchy has
been consistently ignored by historians. Soon after her death, Charles VII
openly acknowledged the debt he owed this remarkable woman in a moving
speech. "The late Yolande, of good memory, queen of Jerusalem and Sicily,
in our youth did us great services in many ways that we hold in perpetual
memory. Our said mother-in-law, after we were excluded from our city of
Paris, received us generously in her lands of Anjou and Maine, and gave us
much advice, support and many services using her goods, people and fortresses to help us against the attacks of our adversaries of England and others." Yolande's grandson, Louis XI, who became known as the Spider King
for his cunning, admired her greatly. The queen of Sicily, he once famously
recalled, "bore a man's heart inside a woman's body."

So accomplished a statesman was Yolande, and so cleverly did she hide her tracks, that the myth that Joan of Arc appeared at Charles's court and convinced the king of his birthright unaided by any mortal being has stood unchallenged for nearly six hundred years. Still, if it is accepted, as it is often said, that without Joan of Arc there would be no France, it is also true that without Yolande of Aragon there would have been no Joan.

Nor does penetrating the mystery of the Maid's introduction to Charles detract in any way from the miraculous nature of her achievement. What is important about Joan is not that she heard voices, or presented the king with a special trinket, but her ferocious courage and unwavering faith. It was her willingness to fight for what she believed against seemingly insurmountable odds that has secured her place in history as an iconic figure. At her core, Joan is testimony to the transcendence of the human spirit.

Joan of Arc was canonized in 1920. She remains an inspiration, not only to the citizens of France, but to oppressed people everywhere.

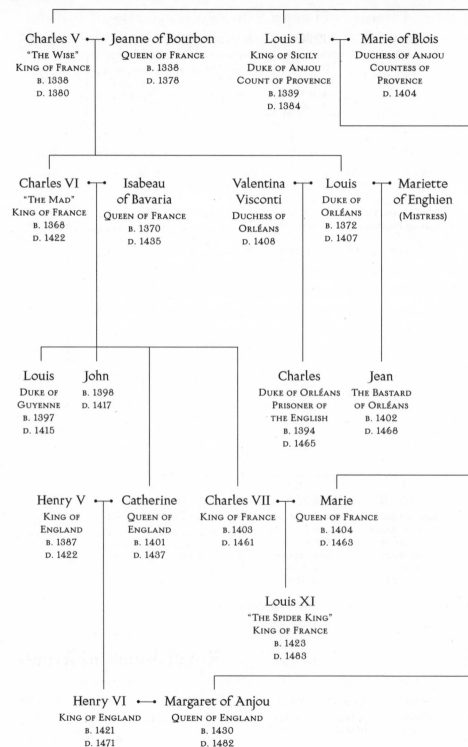

Charles V
"THE WISE"
KING OF FRANCE
B. 1338
D. 1380

Jeanne of Bourbon
QUEEN OF FRANCE
B. 1338
D. 1378

Louis I
KING OF SICILY
DUKE OF ANJOU
COUNT OF PROVENCE
B. 1339
D. 1384

Marie of Blois
DUCHESS OF ANJOU
COUNTESS OF
PROVENCE
D. 1404

Charles VI
"THE MAD"
KING OF FRANCE
B. 1368
D. 1422

**Isabeau
of Bavaria**
QUEEN OF FRANCE
B. 1370
D. 1435

**Valentina
Visconti**
DUCHESS OF
ORLÉANS
D. 1408

Louis
DUKE OF
ORLÉANS
B. 1372
D. 1407

**Mariette
of Enghien**
(MISTRESS)

Louis
DUKE OF
GUYENNE
B. 1397
D. 1415

John
B. 1398
D. 1417

Charles
DUKE OF ORLÉANS
PRISONER OF
THE ENGLISH
B. 1394
D. 1465

Jean
THE BASTARD
OF ORLÉANS
B. 1402
D. 1468

Henry V
KING OF
ENGLAND
B. 1387
D. 1422

Catherine
QUEEN OF
ENGLAND
B. 1401
D. 1437

Charles VII
KING OF FRANCE
B. 1403
D. 1461

Marie
QUEEN OF FRANCE
B. 1404
D. 1463

Louis XI
"THE SPIDER KING"
KING OF FRANCE
B. 1423
D. 1483

Henry VI
KING OF ENGLAND
B. 1421
D. 1471

Margaret of Anjou
QUEEN OF ENGLAND
B. 1430
D. 1482

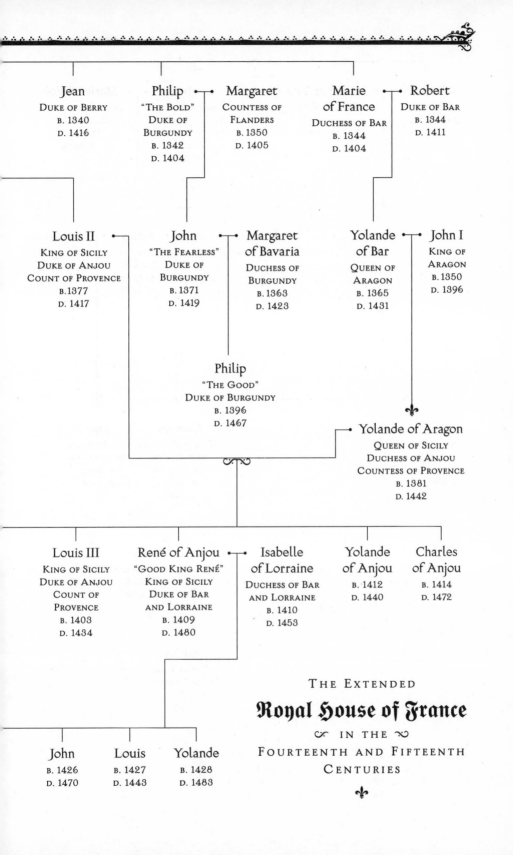

Jean
DUKE OF BERRY
B. 1340
D. 1416

Philip
"THE BOLD"
DUKE OF
BURGUNDY
B. 1342
D. 1404

Margaret
COUNTESS OF
FLANDERS
B. 1350
D. 1405

Marie
of France
DUCHESS OF BAR
B. 1344
D. 1404

Robert
DUKE OF BAR
B. 1344
D. 1411

Louis II
KING OF SICILY
DUKE OF ANJOU
COUNT OF PROVENCE
B.1377
D. 1417

John
"THE FEARLESS"
DUKE OF
BURGUNDY
B. 1371
D. 1419

Margaret
of Bavaria
DUCHESS OF
BURGUNDY
B. 1363
D. 1423

Yolande
of Bar
QUEEN OF
ARAGON
B. 1365
D. 1431

John I
KING OF
ARAGON
B. 1350
D. 1396

Philip
"THE GOOD"
DUKE OF BURGUNDY
B. 1396
D. 1467

Yolande of Aragon
QUEEN OF SICILY
DUCHESS OF ANJOU
COUNTESS OF PROVENCE
B. 1381
D. 1442

Louis III
KING OF SICILY
DUKE OF ANJOU
COUNT OF
PROVENCE
B. 1403
D. 1434

René of Anjou
"GOOD KING RENÉ"
KING OF SICILY
DUKE OF BAR
AND LORRAINE
B. 1409
D. 1480

Isabelle
of Lorraine
DUCHESS OF BAR
AND LORRAINE
B. 1410
D. 1453

Yolande
of Anjou
B. 1412
D. 1440

Charles
of Anjou
B. 1414
D. 1472

John
B. 1426
D. 1470

Louis
B. 1427
D. 1443

Yolande
B. 1428
D. 1483

THE EXTENDED
Royal House of France
↭ IN THE ↭
FOURTEENTH AND FIFTEENTH
CENTURIES

ACKNOWLEDGMENTS

A BOOK THAT SEEKS TO unravel the hopelessly tangled threads of French politics during the latter half of the Hundred Years War, and relies so heavily upon primary sources in French (or, worse, medieval French!), would simply not have been possible for me without the help of my friend Marie-Paule de Valdivia, a native French speaker. Marie-Paule was unerringly patient and encouraging with my own feeble efforts at translation, and is responsible for all of the longer passages, including that marvelous letter from Yolande's agents describing Charles VII's coronation at Reims, which has never been translated fully into English before. I am so proud to be her friend, and so grateful for her elegant phrasing and generosity. Thank you, Marie-Paule.

I am also indebted to Dr. Linda Gray, another close friend, for her help in determining the probable date of Charles VII's conception. It was wonderful to be able to apply Linda's modern medical knowledge and experience to this centuries-long mystery. I had so much fun tackling this problem with her, and we were surely the only two people in the country engaged in a prolonged discussion of medieval menstrual cycles. A thank-you also to her husband, Dr. Greg Soloway, for his aid in researching the various psychoses associated with adolescent delusions or the hearing of voices. Although there was not in the end sufficient evidence to include a definitive diagnosis in the book, his efforts enriched my perspective on Joan and her angels.

Similarly, this book would not have been possible without the insights into Jean of Arras's work provided by Donald Maddox and his wife, Sara Sturm-Maddox, both professors of French and Italian at the University of Massachusetts at Amherst. Their book *Melusine of Lusignan: Founding Fiction in Late Medieval France,* which grew out of an international colloquium commemorating the six hundredth anniversary of the writing of *The Romance of*

Melusine, was an invaluable resource to me. I know they have recently completed a new, more accessible translation of *Melusine,* which I look forward to reading—currently there is no modern translation available. As recognized experts in the field, no two authors are better suited to this task. I am also very grateful to and wish to recognize the work of Dawn Bratsch-Prince, professor of Spanish and department chair at Iowa State University. Professor Bratsch-Prince's scholarship on Yolande of Aragon's mother, Yolande of Bar (Violant in Spanish), added greatly to my understanding of the politics of the court of Aragon, particularly as she very kindly translated some of it from the Spanish for me.

Also necessary to the writing of this book was Sue Madeo, who coordinates the interlibrary loan program at the Westport Public Library and who, as usual, helped me to obtain sources from academic libraries all over the state. And my friend and fellow author Wendy Kann read the book in manuscript for me and pinpointed all the places that needed work, which was a huge help. I am also so grateful to her for her unflagging encouragement and for her suggestions on how to bring the story to life.

I must also profusely thank my editor at Viking, Carolyn Carlson, both for her (greatly appreciated!) enthusiasm for my work and for her incisive read. I have never had more helpful or spot-on editorial suggestions; the manuscript was demonstrably improved by her efforts, and she was always available to toss around ideas. This book was so much fun to do with her. And, of course, I must thank my fabulous agent, Michael Carlisle, who is always fun! Michael saw this book immediately, and has been so encouraging and committed to my work throughout our relationship—I am truly fortunate to have him on my side.

And finally, to my family, on whose love and support I rely every day. To my daughter, Emily, who hunted around in used bookstores to find me a volume of medieval women mystics for Christmas, a special thank-you— that book really helped me to place Joan in historical context. I love you so much and am so proud to be your mother! And to my husband, Larry, who once again put down his own work to walk me (and the dog) through seemingly endless medieval battle plans and political machinations, whose insights greatly enriched this book, and whose belief in me is tangible, thank you, thank you, I love you.

NOTES

xvi "The Sunday . . . because none dared any longer stay in them": Pernoud, *Joan of Arc: By Herself and Her Witnesses*, 72–74.
xvi "day of the herrings": Ibid., 76.
xvi "found themselves squeezed": Ibid., 79.

EPIGRAPHS

xxi "For full fayne": Couldrette, *The Romans of Partenay, or of Lusignen: Otherwise Known as the Tale of Melusine*, 1.
xxi "Consider the effect": Boase, *The Troubadour Revival*, 129–130. Italics added.

CHAPTER 1: The Kingdom of the Gay Science

3 She was born in Barcelona on August 11, 1381: Miron, *The Queens of Aragon: Their Lives and Times*, 217.
5 *The Book in which*: Pedro IV of Aragon, *Chronicle*, Part One, 132.
6 She read voraciously: Baudot, *Les Princesses Yolande et les Ducs de Bar*, 99.
6 the same superior education that she herself . . . had received: On the literacy of the French royal family, Christine de Pizan, a contemporary of Marie's who wrote a biography of Charles V, noted, "By the astute upbringing of his father, he was fully instructed in classical letters such that he understood latin fluently and knew well enough the rules of grammar." ["La sage administracion du père le fist introduire en lettres moult souffisanment et tant que competenment entendoit son latin et suffisanment scavoit les rigles de grammaire."] Baudot, *Les Princesses Yolande et les Ducs de Bar*, 100. Translation by Marie-Paule de Valdivia.

Charles was not the only member of the family to receive this exemplary formal education—it seems that all of his siblings were given the same training, although some benefited from it more than others. One of Charles's brothers, the duke of Berry, would become a famous book collector.

6 a glum letter: Boase, *The Troubadour Revival*, 89.

6 Perhaps to assuage the terrible grief: Bratsch-Prince, "A Queen's Task," 25. Yolande of Aragon had only one brother, Jaume, who lived to be four years old; none of her other siblings survived beyond eight months.

6 "But this was taken to such exaggerated lengths": Boase, *The Troubadour Revival*, 124.

6 "what in bygone days": Ibid., 124.

7 "All earthly things are moved by her": Ibid., 130. "Documents from the royal archives show that [King John] . . . attributed almost miraculous properties to the art of troubadour poetry known as the Gay Science," wrote medieval scholar Roger Boase, ibid., 154.

7 "after having for a long time viewed": Freeman, "A Book of Hours Made for the Duke of Berry," 104.

7 Yolande had his entire library transferred: Kibre, "The Intellectual Interests Reflected in Libraries of the Fourteenth and Fifteenth Centuries," 271.

8 a particularly audacious thief: Senneville, *Yolande d'Aragon*, 39.

8 Convinced that the incident was miraculous: Ibid., 40.

10 "The adventure is this": Sara Sturm-Maddox, "Crossed Destinies: Narrative Programs in the *Roman de Mélusine*," in Maddox and Sturm-Maddox, eds., *Melusine of Lusignan*, 16.

10 "O Lord God!": Couldrette, *The Romans of Partenay, or of Lusignen: Otherwise Known as the Tale of Melusine*, 14.

11 "In God's name, Raymondin": Nadia Margolis, "Myths in Progress: A Literary-Typological Comparison of Melusine and Joan of Arc," in Maddox and Sturm-Maddox, eds., *Melusine of Lusignan*, 247.

11 "huge mouth and large great nostrils": Couldrette, *The Romans of Partenay*, 46.

11 "though he could see more clearly": Ibid., 49.

12 "Evil was the hour": Laurence de Looze, "'La fourme du pié toute escripte': Melusine and the Entrance into History," in Maddox and Sturm-Maddox, eds. *Melusine of Lusignan*, 126, 127, 131.

12 "Melusine came to Lusignan": Maddox and Sturm-Maddox, eds., *Melusine of Lusignan*, 1.

12 "if not in the air": Ibid., 130.

12 "to tell the last English tenant": Stephen G. Nichols, "Melusine Between Myth and History: Profile of a Female Demon," in Maddox and Sturm-Maddox, eds., *Melusine of Lusignan*, 159.

13 "It is in Jean d'Arras": Ibid., 162.

14 printed in Geneva in 1478: Couldrette, *The Romans of Partenay*, x.

14 Significantly, in 1444 the court of Lorraine: Baudot, *Les Princesses Yolande et les Ducs de Bar,* 364.

14 "And to the pleasure": Couldrette, *The Romans of Partenay,* ix.

14 "for the amusement of Marie of France": Baudot, *Les Princesses Yolande et les Ducs de Bar,* 121.

15 "political education of the children": Ibid., 123.

15 Jean of Arras even based two: Ibid., 363.

15 "Very noble lord dauphin": Pernoud and Clin, *Joan of Arc: Her Story,* 22.

CHAPTER 2: To Be a Queen

16 In 1388, when John impatiently threatened: Bisson, *The Medieval Crown of Aragon,* 123.

16 "She was very interested in the affairs of state": ["Que s'interessava molt pels afers de l'estat I volia tenir sempre al seu costat, valent-se de les arts d'una dona que se sap estimada, el seu marit."] Bratsch-Prince, "A Queen's Task," 24. Translation by Dawn Bratsch-Prince.

18 "400 lances": Senneville, *Yolande d'Aragon,* 23.

18 "And for certain this lady": ["Et pour certain ceste dame avoit bien l'astuce de sçavoir congnoistre céulx qui luy povoient servir et ayder. Et quant elle les congnoissoit, elle avoit bien la grâce de les gaigner et retenir, car elle estoit libéralle, gracieus et affable. Et oultre estoit songneuse, diligent, et en magnanimité de cueur et virilles entre-prinses excédoit maintz princes de son temps, parquoy elle estoit de chascun fort crainte, prisée et estimée."] Bourdigné, *Chroniques d'Anjou et du Maine,* 121. Translation by Marie-Paule de Valdivia.

19 by knighting Louis II at a grand celebration: For details of the knighting ceremony see *Chronique du Religieux de Saint-Denys,* vol. 1, 589–599.

19 the pope crowned twelve-year-old Louis II king: For details of the coronation ceremony see Bourdigné, *Chroniques d'Anjou et du Maine,* 117, and Senneville, *Yolande d'Aragon,* 24.

20 To extricate the crown of Aragon: Senneville, *Yolande d'Aragon,* 27.

20 Charles VI hastily offered the hand of his own daughter: Famiglietti, *Royal Intrigue,* 36.

22 "This princess captivated all eyes": ["Cette princess captivait tous les regards par sa rare beauté, par les charmes de son visage et par l'air de dignité répandu sur toute sa personne. C'était en un mot un véritable trésor de grâces. Au dire des gens, sages, la nature avait pris plaisir à la former et l'avait comblée de toutes les perfections; il ne suffira de dira qu'aucune femme ne méritait de lui être comparée."] *Chronique du Religieux de Saint-Denys,* vol. 1, 773. Translation by Marie-Paule de Valdivia.

22 "one of the most beautiful creatures": Kekewich, *The Good King,* 15, footnote 11.

23 "with all expressions of honor and joy": Senneville, *Yolande d'Aragon,* 30.

25 "it was joyful to see": ["ilz estoient si joyeulx de veoir la fervente et cordialle amour qui estoit entre ces deux jeunes gens"] Bourdigné, *Chroniques d'Anjou et du Maine,* 123.

26 "For twenty-two years": ["Pendant vingt-deux ans en effect elle administra avec tant d'ordre et de prévoyance les revenus de la Provence, de l'Anjou et du Maine, qu'elle put soutenir à ses frais, un nom de son fils aîné Louis, la guerre de Naples commencée par son père, tout en donnant à ce fils de quoi tenir en état de roi. Ses conseillers intimes assurent qu'elle amassa sur les revenus de ses domaines un trésor particulier de deux cent mille écus d'or."] *Chronique du Religieux de Saint-Denys,* vol. 2, 215. Translation by Marie-Paule de Valdivia.

27 "When her last hour approached": ["Voyant approcher sa dernière heure, elle reçut devotement les sacrements de l'Église; après quoi elle fit venir son fils et lui révéla ce secret. Le jeune prince justement étonné lui demanda avec douceur pourquoi, dans le temps où il avait été presque réduit à la détresse, elle ne l'avait pas secouru plus généreusement. Elle lui répondit qu'elle avait craint de le voir prisonnier, et qu'elle avait toujours voulu lui tenir cet argent en réserve, pour lui épargner la honte de mendier sa rançon de tour côtés."] Ibid., 215. Translation by Marie-Paule de Valdivia.

CHAPTER 3: The Mad King of France

29 "The Duke of Burgundy": Froissart, *Chronicles of England, France, Spain and the Adjoining Countries,* vol. 1, 295.

29 "The clattering on the helmets": Ibid., 260–261.

32 "I feel I have not long to live": Ibid., 190.

33 "Tell my uncle, the Duke of Burgundy": Bearne, *Pictures of the Old French Court,* 117.

34 "with many thanks": Kitchin, *A History of France,* 484.

34 "The bells were ringing": ["Les cloches furent mises en branle, et pour faire connaitre à tous les Français le nouvel et joyeux événement survenu dans la ville, on envoya de tous côtés, au nom du roi, des courriers chargés de répandre dans le royaume l'heureuse nouvelle de la naissance du prince."] *Chronique du Religieux de Saint-Denys,* vol. 1, 733. Translation by Marie-Paule de Valdivia.

35 "with much diligence": ["avec beaucoup de zèle"] Ibid., 735.

35 "The first words the King said": Froissart, *Chronicles of England, France, Spain and the Adjoining Countries,* vol. 2, 94–95.

36 "He had been the whole summer": Ibid., 99.

36 "unbecoming to royalty": Famiglietti, *Royal Intrigue,* 2.

36 "Go no further, great king": Ibid., 2.

36 "Advance, advance": Froissart, *Chronicles of England, France, Spain and the Adjoining Countries,* vol. 2, 100.

38 "when . . . she [Isabeau] approached": Gibbons, "Isabeau of Bavaria, Queen of France," 61, footnote 41.

39 openly conducting an affair: For recent scholarship on the issue of Isabeau's infidelity, see Famiglietti, *Royal Intrigue,* 44.

40 "They [Isabeau and the duke of Orléans] could be reproached": Gibbons, "Isabeau of Bavaria, Queen of France," 63, footnote 49.

40 "sounder part": Famiglietti, *Royal Intrigue,* 28.

40 And the next year . . . gemstone that had caught his eye: Ibid., 39.

41 so affected by this death: *Chronique du Religieux de Saint-Denys,* vol. 2, 731.

42 "I am the Duc d'Orléans!": Bearne, *Pictures of the Old French Court,* 238.

CHAPTER 4: Civil War

44 "Ah, cousin": ["Ah, cousin, vous avez fait un mauvais acte!"] Bourdigné, *Chroniques d'Anjou et du Maine,* 135.

45 "About the end of August": *A Parisian Journal,* 52.

45 "The King of France arrived with his army": Ibid., 66–67.

46 "Know with certainty": Famiglietti, *Royal Intrigue,* 118.

47 It is a simple matter . . . from the guest list: For the guest list for the marriage ceremony see *Chronique du Religieux de Saint-Denys,* vol. 3, 231. ["La cérémonie se fit au château royal du Louvre, en présence de l'auguste reine, de Louis, roi de Sicile, des ducs de Guienne et d'Orléans, des comtes de Vertus, d'Eu et d'Armagnac."]

48 Yolande received six hanaps . . . and a ring from the queen of France: Beaucourt, *Histoire de Charles VII,* tome I, 16, footnote.

48 "Three months": ["Depuis trois mois"] *Chronique du Religieux de Saint-Denys,* vol. 2, 294.

50 "Alarm! Alarm!": Beaucourt, *Histoire de Charles VII,* tome I, 11.

51 "For the great love of nourishment": Besant, *Essays and Historiettes,* 6.

52 "Bonne Mère": Senneville, *Yolande d'Aragon,* 89.

53 "Then, by moving it to and fro": Barker, *Agincourt,* 32.

53 a meeting between the French and the English in July 1415: For details of this meeting, see Jacob, *The Fifteenth Century,* 142.

54 "simply did not happen": Barker, *Agincourt,* 69.

54 "looking like a couple of baby owls": Ibid., 59.

56 "their numbers were so great": Ibid., 247.

56 "There is no doubt": Ibid., 250.

57 the sickening waste of human life: For the estimated number of French dead at Agincourt see Famiglietti, *Royal Intrigue,* 168, and Barker, *Agincourt,* 299. For the number of English dead, see Barker, *Agincourt,* 304.

CHAPTER 5: A New Dauphin

59 John the Fearless's reaction: "In fact, John was happy to watch the flower of the Armagnacs lose their lives 'for France' at the battle of Agincourt." Jones, ed., *The New Cambridge Medieval History*, vol. 6, 585.

62 "he clasped [Charles] many times in his arms": ["On rapporte qu'il serra plusieurs fois le Dauphin dans ses bras, en lui recommandant de ne jamais se fier au duc de Bourgognes, mais d'employer cependant tous les moyens possibles pour vivre en bonne intelligence avec lui."] La Marche, *Le Roi René*, 34.

63 In his will: For details of Louis II's will see ibid., 34.

64 "the Queen was deprived of everything": *A Parisian Journal*, 103.

64 "the consent of our very dear lord": Senneville, *Yolande d'Aragon*, 110.

65 "persons of low rank": Famiglietti, *Royal Intrigue*, 184.

66 "Indeed, it is perfectly true": *A Parisian Journal*, 107.

67 "Then Paris was in an uproar": Ibid., 112.

68 "Vive le duc de Bourgogne!": Ibid., 113.

69 "to the great annoyance": Ibid., 112.

69 "The people, bitterly inflamed": Ibid., 114.

70 "until we have had the advice": Vale, *Charles VII*, 23, and Beaucourt, *Histoire de Charles VII*, Tome I, 101.

70 "We have not nurtured": Senneville, *Yolande d'Aragon*, 119.

70 "I know very well": Vale, *Charles VII*, 26.

71 "Those who get power": Ibid.

71 "the kiss of peace": Famiglietti, *Royal Intrigue*, 190.

CHAPTER 6: Childhood in Domrémy

77 "In my town they called me Jeannette": Pernoud, *Joan of Arc: By Herself and Her Witnesses*, 15.

77 "As far as I know": Ibid.

77 "Jacques Tarc": Smith, *Joan of Arc*, 11.

77 "dressed in poor clothes": Ibid., 49.

77 "[I] knew neither A nor B": Ibid., 10.

78 "It was from my mother": Pernoud, *Joan of Arc: By Herself and Her Witnesses*, 16–17.

78 "This girl spoke terribly well": Pernoud and Clin, *Joan of Arc: Her Story*, 28.

79 "When I was quite big": Pernoud, *Joan of Arc: By Herself and Her Witnesses*, 20.

79 "Life [in Domrémy] was like the countryside": Smith, *Joan of Arc*, 13.

80 "Did the people of Domrémy": Pernoud, *Joan of Arc: By Herself and Her Witnesses*, 20.

80 "Bar and Lorraine could provide invaluable links": Kekewich, *The Good King*, 21.

81 "Yolande had pulled off a double *coup*": Ibid.

81 "Now it is true": ["Or est vray que ledit cardinal donna et fist son héritier dudit Regné son nepveu, et luy donna et délaissa la duchie de Bar et pluiseurs aultres belles seignouries; et par le moyen d'icelles seignouries, et aussi qu'il estoit filz de roy, issu de la très crestienne maison de France, la fille et héritière de la duchie de Lorrayne luy fut donnée en mariage; qui fut ung grant bien pour les duchies de Bar et de Lorraine; car, de long temps avoit eu en icelles seignouries guerres et divisions, qui par icelluy mariage furent en paix et unies soubz ung seul seigneur."] *Chronique de Jean Le Févre, Seigneur de Saint-Remy: 1420–1435,* tome second, 258.

82 "that he should give me his son": Pernoud and Clin, *Joan of Arc: Her Story,* 19.

83 "In your extreme youth": Pernoud, *Joan of Arc: By Herself and Her Witnesses,* 20.

84 "*Item,* In view of the horrific and enormous crimes": ["*Item,* vu les horribles et énormes délits commis dans ledit royaume de France par Charles, soi-disant dauphin de Viennois, il est entendu que ni nous, ni notredit fils Henri, ni notre très-cher fils le duc de Bourgogne, ne traiterons aucunement de paix ou d'alliance avec ledit Charles."] *Chronique du Religieux de Saint-Denys,* vol. 3, 429. See also Gibbons, "Isabeau of Bavaria," 70, footnote, for translation.

84 "One should not take account": Vale, *Charles VII,* 31.

85 "He didn't willingly arm himself": Ibid., 35.

86 "All the people in the streets": *A Parisian Journal,* 181–182.

86 "Thus his body was borne along": Ibid.

86 "'God grant life to Henry'": ["'Dieu donne vie à Henri, par la grâce de Dieu, roi de France et d'Angleterre, notre souverain Seigneur.' Alors, les hérauts redres- sèrent leurs masses et crièrent d'une seule voix: 'Vive le roi! Vive le roi!'"] Senne- ville, *Yolande d'Aragon,* 161.

86 "and there were many heralds": Waurin, *A Collection of the Chronicles and Ancient Histories of Great Britain, Now Called England,* 3.

86 "Then there was raised a banner": Ibid.

87 "French historians have speculated": Smith, *Joan of Arc,* 21.

88 "the king of Bourges": Vale, *Charles VII,* 3.

88 "In the town of Maxey": Pernoud, *Joan of Arc: By Herself and Her Witnesses,* 20.

88 "to a fortified place": Ibid.

88 "Jeannette would go often": Ibid., 16–17.

89 "She was brought up in the Christian religion": Ibid., 17.

89 "the captain-general of the armies of heaven": Smith, *Joan of Arc,* 32.

89 she would have learned about the lives of these saints: Wood, *Joan of Arc and Richard III,* 133–134. Wrote Professor Wood, "It seems far from coincidental that the feast days of these three saints are celebrated in autumn or that they follow each other in suggestive sequence: Michael on September 29, Margaret on Octo- ber 8, and Catherine on November 25. For in that sequence, and in the saintly attributes that would have been stressed in sermons and homilies, there emerge a host of problems with which Joan would have strongly identified as well as tales

of success in surmounting them that suggested personal qualities which would prove central to her maturing sense of being."

91 "In this same year": Waurin, *A Collection of the Chronicles and Ancient Histories of Great Britain, Now Called England*, 15.

91 "The said English": Ibid., 16.

91 "There can be little doubt": Vale, *Charles VII*, 35.

92 "France, ruined by a woman": ["Prophetisatum fuit quod Francia per mulierem deperderetur et per unam virginem de Marchiis Lotharingiae restauraretur."] Quicherat, *Procès*, III, 83. See also Vale, *Charles VII*, 50, footnote 4.

92 "a Maid [a virgin] would come": Pernoud and Clin, *Joan of Arc: Her Story*, 30.

CHAPTER 7: The Angels Speak to Joan

94 "The first time that I heard the voice": Pernoud, *Joan of Arc: By Herself and Her Witnesses*, 23–24.

95 "When I was thirteen years old": Ibid., 30.

95 "What made you cause . . . no promise whatever": Ibid., 23.

95 "I obeyed them [her parents] in all things": Ibid.

95 "The first time I had great doubt": Ibid., 31.

96 "How was it that you recognized . . . that it was him": Ibid.

96 "When I was still in the house": Ibid., 23.

97 "I believed it quite quickly": Ibid., 31.

97 "What doctrines . . . in the Kingdom of France": Ibid.

97 "We should not let any": ["que en icelle on ne laisse entrer aucunes gens d'armes plus fors que les gens de la ville, soit le Roy nostre sire, le président en sa compaignie, qui de lui a le principal gouvernement, ou autres de ses gouverneurs qui perturbent et empeschent la dicte paix, et lesquelx monseigneur de Richemont, connestable de France, et la dicte Royne entendent à mettre briefvement hors de la compaignie et gouvernement du Roy"] Beaucourt, *Histoire de Charles VII*, tome II, 95.

98 "a fat man of about forty": ["un gros homme d'une quarantaine d'années"] Lavisse, *Histoire de France Depuis les Origines*, tome quatrième, 25.

98 "Dear cousin": Vale, *Charles VII*, 39–40.

99 the duke of Bedford very publicly summoned a war council: For more on the war council see Ramsay, *Lancaster and York*, 378; also Stevenson, *Letters and Papers Illustrative of the Wars of the English in France*, vol. 2, part 2, 533.

99 "The voice told me": Pernoud, *Joan of Arc: By Herself and Her Witnesses*, 30.

99 "As for my father and my mother": Ibid., 32.

99 "I went to my uncle's": Ibid., 32–33.

100 "I went myself to fetch Joan": Ibid., 33.

100 "Joan the Maid came to Vaucouleurs": Ibid., 33–34.

100 "This Robert several times told me": Ibid., 33.

101 the war intervened: For more on the campaign in Champagne see Pernoud and Clin, *Joan of Arc: Her Story*, 17, and Stevenson, *Letters and Papers Illustrative of the Wars of the English in France*, vol. 2, part 2, 531, 535.

102 "the queen of Sicily and those whom she was pleased to designate": ["[I]ls demandaient que la reine de Sicile et ceux qui'il lui plairait de désigner, fussent chargés de veiller à l'exécution des délibérations prises."] Beaucourt, *Histoire de Charles VII*, tome II, 166.

103 "How this Herry in the eight degree": McKenna, "Henry VI of England and the Dual Monarchy," 153.

104 "never again had joy in her heart": Famiglietti, *Royal Intrigue*, 44.

104 "at the beginning of the month of June": ["Au commencement du mois de juin, le duc de Bourgogne, ayant appris la guérison du roi."] *Chronique du Religieux de Saint-Denys*, vol. 2, 35.

104 "you are the son of a king": ["Tu es fils de roi."] Senneville, *Yolande d'Aragon*, 207. Senneville remarks upon the similiarity between Yolande's words and those used by Joan of Arc at her initial meeting with Charles.

104 "saying nothing, but begging God": Vale, *Charles VII*, 52.

105 "I must be at the King's side": Pernoud, *Joan of Arc: By Herself and Her Witnesses*, 35.

106 "the prosperity of the king's arms": Wood, *Joan of Arc and Richard III*, 138.

106 "The voice told me": Pernoud, *Joan of Arc: By Herself and Her Witnesses*, 30.

106 "At the time when Joan sought to leave the town": Ibid., 36.

107 "not thus that they should depart": Pernoud and Clin, *Joan of Arc: Her Story*, 18.

107 "The register of the Archives of La Meuse": France, *The Life of Joan of Arc*, vol. 1, 93, footnote 1.

108 "I saw Robert de Baudricourt": Smith, *Joan of Arc*, 50.

108 "When Joan the Maid came": Pernoud, *Joan of Arc: By Herself and Her Witnesses*, 35.

108 "I asked her if she wanted to go in her own clothes": Ibid.

109 "The Duke of Lorraine required": Ibid., 38.

109 René sat in on this audience: His biographer Margaret Kekewich wrote that René "probably saw her [Joan] when she presented herself . . . at Nancy early in 1429 and asked the duke to send him with men-at-arms to escort her into France." Kekewich, *The Good King*, 24. A. Lecoy de la Marche, René's definitive biographer, citing primary documentation, also placed René in Nancy during this time period, and agreed that he was most likely present at this audience. See La Marche, *Le Roi René*, tome premier, 69.

109 "had told him [the duke] that he was behaving badly": Pernoud, *Joan of Arc: By Herself and Her Witnesses*, 38.

110 "Precisely because her assumptions accorded so well": Wood, *Joan of Arc and Richard III*, 139.

110 "Robert twice refused and repulsed me": Pernoud, *Joan of Arc: By Herself and Her Witnesses*, 34.

111 "Robert de Baudricourt caused those": Ibid., 39.

Chapter 8: Joan Meets the Dauphin

112 "When I arrived at the town": Pernoud and Clin, *Joan of Arc: Her Story*, 15.

112 "because of the Burgundian and English soldiers": Pernoud, *Joan of Arc: By Herself and Her Witnesses*, 39.

113 "Afterwards I heard those who took her": Ibid.

113 "every night she lay down": Ibid., 39–40.

113 "She never swore": Ibid., 40.

113 "The Maid always told us to have no fear": Ibid.

113 "I sent letters to my King": Ibid., 48.

114 "I know that, when Joan arrived in Chinon": Ibid., 48–49.

114 "There is no evidence of opposition": Vale, *Charles VII*, 50.

114 "Orliac [a noted French historian] assigns a major role": Kekewich, *The Good King*, 25.

115 "When she [Joan] entered the castle": Pernoud, *Joan of Arc: By Herself and Her Witnesses*, 49.

115 "There were more than three hundred knights": Ibid., 47.

115 "When the King knew that she was coming": Ibid., 49.

115 "It was essential": Vale, *Charles VII*, 51.

116 "When I entered my King's room": Pernoud, *Joan of Arc: By Herself and Her Witnesses*, 46.

116 "I was myself present at the castle": Pernoud and Clin, *Joan of Arc: Her Story*, 22.

116 "when a messenger came to tell me": Ibid., 26.

116 "When [the king] saw her, he asked Joan her name": Ibid., 23.

117 "In God's name": Pernoud, *Joan of Arc: By Herself and Her Witnesses*, 55–56.

117 "the secret prayer": Wood, *Joan of Arc and Richard III*, 148.

118 "I say to you, on behalf of the Lord": Pernoud and Clin, *Joan of Arc: Her Story*, 23.

118 "the king seemed radiant": Ibid.

118 "To introduce a prophetess to the impressionable Charles": Vale, *Charles VII*, 50.

118 "Joan came to the king's mass": Pernoud and Clin, *Joan of Arc: Her Story*, 27.

119 "Joan ran about charging with a lance": Ibid.

120 "I asked her what language": Ibid., 29.

120 "Finally, it was concluded": Ibid., 30.

120 "In her, Joan, we find": Ibid.

121 "I heard it said that Joan": Ibid., 30–31.

121 "The Master's report having been made": Pernoud, *Joan of Arc: By Herself and Her Witnesses*, 58–59.

122 "on which was painted": Ibid., 60.

122 "An arms merchant of Tours": Ibid., 61–62.

122 "Laden in the town of Blois": Ibid., 81.

123 Joan was by no means the only visionary: For the number of people claiming visions in 1428 see Senneville, *Yolande d'Aragon*, 204.

123 "dressed in cloth-of-gold": Smith, *Joan of Arc,* 36.

123 "I answered this Catherine": Pernoud, *Joan of Arc: By Herself and Her Witnesses,* 142.

123 "When Joan left Blois": Pernoud and Clin, *Joan of Arc: Her Story,* 38–39.

CHAPTER 9: The Maid of Orléans

125 "Jhesus-Maria, King of England": Pernoud, *Joan of Arc: By Herself and Her Witnesses,* 70.

126 "Really the *bastilles* were not to blame": Lang, *The Maid of France,* 68.

127 "God knoweth by what advis": Ibid., 65.

128 "was rendered possible": Burne, *The Agincourt War,* 238.

128 "'Are you the Bastard of Orléans . . . the King of Heaven'": Pernoud and Clin, *Joan of Arc: Her Story,* 39–40.

129 "Forthwith I had the sails hoisted": Pernoud, *Joan of Arc: By Herself and Her Witnesses,* 82.

129 "I then implored her": Ibid., 82.

129 "Came to receive her": Ibid., 83–84.

130 "Joan went to see the Bastard": Ibid., 84.

130 "go away in God's name": Pernoud and Clin, *Joan of Arc: Her Story,* 42.

130 "Glasdale and those of his company": Pernoud, *Joan of Arc: By Herself and Her Witnesses,* 84.

131 "It seems to me": Ibid., 82.

131 "Joan's contribution": Burne, *The Agincourt War,* 244.

131 "The fact that Fort St. Loup": Ibid., 240.

131 "Ah, bleeding boy": Pernoud, *Joan of Arc: By Herself and Her Witnesses,* 86.

132 "The English were preparing their defense": Ibid.

132 "She wept much upon them": Ibid., 86–87.

132 "You, Englishmen, who have no right": Ibid., 87.

132 "Read, it is news!": Ibid.

132 "Joan began to sigh": Ibid.

133 "When they perceived": Ibid., 89.

134 "was afraid and wept": Ibid., 90.

134 "The assault lasted from the morning": Ibid.

134 "And Joan, moved by pity": Ibid., 92.

134 "expressing joy in every way": Pernoud and Clin, *Joan of Arc: Her Story,* 48.

136 "if the English assaulted them": Ibid., 49.

136 "From the King . . . the doing of all these things": Pernoud, *Joan of Arc: By Herself and Her Witnesses,* 97.

137 "Noble Dauphin, hold not such": Ibid., 110.

137 "I remember that": Ibid., 109.

138 "All rallied to her opinion": Ibid.

138 "Lady, fear not": Ibid., 114.

138 "And arrived the Monday at Selles": Ibid., 111.

139 "If it be so": Ibid., 100.

139 "about twelve hundred lances": Ibid., 113.

140 "Be not afraid of any armed host": France, *The Life of Joan of Arc*, vol. 1, 349.

140 "Ah, gentle Duke, wast thou afeared?": Pernoud, *Joan of Arc: By Herself and Her Witnesses*, 114.

140 "That machine . . . will kill thee": Ibid., 114.

140 "Are you a gentleman?": France, *The Life of Joan of Arc*, vol. 1, 354.

141 "And while the English [at Beaugency] were retreating": Pernoud, *Joan of Arc: By Herself and Her Witnesses*, 115–116.

141 "Then the lord Duke of Alençon": Ibid., 117.

143 "And before he had gone": Ibid., 119.

143 "By the renown of Joan the Maid": Ibid., 112.

143 "The French did not give the English archers time": Jacob, *The Fifteenth Century*, 247.

144 "All that [pursuing the English to Paris] means nothing to me": Smith, *Joan of Arc*, 74.

144 "told the King to advance boldly": Pernoud, *Joan of Arc: By Herself and Her Witnesses*, 124.

144 "Loyal Frenchmen, come out": Ibid., 121.

144 "they would pay to the King": Ibid.

144 "So many came": ["Eu autant de gens que c'est chose infinite a escrire et auxi la grande joye que chacun en avoit."] *Les Deux Procès de Condamnation, les Enquêtes et la Sentence de Réhabilitation de Jeanne d'Arc*, 323.

145 "Our Queens and most dread Ladies . . . God knows you were missed": [The full letter reads: "Nos souveraines et très redoutées dames, plaise vous scavoir que yer le Roy arriva en cest ville de Rains ouquel il a trouvé toute et plein obéissance. Aujourd'huy il a esté sacré et couronné et a esté moult belle chose à voir le beau mystère, car il a esté auxi solempnel et accoustré de toutes les besongnes y appartenans auxi bien et si convenablement pour faire la chose tant en abis royaux et autres choses à ce nécessaires comme s'il eust mandé un an auparavant, et y a eu autant de gens que c'est chose infinie a escrire et auxi la grande joye que chacun en avoit. . . .

"Messeigneurs le duc d'Alençon, le comte de Clermont, le conte de Vendosme, les seigneurs de Laval et la Trimoille y ont esté en abis royaux; et monseigneur d'Alençon a fait le Roy chevalier et les dessusditz représentoient les pairs de France; monseigneur d'Albret a tenu l'espée durant ledit mystère devant le Roy et pour les pairs d'Église y estoient avec leurs croces et mitres, messeigneurs de Rains, de Chalons qui sont pairs; et en lieu des autres, les evesques de Seez et d'Orléans et deux autres prélas, et mondit seigneur de Rains y a fait ledit mystère et sacre qui luy appartient.

"Pour aller querir la sainte ampolle en l'abaye de Saint-Remy et pour la apporter en l'église de Nostre-Dame où a esté fait le sacre, fut ordonnez le mareschal de Bossac, les seigneurs de Rays, Graville et l'admiral avec leurs quatre bannières que chacun portoit en sa main, armez de toutes pièces et à cheval, bien accompagnez pour conduire l'abbé dudit lieu qui apportoit ladite ampolle; et entrènt à cheval en ladite grande église et descendirent à l'entrée du chœur et en ceste stat l'ont rendue après le service en ladite abbaye; le service a duré depuis neuf heures jusqu'à deux heures. Et à l'heure que le Roy fut sacré et auxi quand l'on lui assist la couronne sur la teste, tout homme cria Noël! et trompettes sonnèrent en telle manière qu'il sembloit que les voultes de l'église se deussent fendre.

"Et durant ledit mystère, la Pucelle s'est tousjours tenue joignant du Roy, tenant son estendart en sa main. Et estoit moult belle chose de voir les belles manières que tenoit le Roy et aussi la Pucelle. Et Dieu sache si vous y avez esté souhaitées.

"Aujourdhuy ont esté faitz par le Roy contes le sire de Laval et le sire de Sully et Rays mareschal. . . . Demain s'en doibt partir le Roy tenant son chemin vers Paris. On dit en ceste ville que le duc de Bourgongne y a esté et s'en est retourné à Laon où il est de present; il a envoyé si tost devers le Roy qu'il arriva en ceste ville. A ceste heure, nous espérons que bon traité y trouvera avant qu'ils partent. La Pucelle ne fait doubte qu'elle ne mette Paris en l'obéissance.

"Audit sacre, le Roy a fait plusieurs chevaliers et auxi lesdits seigneurs pairs en font tant que marveilles. Il y en a plus de trois cents nouveaux.

"Nos souveraines et redoubtées Dames, nous prions le benoist Saint-Esprit qu'il vous donne bonne vie et longue.

"Escript à Rains, ce dimanche XVII de Juillet. Vos très humbles et obéissans serviteurs, Beauveau, Moréal, Lussé."] Ibid., 322–324.

146 "Tomorrow the king must leave": Ibid., 323.

147 "Why was your standard": Pernoud, *Joan of Arc: By Herself and Her Witnesses*, 125.

CHAPTER 10: Capture at Compiègne

148 "I shall last a year": Pernoud, *Joan of Arc: By Herself and Her Witnesses*, 141.

148 "The food was shocking": *A Parisian Journal*, 272.

149 "Most redoubted lord": Vaughan, *Philip the Good*, 24.

150 "a show of hands": *A Parisian Journal*, 237–238.

150 "by the command of my lord": Stevenson, *Letters and Papers Illustrative of the Wars of the English in France*, vol. 2, part 1, 101–102.

150 "promised . . . on their faith": *A Parisian Journal*, 238.

151 "as much because some felt": Pernoud, *Joan of Arc: By Herself and Her Witnesses*, 133.

151 "make good firm peace": Ibid., 128.

151 "We, John of Lancaster": Ibid., 131–132.

152 "On the Friday following the 26th day of August": Pernoud and Clin, *Joan of Arc: Her Story*, 76.

152 "well accompanied by soldiers": Kekewich, *The Good King*, 25.

153 "The assault, which was very cruel": Pernoud, *Joan of Arc: By Herself and Her Witnesses*, 135.

153 "Yield to us quickly": Ibid.

154 "Here's for you!": Ibid.

154 "A little after four o'clock": Ibid.

154 "In September": Ibid.

155 "changeability, defiance, and above all, envy": Pernoud and Clin, *Joan of Arc: Her Story*, 79.

155 "Messire Regnault de Chartres": Pernoud, *Joan of Arc: By Herself and Her Witnesses*, 142.

155 "the sire de la Trémoïlle sent Joan": Ibid., 145.

156 "When Joan had been there a space of time": Ibid.

156 "It was at the request of the men of war": Ibid., 134.

156 "did not wish to pay attention": Pernoud and Clin, *Joan of Arc: Her Story*, 91.

157 "The King being in the town": Pernoud, *Joan of Arc: By Herself and Her Witnesses*, 147.

158 "resolute to undergo every risk": Pernoud and Clin, *Joan of Arc: Her Story*, 83.

159 "with a doublet of rich cloth-of-gold": Ibid., 86.

159 "well-accompanied by many noble men": Ibid.

159 "and more assistance flowed towards the Burgundians": Ibid., 87.

159 "The Maid, going beyond the nature": Ibid.

159 "an archer, a rough man": Pernoud, *Joan of Arc: By Herself and Her Witnesses*, 151.

160 "were very joyous at it": Ibid., 152.

160 "by the pleasure of our blessed Creator": Pernoud and Clin, *Joan of Arc: Her Story*, 90.

160 "more joyful than if he had had a King": Pernoud, *Joan of Arc: By Herself and Her Witnesses*, 151.

161 "had become full of pride": Pernoud and Clin, *Joan of Arc: Her Story*, 91.

162 "God's will is inscrutable": Marina S. Brownlee, "Interference in *Mélusine*," in Maddox and Sturm-Maddox, eds., *Melusine of Lusignan*, 233.

162 "I have never been a prisoner": Pernoud, *Joan of Arc: By Herself and Her Witnesses*, 154.

163 "The demoiselle of Luxembourg and the lady of Beaurevoir": Ibid., 156.

CHAPTER 11: The Trial of Joan of Arc

164 "You say that you are my judge": Pernoud, *Joan of Arc: By Herself and Her Witnesses*, 182.

166 "Whereas all faithful Christian princes": Ibid., 157.

168 "It is by this that it is required": Ibid., 157–158.

168 "they should not for anything": Ibid., 158.

169 "The lady of Luxembourg asked": Pernoud and Clin, *Joan of Arc: Her Story*, 93.

169 "I would rather die": Ibid., 96–97.

169 "What was the reason you jumped": Ibid., 96.

170 "The Bishop of Beauvais whom I saw": Pernoud, *Joan of Arc: By Herself and Her Witnesses*, 160.

170 "And I know for certain": Pernoud and Clin, *Joan of Arc: Her Story*, 104.

170 "fastened by the neck": Ibid., 105.

171 "Englishmen of the lowest rank": Ibid., 104.

171 "in a secret place": Pernoud, *Joan of Arc: By Herself and Her Witnesses*, 169.

171 "had the warders and others": Ibid.

171 "nothing concerning Joan": Ibid.

171 "he was a traitor": Ibid., 168.

171 "as much for the serenity": Pernoud and Clin, *Joan of Arc: Her Story*, 108.

172 "The assessors with the judges": Pernoud, *Joan of Arc: By Herself and Her Witnesses*, 170.

172 "At the beginning of the trial": Ibid., 171.

172 "On this subject": Ibid.

172 "[He] pretended to be of the Maid's own country": Ibid., 172.

172 "In fact, at the beginning of the trial": Ibid.

173 "to speak the truth": Ibid., 180.

173 "it may happen that you will ask": Ibid.

173 "About my father and mother": Pernoud and Clin, *Joan of Arc: Her Story*, 109.

174 "This voice which you say . . . may God keep me in it": Pernoud, *Joan of Arc: By Herself and Her Witnesses*, 183.

174 "Asked about the tree . . . there or anywhere else": Smith, *Joan of Arc*, 111.

174 at least seventy recorded cases of witchcraft: For more on recorded trials of witchcraft, see Kieckhefer, *European Witch Trials*.

175 "It has long been clear": Russell, *Witchcraft in the Middle Ages*, 261–262.

175 "erred with fairies": Smith, *Joan of Arc*, 114.

175 "She said that she had heard it": Ibid., 112.

176 "Do you think that God": Pernoud, *Joan of Arc: By Herself and Her Witnesses*, 188.

176 "Why should it have been cut off?": Ibid.

176 "I have always told you": Ibid.

176 "How do you know . . . nothing but by God's commandment": Ibid., 184–185.

176 "She was right subtle": Ibid., 193.

177 "Since your voices have told you . . . a great treasure": Ibid., 191.

177 "which the laws of God": Murray, *Jeanne d'Arc, Maid of Orleans, Deliverer of France*, 354.

177 "If the Church Militant . . . God being first served": Pernoud and Clin, *Joan of Arc: Her Story*, 124.

178 "Truly, if you pull": Ibid., 127.

178 "If you have the sacraments . . . about that submission": Pernoud, *Joan of Arc: By Herself and Her Witnesses*, 203.

178 "The earl of Warwick": Pernoud and Clin, *Joan of Arc: Her Story*, 125.

179 "for her own good": Smith, *Joan of Arc*, 157.

179 "O Royal House of France!": Pernoud and Clin, *Joan of Arc: Her Story*, 130.

179 "I appeal to God": Ibid., 131.

179 "Do it now": Ibid.

179 "a great murmur arose": Ibid., 130.

179 "I, Joan, called the Maid": Smith, *Joan of Arc*, 165.

180 "in future she would neither carry arms": Pernoud and Clin, *Joan of Arc: Her Story*, 131.

180 "The king has spent his money very badly": Ibid.

180 "it would go badly": Ibid., 132.

180 "some of you men": Ibid.

180 "Take her back": Ibid.

181 "Gentlemen, you know that it is forbidden": Pernoud, *Joan of Arc: By Herself and Her Witnesses*, 219.

181 "You said, upon the scaffold . . . I will do nothing about it": Ibid., 222.

181 "Farewell, it is done": Ibid.

182 "'Alas! Do they treat me'": Ibid., 228.

182 "Bishop, I die by you": Ibid.

182 "We declare that thou, Joan": Ibid., 230.

183 "By this sentence": Smith, *Joan of Arc*, 172.

184 "imploring and invoking": Pernoud and Clin, *Joan of Arc: Her Story*, 136.

184 "Once in the fire": Ibid.

184 "because they feared": Pernoud, *Joan of Arc: By Herself and Her Witnesses*, 233.

184 "We are all lost": Ibid.

CHAPTER 12:   Of Politics and Prisoners

188 "the prelates, dukes, counts": Pernoud and Clin, *Joan of Arc: Her Story*, 141.

188 "She rode with the King every day": *A Parisian Journal*, 262–263.

189 "our adversary of Burgundy": Vaughan, *Philip the Good*, 63.

189 "has, for some time": Pernoud, *Joan of Arc: By Herself and Her Witnesses*, 146–147.

192 "When the constable came": ["Quand le connétable vint, au nom de son frère, trouver Yolande, accompagné du comte d'Etampes et d'ambassadeurs bretons, pour obtenir son agrément, elle entra dans une violente colère, et peu s'en fallut que les choses n'en vinssent à une guerre déclarée."] G. du Fresne de Beaucourt, *Histoire de Charles VII*, tome II, 272.

193 "the great, notable, profitable and agreeable": Ibid., 275.

194 "a brave knight of great heart": Kekewich, *The Good King*, 27.

195 "he had so many men": Ibid., 28.

195 "Intelligence of this defeat": *The Chronicles of Enguerrand de Monstrelet*, vol. 1, 598.

198 "It is . . . true, most redoubted lord": Vaughan, *Philip the Good*, 25.

198 "And firstly, with regard to . . . as ought reasonably to be satisfactory": Stevenson, *Letters and Papers Illustrative of the Wars of the English in France*, vol. 2, part 1, 188–192.

199 "Notwithstanding all letters": Ibid., 198–199.

199 "it is he who does and decides everything": Vaughan, *Philip the Good*, 169.

200 Rather, he went to see his mother: For the specifics of René's visit to his mother, see La Marche, *Le Roi René*, tome premier, 103, and Senneville, *Yolande d'Aragon*, 247.

CHAPTER 13: The Queen Takes Control

202 "La Trémoïlle's . . . one thought": Perroy, *The Hundred Years War*, 292.

202 "The duke of Bedford expected": *The Chronicles of Enguerrand de Monstrelet*, vol. 1, 615.

203 "They made him prisoner": Ibid., 621.

204 "Yolande [of Aragon] resumed all her lost ascendancy": Perroy, *The Hundred Years War*, 292.

204 the duke of Burgundy . . . ordered his representatives: Of the duke of Burgundy's negotiators' sudden separation at the council in Basel, medieval historian Joycelyne Dickinson wrote, "This appears to have been the first occasion on which the duke showed his hand . . . as a separate power with separate interests, which could no longer be served by identification with those of England." Dickinson, *The Congress of Arras, 1435*, 122.

204 "The war got worse and worse": *A Parisian Journal*, 289–290.

205 "disobedient rebel, self-styled duke of Burgundy": Vaughan, *Philip the Good*, 71.

205 "At length the duchess came . . . and in distress": *The Chronicles of Enguerrand de Monstrelet*, vol. 1, 633–634.

207 "Charles, by the grace of God, king of France": Vaughan, *Philip the Good*, 100.

207 "The king [Charles] will declare": *The Chronicles of Enguerrand de Monstrelet*, vol. 2, 10.

208 "Within a few days": Ibid., vol. 1, 634.

208 Yolande maintained her influence: Of Yolande's influence over the Congress of Arras, Joycelyne Dickinson observed: "It is . . . clear that . . . the queen of Sicily, actively concerned for her son the duke of Bar and perhaps also for the interests of her son-in-law Charles VII, sent no mere observers to Arras, but [was]

directly associated with the official French embassy, at least in sessions with the mediators." Dickinson, *The Congress of Arras, 1435,* 12.

210 "The English ambassadors were not well pleased": *The Chronicles of Enguerrand de Monstrelet,* vol. 2, 6.

212 "for they had perceived": Ibid., 8.

212 "acknowledge our aforesaid lord king": Ibid., 16.

212 "All persons were very much surprised": Ibid., 20.

213 "When the French or Armagnacs realized": *A Parisian Journal,* 299.

213 "let us into Paris peacefully . . . agreed to let them into the town": Ibid., 302–303.

214 "My good friends": Ibid., 305.

214 "The Parisians loved them for this": Ibid., 306.

214 "in very grand state": *The Chronicles of Enguerrand de Monstrelet,* vol. 2, 55.

215 "Thus nobly accompanied": Ibid.

215 "The crowd of common people": Ibid., 57.

CHAPTER 14: The Road to Rouen

220 "expressing a confidence": ["qui mettait toute sa confiance en elle après Dieu"] La Marche, *Le Roi René,* tome premier, 119.

222 "a brave prince": Kekewich, *The Good King,* 30.

223 "In this year": *The Chronicles of Enguerrand de Monstrelet,* vol. 2, 88.

223 "they could not agree": Ibid.

224 "While these negotiations were pending": Ibid., 100.

225 "For . . . the king [Charles VII] had been informed": Ibid., 105.

225 "King Charles of France now assembled": Ibid., 106.

227 "Were I certain of death": Kekewich, *The Good King,* 65.

228 "dazzling": ["éblouissante"] Senneville, *Yolande d'Aragon,* 308.

228 "The most beautiful": ["le plus bel et le meilleur a esté employé pour la fait du royaume d'Italie et baillé au roy Loys"] Ibid., 309.

230 "I will reveal my secret to no one": Seward, *The Hundred Years War,* 242.

230 "our dear uncle of France": Perroy, *The Hundred Years War,* 310.

231 "The meetings for peace": *The Chronicles of Enguerrand de Monstrelet,* vol. 2, 136–137.

231 "The marriage of Margaret was concluded": ["le mariage de Marguerite fut conclu . . . dans l'intérêt de Charles VII et sur sa demande"] La Marche, *Le Roi René,* tome premier, 127.

233 bestowed upon Charles VII a beautifully bound volume: For information about the copy of *Melusine* given to Charles VII, see Baudot, *Les Princesses Yolande et les Ducs de Bar,* 364.

234 "As heretofore Joan the Maid": Pernoud and Clin, *Joan of Arc: Her Story,* 149.

CHAPTER 15: The Rehabilitation of Joan of Arc

235 "I know well": Pernoud, *Joan of Arc: By Herself and Her Witnesses,* 188.

235 this explanation gives Charles far too much credit: Of Charles's motivation concerning the inquiry into Joan's condemnation, medieval scholar M. G. A. Vale wrote, "The wording of the king's order to Bouillé suggests two motives: first, a desire to ascertain the facts about the trial; secondly, to use those facts, if possible, against the English, who were still holding part of Normandy, as well as Gascony, in February 1450." Vale, *Charles VII,* 60.

237 "an iniquitous, scandalous sentence": Ibid., 62.

238 "[acted] more through love of the English": Ibid.

238 "Do you know . . . keep me in it": Pernoud, *Joan of Arc: By Herself and Her Witnesses,* 183.

239 "I know that the matter": Vale, *Charles VII,* 63.

240 "the preceding and other points": Pernoud and Clin, *Joan of Arc: Her Story,* 154.

240 "Although many persons could be plaintiffs": Pernoud, *Joan of Arc: By Herself and Her Witnesses,* 264.

240 "a tribunal of rehabilitation": Vale, *Charles VII,* 65.

241 "loved to converse upon legal matters": Pastor, *The History of the Popes,* vol. 2, 332. The university referred to here was not the University of Paris but the University of Lérida, but the point is that Calixtus very much appreciated scholarship.

241 "I had a daughter": Pernoud and Clin, *Joan of Arc: Her Story,* 156–157.

243 "Bearing in her hand her standard": Pernoud, *Joan of Arc: By Herself and Her Witnesses,* 82.

243 "Many of the King's men": Ibid., 117.

244 "Then the Maid came": Ibid., 122.

244 "Willingly did she . . . punctual in ringing": Ibid., 18–20.

244 "I call upon God": Ibid., 194.

244 "It pleased God thus to do": Ibid.

244 "As for the Church": Ibid., 173.

244 "And me, I tell you": Ibid., 181.

246 "In consideration of the request": Ibid., 269.

246 "And thereafter my voices say to me": Ibid., 191.

EPILOGUE

247 "both small and great": *The Chronicles of Enguerrand de Monstrelet,* vol. 2, 225.

247 "The attack commenced": Ibid.

247 "he was put to death": Ibid.

248 "to watch all the coastline daily": Vale, *Charles VII,* 125.

248 "The late Yolande": Kekewich, *Good King René,* 18.

248 "bore a man's heart": Senneville, *Yolande d'Aragon,* 105.

SELECTED BIBLIOGRAPHY

Abulafia, David, ed. *The French Descent into Renaissance Italy, 1494–95: Antecedents and Effects*. Farnham, Surrey, UK: Variorum, 1995.

Allmand, C. T. "The Lancastrian Land Settlement in Normandy, 1417–50." *Economic History Review*, New Series, 21, no. 3 (December 1968): 461–479.

Bailey, Michael D. *Battling Demons: Witchcraft, Heresy, and Reform in the Late Middle Ages*. University Park: Pennsylvania State University Press, 2003.

Barker, Juliet. *Agincourt: Henry V and the Battle That Made England*. New York: Little, Brown, 2005.

Baudot, Jules. *Les Princesses Yolande et les Ducs de Bar de la Famille des Valois*. Paris: Alphonse Picard et Fils, 1900.

Bearne, Catherine. *Pictures of the Old French Court: Jeanne de Bourbon, Isabeau de Bavière, Anne de Bretagne*. London: T. Fisher Unwin, 1900.

Beaucourt, G. du Fresne de. *Histoire de Charles VII*. Paris: Librairie de la Société Bibliographique, 1881.

Besant, Walter. *Essays and Historiettes*. London: Chatto & Windus, 1903.

Bisson, T. N. *The Medieval Crown of Aragon: A Short History*. Oxford: Clarendon Press, 1991.

Boase, Roger. *The Troubadour Revival: A Study of Social Change and Traditionalism in Late Medieval Spain*. London: Routledge & Kegan Paul, 1978.

Bourdigné, Jehan de. *Chroniques d'Anjou et du Maine*. Angers: Imprimerie de Cosnier et Lachèse, 1842.

Bratsch-Prince, Dawn. "A Queen's Task: Violant de Bar and the Experience of Royal Motherhood in Fourteenth-Century Aragón." *La corónica* 27, no. 1 (Fall 1998): 21–34.

Brockington, Ian. "Menstrual Psychosis." *World Psychiatry: Official Journal of the World Psychiatric Association* 4, no. 1 (February 2005): 9–17. http://www.ncbi.nlm.nih.gov/pms/articles/PMC1414712.

Burne, Alfred H. *The Agincourt War: A Military History of the Latter Part of the Hundred Years War from 1369 to 1453*. Fair Lawn, NJ: Essential Books, 1956.

Chartier, Jean. *Chronique de Charles VII, Roi de France*. Paris: Chez P. Jannet, 1858.

Chronique de Jean Le Févre, Seigneur de Saint-Remy: 1420–1435. Tome second. Edited by François Morand. Paris: Librairie de la Société de l'Histoire de France, 1881.

Chronique du Religieux de Saint-Denys, publiée en latin et traduite par M. L. Bellaguet, 1842. Paris: Éditions du Comité des travaux historiques et scientifiques, 1994.

Couldrette. *The Romans of Partenay, or of Lusignen: Otherwise Known as the Tale of Melusine; Translated from the French of La Coudrette (before 1500 A.D.).* Revised by the Reverend Walter W. Skeat. Rye Brook, NY: Elibron Classics, 2005. Unabridged facsimile of the edition published in 1866 by Kegan Paul, Trench, Trübner, London.

Dickinson, Joycelyne Gledhill. *The Congress of Arras, 1435: A Study in Medieval Diplomacy.* New York: Biblo and Tannen, 1972.

Evans, Joan. *Dress in Mediaeval France.* Oxford: Clarendon Press, 1952.

Famiglietti, R. C. *Royal Intrigue: Crisis at the Court of Charles VI, 1392–1420.* New York: AMS Press, 1986.

Favier, Jean. *Gold and Spices: The Rise of Commerce in the Middle Ages.* New York: Holmes & Meier, 1998.

Fraioli, Deborah A. *Joan of Arc: The Early Debate.* Woodbridge, Suffolk, UK: Boydell Press, 2000.

France, Anatole. *The Life of Joan of Arc: A Translation by Winifred Stephens in Two Volumes.* New York: John Lane Company, 1908.

Freeman, Margaret B. "A Book of Hours Made for the Duke of Berry." *Metropolitan Museum of Art Bulletin,* New Series, 15, no. 4 (December 1956): 93–104.

Froissart, Sir John. *Chronicles of England, France, Spain and the Adjoining Countries from the Latter Part of the Reign of Edward II to the Coronation of Henry IV.* Translated from the French by Thomas Jones. 2 vols. Revised edition. London: Colonial Press, 1901.

Furlong, Monica. *Visions and Longings: Medieval Women Mystics.* Boston: Shambhala, 1996.

Gibbons, Rachel. "Isabeau of Bavaria, Queen of France (1385–1422): The Creation of an Historical Villainess: The Alexander Prize Essay." *Transactions of the Royal Historical Society,* 6th series, 6 (1996): 51–73.

Hay, Denys. *Europe in the Fourteenth and Fifteenth Centuries.* New York: Holt, Rinehart and Winston, 1966.

Hillgarth, J. N. *The Spanish Kingdoms: 1250–1516.* 2 vols. Oxford: Clarendon Press, 1976–78.

Hookham, Mary Ann. *The Life and Times of Margaret of Anjou, Queen of England and France; and of Her Father, René the Good.* Vol. 1. London: Tinsley Brothers, 1872.

Jacob, E. F. *The Fifteenth Century, 1399–1485.* Oxford: Oxford University Press, 1993.

Jones, Michael, ed. *The New Cambridge Medieval History,* vol. 6, *c. 1300–c. 1415.* Cambridge: Cambridge University Press, 2000.

Journal d'un Bourgeois de Paris de 1405 à 1449. Texte français moderne de Jacques Mégret. Paris: Horizons de France, 1944.

Kekewich, Margaret L. *The Good King: René of Anjou and Fifteenth-Century Europe.* New York: Palgrave Macmillan, 2008.

Kibre, Pearl. "The Intellectual Interests Reflected in Libraries of the Fourteenth and Fifteenth Centuries." *Journal of the History of Ideas* 7, no. 3 (June 1946): 257–297.

Kieckhefer, Richard. *European Witch Trials: Their Foundations in Popular and Learned Culture, 1300–1500.* Berkeley: University of California Press, 1976.

Kitchin, G. W. *A History of France.* 2nd ed. Vol. 1. Oxford: Clarendon Press, 1881.

la Marche, A. Lecoy de. *Le Roi René: Sa Vie, Son Administration, Ses Travaux Artistiques et Littéraires.* Tome premier. Paris: Librairie de Firmin-Didot Frères, Fils et Cie, 1875.

Lang, Andrew. *The Maid of France: Being the Story of the Life and Death of Jeanne d'Arc.* London and New York: Longmans, Green, 1908.

Lavisse, Ernest. *Histoire de France Depuis les Origines Jusqu'à la Révolution.* Tome quatrième, *Charles VII, Louis XI et les Premières Années de Charles VIII (1422–1492)* par Ch. Petit-Dutaillis. Paris: Librairie Hachette et Cie, 1902.

Leff, Gordon. *Paris and Oxford Universities in the Thirteenth and Fourteenth Centuries: An Institutional and Intellectual History.* New York: Robert E. Krieger Publishing, 1975.

Léonard, Émile G. *Les Angevins de Naples.* Paris: Presses Universitaires de France, 1954.

Les Deux Procès de Condamnation, les Enquêtes et la Sentence de Réhabilitation de Jeanne d'Arc. Tome premier. Paris: Henri Plon, Imprimeur-Éditor, 1868.

Lettres Historiques des Archives Communales de la Ville de Tours Depuis Charles VI Jusqu'à la Fin du Règne de Henri IV, 1416–1594. Tours: Imprimerie ad Mame et Cie, 1861.

Lewis, P. S. *Later Medieval France: The Polity.* New York: St. Martin's Press, 1968.

———. *The Recovery of France in the Fifteenth Century.* New York: Harper & Row, 1971.

McKenna, J. W. "Henry VI of England and the Dual Monarchy: Aspects of Royal Political Propaganda, 1422–1432." *Journal of the Warburg and Courtauld Institutes* 28 (1965): 145–162.

Maddox, Donald, and Sara Sturm-Maddox, eds. *Melusine of Lusignan: Founding Fiction in Late Medieval France.* Athens: University of Georgia Press, 1996.

Miron, E. L. *The Queens of Aragon: Their Lives and Times.* London: Stanley Paul, 1913.

Miskimin, Harry A. *Money and Power in Fifteenth-Century France.* New Haven, CT: Yale University Press, 1984.

Monstrelet, Enguerrand de. *The Chronicles of Enguerrand de Monstrelet; Containing an Account of the Cruel Civil Wars Between the Houses of Orleans and Burgundy.* 2 vols. Translated by Thomas Johns. London: Henry G. Bohn, 1853.

Munro, John H. "An Economic Aspect of the Collapse of the Anglo-Burgundian Alliance, 1428–1442." *English Historical Review* 85, no. 335 (April 1970): 225–244.

Murray, T. Douglas. *Jeanne d'Arc, Maid of Orleans, Deliverer of France: Being the Story of Her Life, Her Achievements, and Her Death, As Attested on Oath and Set Forth in the Original Documents.* New York: McClure, Phillips, 1902.

O'Callaghan, Joseph F. *A History of Medieval Spain.* Ithaca, NY: Cornell University Press, 1975.

A Parisian Journal, 1405–1449. Translated from the anonymous *Journal d'un Bourgeois de Paris* by Janet Shirley. Oxford: Clarendon Press, 1968.

Partner, Peter. *The Papal State Under Martin V: The Administration and Government of the Temporal Power in the Early Fifteenth Century.* London: British School at Rome, 1958.

Pastor, Ludwig. *The History of the Popes, from the Close of the Middle Ages*. Vol. 2. London: John Hodges, 1891.

Pedro IV of Aragon. *Chronicle*. Translated by Mary Hillgarth. Toronto: Pontifical Institute of Mediaeval Studies, 1980.

Pernoud, Régine. *Joan of Arc: By Herself and Her Witnesses*. Lanham, MD: Scarborough House, 1982.

Pernoud, Régine, and Marie-Véronique Clin. *Joan of Arc: Her Story*. Revised and translated by Jeremy duQuesnay Adams. New York: St. Martin's Griffin, 1999.

Perroy, Edouard. *The Hundred Years War*. New York: Capricorn, 1965.

Pirie, Valérie. *The Triple Crown: An Account of the Papal Conclaves from the Fifteenth Century to the Present Day*. Wilmington, NC: Consortium Books, 1976.

Quicherat, J., ed. *Procès de Condamnation et de Réhabilitation de Jeanne d'Arc*. 5 vols. Paris: Société de l'Histoire de France, 1841–49.

Ramsay, Sir James Henry. *Lancaster and York: A Century of English History, A.D. 1399–1485*. Oxford: Clarendon Press, 1892.

Revue Historique, Littéraire et Archéologique de l'Anjou, Publiée sous les Auspices du Conseil Général, Huitième Année. Tome quinzième. Angers: Imprimerie-Librairie de E. Barassé, 1876.

Russell, Jeffrey Burton. *Witchcraft in the Middle Ages*. Ithaca, NY: Cornell University Press, 1972.

Senneville, Gérard de. *Yolande d'Aragon: La Reine Qui a Gagné la Guerre de Cent Ans*. Paris: Perrin, 2008.

Seward, Desmond. *The Hundred Years War: The English in France, 1337–1453*. New York: Penguin, 1978.

Smith, John Holland. *Joan of Arc*. New York: Charles Scribner's Sons, 1973.

Spufford, Peter. *Money and Its Use in Medieval Europe*. Cambridge: Cambridge University Press, 1988.

Stevenson, Joseph. *Letters and Papers Illustrative of the Wars of the English in France During the Reign of Henry the Sixth King of England*. London: Elibron Classics, 2007.

Vale, M. G. A. *Charles VII*. Berkeley: University of California Press, 1974.

Vaughan, Richard. *Philip the Good: The Apogee of Burgundy*. Woodbridge, Suffolk, UK: Boydell Press, 2002.

Villeneuve Bargemont, F. L. de. *Histoire de René D'Anjou, Roi de Naples, Duc de Lorraine et Comte de Provence*. Tome premier. Paris: Chez J. J. Blaise, 1825.

Waugh, Scott L., and Peter D. Diehl, eds. *Christendom and Its Discontents: Exclusion, Persecution, and Rebellion, 1000–1500*. Cambridge: Cambridge University Press, 1996.

Waurin, John de, Lord of Forestel. *A Collection of the Chronicles and Ancient Histories of Great Britain, Now Called England, from A.D. 1422 to A.D. 1431*. Translated by Edward L. C. P. Hardy. London: Published by the Authority of the Lords Commissioners of Her Majesty's Treasury, Eyre and Spottiswoode, 1891.

Willard, Charity Cannon. *Christine de Pizan: Her Life and Works*. New York: Persea Books, 1984.

Wirth, Robert, ed. "Primary Sources and Context Concerning Joan of Arc's Male Clothing." Historical Academy for Joan of Arc Studies, 2006. http://primary -sources-series.joan-of-arc-studies.org/PSS021806.pdf.

Wood, Charles T. *Joan of Arc and Richard III: Sex, Saints, and Government in the Middle Ages*. Oxford: Oxford University Press, 1988.

ILLUSTRATION CREDITS

xix *Portrait of Joan of Arc carrying her sword and banner.* Miniature drawn in the margin of a register recording the raising of the siege of Orléans, May 8, 1429, by a clerk, Clement de Fauquembergue, fifteenth century. Paris, Archives nationales. Photo credit: Luisa Ricciarini/Leemage.

1 *The queen distributes prizes to the victor at the tournament.* Barthelemy d'Eyck, miniature from ms. 2695, "Le Livre des Tournois de René d'Anjou," 1460. Paris, Bibliothèque nationale. Photo credit: Josse/Leemage.

13 *Raymondin spies on his wife, Melusine, in the bath.* Engraving from folio 142, "Histoire de Melusine" by Jean of Arras, 1478. Paris, Bibliothèque nationale. Photo credit: Josse/Leemage.

23 *Portrait of Louis I of Anjou (1339–1384), king of Naples and count of Provence, and Marie of Blois (1345–1404), countess of Provence.* Aix-en-Provence, Musée Arbaud. Photo credit: Jean Bernard/Leemage.

37 *The madness of Charles VI (1368–1422).* From the *Chroniques de Enguerrand de Monstrelet* (1400–1453). Paris, Bibliothèque nationale. Photo credit: Josse/Leemage.

49 *Louis II of Anjou and Yolande of Aragon greet their future son-in-law, who became Charles VII.* Miniature from the *Chroniques de Jean Froissart,* folio 321v, fifteenth century. Paris, Bibliothèque nationale. Photo credit: Josse/Leemage.

57 *The battle of Agincourt.* Miniature from the manuscript "Vigiles du roi Charles VII" by Martial d'Auvergne, 1484. Paris, Bibliothèque nationale. Photo credit: Josse/Leemage.

68 *The Hundred Years War: massacre of the Armagnacs by the Burgundians during the civil war.* Miniature from the manuscript "Vigiles du roi Charles VII" by Martial d'Auvergne, 1477–1483. Paris, Bibliothèque nationale. Photo credit: Josse/Leemage.

75 *Portrait of Joan of Arc carrying her sword and banner.* Drawn in the margin of a register recording the raising of the siege of Orléans, May 8, 1429, by a clerk, Clement de

Fauquembergue. Miniature, fifteenth century. Paris, Archives nationales. Photo credit: Luisa Ricciarini/Leemage.

87 *Portrait of Charles VII, king of France.* Painting by Jean Fouquet, 1444. Paris, Musée du Louvre. Photo credit: Josse/Leemage.

119 *Joan of Arc before King Charles VII.* Miniature from the manuscript "Vigiles du roi Charles VII" by Martial d'Auvergne, 1477–1483. Paris, Bibliothèque nationale. Photo credit: Josse/Leemage.

135 *The French raise the siege of Orléans and enter the city on May 8, 1429.* Miniature from the manuscript "Vigiles du roi Charles VII" by Martial d'Auvergne, 1484. Paris, Bibliothèque nationale. Photo credit: MP/Leemage.

146 *Coronation of Charles VII by the archbishop of Reims.* Miniature from the manuscript "Vigiles du roi Charles VII" by Martial d'Auvergne, 1477–1483. Paris, Bibliothèque nationale. Photo credit: Josse/Leemage.

160 *The Hundred Years War: Joan of Arc is taken prisoner at Compiègne.* Miniature from the manuscript "Vigiles du roi Charles VII" by Martial d'Auvergne, 1484. Paris, Bibliothèque nationale. Photo credit: Josse/Leemage.

183 *Joan of Arc is tied to the stake.* Miniature from the manuscript "Vigiles du roi Charles VII" by Martial d'Auvergne, 1484, folio 71. Paris, Bibliothèque nationale. Photo credit: Josse/Leemage.

185 *The Hundred Years War: the battle of Formigny.* Miniature from the manuscript "Vigiles du roi Charles VII" by Martial d'Auvergne, 1484. Paris, B.N. Photo credit: Josse/Leemage.

193 *Portrait of King René of Anjou, also known as René I of Naples and also René of Sicily in his cabinet.* Fifteenth-century miniature engraving. Photo credit: Selva/Leemage.

206 *Portrait of Philip III of Burgundy, known as Philip the Good.* Illustration by Wavrin, Master of London, 1481–1486. Shelfmark Harl 6199, folio 57v, British Library. Photo credit: Heritage Images/Leemage.

215 *The Hundred Years War: Charles VII, king of France, enters Paris after the reconquest of the city from the English in November 1437.* Miniature from the manuscript "Vigiles du roi Charles VII" by Martial d'Auvergne, 1484. Paris, B.N. Photo credit: Heritage Images/Leemage.

229 *Yolande of Aragon.* Stained glass window at the cathedral of Saint-Julien du Mans, fifteenth century. Photo credit: Selva/Leemage.

245 *Portrait of Joan of Arc.* Miniature from the "Poesies of Charles d'Orléans," fifteenth century. Paris, Archives nationales. Photo credit: Josse/Leemage.

INDEX